ROUTLEDGE LIBRARY EDITIONS:
THE ADOLESCENT

Volume 16

ADOLESCENT BOYS OF
EAST LONDON

ADOLESCENT BOYS OF EAST LONDON

PETER WILLMOTT

Routledge
Taylor & Francis Group

LONDON AND NEW YORK

First published in 1966 by Routledge & Kegan Paul Ltd

This edition first published in 2023
by Routledge
4 Park Square, Milton Park, Abingdon, Oxon OX14 4RN

and by Routledge
605 Third Avenue, New York, NY 10158

Routledge is an imprint of the Taylor & Francis Group, an informa business

ISBN: 978-1-032-37655-4 (Set)
ISBN: 978-1-032-38491-7 (Volume 16) (hbk)
ISBN: 978-1-032-38501-3 (Volume 16) (pbk)
ISBN: 978-1-003-34534-3 (Volume 16) (ebk)

DOI: 10.4324/9781003345343

Publisher's Note
The publisher has gone to great lengths to ensure the quality of this reprint but points out that some imperfections in the original copies may be apparent.

Disclaimer
The publisher has made every effort to trace copyright holders and would welcome correspondence from those they have been unable to trace.

ADOLESCENT BOYS
OF EAST LONDON

PETER WILLMOTT

LONDON
ROUTLEDGE & KEGAN PAUL

First published 1966
by Routledge & Kegan Paul Ltd
Broadway House, 68–74 Carter Lane
London, E.C.4

Printed in Great Britain
by Cox and Wyman Ltd
London, Fakenham and Reading

CONTENTS

INTRODUCTION

The study reported in this book was an attempt to unravel some apparent contradictions. One was that what my colleagues and I had observed of local boys in the course of other research in East London seemed at variance with much of what was written and said about contemporary youth – about the hooliganism and violence, the 'insecure offenders',[1] the 'delinquent generation'. The second problem was about the delinquency that did go on, for there clearly was some: the late-night battle in the alleyway next to the Institute of Community Studies, when knives had flashed, the girl raped in Victoria Park by a gang of teenagers, the shops broken into, motor scooters stolen, telephone boxes put out of order, windows aimlessly smashed. Such things might be relatively rare, but they raised some crucial questions – what sort of local boys did these things, and where did this behaviour fit into the way of life of local adolescents generally?

These questions pointed to another study in Bethnal Green[2] to add to some earlier research that had been done in the same place. We would look out from our own doorstep once more, this time at adolescence, against the background of a set of family and community patterns about which we already knew something. The emphasis would be on normality, on ordinary youths. Hence this book: an attempt, based mainly on interviews with boys living in one district of East London, to examine the processes of male adolescence. In general girls pose less of a problem to adult society; partly for this reason, partly because resources were limited, we decided to confine the study to boys.

In the main series of interviews, 14 has been taken as the lower age limit, 20 as the top. This age range coincides with that catered for by the youth service; it also starts conveniently with boys in their last year of compulsory schooling and goes up to the brink

[1] See Fyvel, T. R., *The Insecure Offenders*. Full references are given in Appendix 5 to all works cited. Titles in italics are books, and those in inverted commas articles.
[2] Note that Bethnal Green is no longer a distinct local authority area; from April 1965 it became part of the London Borough of Tower Hamlets.

of their legal – and electoral – entry into manhood. By definition, adolescence is a period of transition; it bridges the years between childhood and adulthood. The transformation that occurs within the span of six years was illustrated by some of the immediately apparent differences between the younger and older boys we interviewed. Most of the 14 year olds were small, with slim hips, smooth cheeks and soft voices. To many of them the *Beano Annual* or a plastic racing car was as engrossing as the latest hit record or the newest style in shirts. They giggled at some questions in the interview, were puzzled by others. At the other end of the scale, the 20 year olds were full-grown men, who pondered their answers and talked seriously of their work, their friends, their views on youth and age and, often, the plans for their approaching marriage or the problem of saving a deposit for a house. They were different not only from their younger fellows but also from their former selves – as we could sometimes observe when boys seen at the start of the study were met a few years later or when, as happened once or twice, we found that the tall young man we were talking to was the boisterous, short-trousered schoolboy who had rushed into the home when his own parents were being interviewed, seven or eight years earlier, during our first research in Bethnal Green.

We started the present study in 1959. Over the following five years my colleagues and I carried out intermittent series of interviews with over a hundred adolescent boys living in Bethnal Green. Sixty of them were interviewed in their homes, with a relatively 'open' or unstructured questionnaire. Others were contacted by less formal and less systematic means. We got talking to some in youth clubs, cafés and pubs. We re-interviewed some of those seen in their homes and invited them to bring along their friends. We built up a series of 'chains' of informants. The most rewarding discussions took place at the Institute of Community Studies itself. Boys came to the office at evenings or week-ends – sometimes alone, often in groups; some just once, most twice or more – and in the presence of a tape-recorder talked over their opinions and experiences. By 1964 we had collected a cupboard-full of tapes (and typed transcripts), together with files of interview reports. At this stage, therefore, we had a good deal of impressionistic and illustrative material, but almost nothing in the way of statistical information.

For this reason we set out to interview the main sample which is the source of most of the figures in the book; this was done in the summer of 1964.[3] Since there is no recognized 'sampling frame' from which to pick a cross-section of boys, we had to adopt a rather laborious method. We drew from the electoral register a sample of 2,300 addresses in Bethnal Green, and called at these to see if any boys aged 14 to 20 inclusive were living there; we then tried to contact and interview any who were. At the 2,300 addresses, there were altogether 279 young men reported as of the right age. Some refused an interview and a few could not be contacted; but we succeeded in interviewing 246. This was nearly nine out of ten of all those traced, so the sample is a reasonably representative cross-section of boys between 14 and 20 living in the survey district.

Apart from a few of these interviews that I did myself, this phase of interviewing was done by a team of ten young men specially recruited for the job. All were under 25, all had a sympathetic and as it seemed to me 'classless' manner – half were Australians or New Zealanders.[4] They not only had relatively few refusals or other failures; they were reasonably successful in another way, too. In our earlier attempts to interview boys in their homes, it seemed that when other people, particularly parents, were present, this not surprisingly sometimes influenced the boys' answers. The interviewers were asked to see the boys alone wherever possible – if necessary, specifically asking for this and tactfully explaining why. This they usually managed to do; altogether nearly nine out of ten of the boys were seen by themselves.[5]

The boys in this sample were also asked if they were willing to keep a detailed week's diary for us (for a small fee) or to come to

[3] Further details about this main survey are given in Appendix 1, and the interview schedule and interviewers' instructions are reproduced in Appendix 2.
[4] As Gorer points out: 'There are numerous advantages in being a foreigner to the society one is studying; one is unplaced socially, for one's foreignness masks the lesser differences of class or region . . .' (Gorer, G., *Exploring English Character*, p. 1).
[5] We obviously wanted to see whether the one in ten who were interviewed with others gave different answers from those seen alone. There were some apparent differences but the numbers were too small for us to be sure whether they merely reflected sampling variations. Since the differences were not all that sharp, we decided that it was proper to include the tenth with the rest of the sample in all our analyses, and this is what we did.

the Institute, if asked, for further talk. About three-quarters said they would do both. From these we picked a sub-sample of forty-two, who were invited to write their diary for a particular week in June 1964: in the event, thirty wrote completed diaries, and these have been drawn on in writing the book, together with another five that we specially commissioned later from school-boys.[6] We also asked about twenty selected boys to come to the Institute for still more tape-recorded interviews, and these have been used as well. Finally, we 'observed' local boys wherever we could – in the streets, the parks, the cafés, youth clubs and so on.

One limitation of the design of the main survey should be stated. Any study of processes can be done in two ways: it can compare people of different ages at the same point in time, as we have done with our sample of 246, or it can follow through the same people, interviewing them at different ages (a 'longitudinal' study). The advantage of the second method is that it reduces the risk of confusing changes in society over time with changes in people's own lives as they get older. When I compare, as I do in later chapters, boys of 14 and 15 with those of 19 and 20, I cannot be sure that the older boys did, when they were 14 or 15, what the younger ones do now. But the 'longitudinal' study has its own difficulties; people are likely to drop out during the course of the research, and the consciousness that they are being studied may influence the behaviour and attitudes of those who stay in. Thus the arguments are fairly evenly balanced. Because we were working on the research over a period of five years, we were in fact able to see some of the same boys at various stages between 14 and 20. Though this was not done systematically, these contacts suggested – like our general observation in Bethnal Green during the years – that the statistical comparisons of boys at different ages were not giving a misleading impression.

I must add the familiar warning that what people say may be at odds with what they actually do. More important still, the reader should bear in mind that this was not simply, even mainly, a statistical study. The tape-recorded conversations, the freer interviews, the diaries and our observation in the district all play a part in the account that follows. The sample survey provided a mass of quantitative information, but some questions were not

[6] A sample diary, and the instructions to boys who agreed to keep them, are given in Appendix 3.

4

– could not be – included in it, and we therefore have no reliable figures on them. Sometimes, too, the sub-groups within the sample of 246 were too small for us to speak with any authority. On other topics, we were fairly confident that we knew what had happened, but not why or how. The non-statistical material has therefore been drawn upon freely, not just to illustrate statistical findings (though this has been done), but also to help in interpreting, in speculating, in trying to understand.

The conventions I have followed may help the reader to recognize the degree of authority with which different statements are made. First, I have adopted the usual statistical procedure over possible sampling errors, so that when figures are presented it can normally be assumed that the chances are at least nineteen out of twenty that a similar result would apply to the whole population from which the sample was taken – that is, Bethnal Green boys then aged 14 to 20. If the numbers were too low or the differences under discussion too small for this degree of confidence, I have drawn attention to the fact. On the whole, when venturing beyond the statistical evidence, I have used a more speculative form of words – 'it seems', 'the impression is', 'a possible interpretation' and so on.[7]

The reader will note that the book contains many direct quotations. This seemed particularly important in a study of adolescence. By allowing the boys to speak for themselves, in their own words, I hope to communicate to adult readers something of how they see their lives, how they feel about what is happening to them. But in drawing so liberally upon them, it is the more essential to ensure that particular boys cannot be identified from the text. I have given everybody a fictitious name; where both first and surname are quoted, these may correspond by chance to the names of real people, but this is purely coincidental. As well as changing names, other details have been altered. In particular, the more detailed 'portraits' of some boys are not in fact of individual people; they are composite descriptions, incorporating elements from several. These precautions may mislead – in the sense that what I have deemed unimportant details, and therefore changed, may actually be crucial. I hope not.

The subsequent chapters try to illuminate two broad sets of questions about adolescence in East London. The first are about

[7] 'Statistical significance' is discussed in Appendix 1, pp. 184–185.

the process itself, for the generality of local boys. What are the changes in social relationships during these crucial years and how are they worked through? How much strain does maturation impose: are delinquency, violence, hooliganism common expressions of tension and of conflict with adult society? Does adolescence, for some reason, present more of a problem now than it used to? What is the role of the family in the process? And what of other institutions – school, work and youth clubs, for instance; which, if any, ease the transition and which hinder it?

The second set of questions concern variations between the boys themselves. They clearly differ in ability, in schooling, in the kind of jobs they do, in their values, ambitions and hopes. Is it possible to distinguish different types of boy – and characteristically different patterns of response to growing up in a district like this?

The structure of the book is straightforward, and naturally reflects these questions. After Chapter I, which describes something of the district and the place of the boys in it, the next three chapters concentrate on the processes of adolescence, dealing in turn with the principal 'informal groupings' to which the boys belong. The second half of the book looks at various institutions of the wider society, asking what part they play and how the boys fit in; these chapters bring out particularly some of the differences in adolescent responses to the outside world.

The research reported in this book was financed by a grant from the Ford Foundation and, as part of their general support to the Institute, by the Joseph Rowntree Memorial Trust and later the Nuffield Foundation. I am grateful to these three bodies.

The study owes even more to the work of others than the previous Institute projects with which I have been associated. Raphael Samuel, before leaving to take up teaching at Ruskin College, Oxford, carried the main burden of the research in its early phases, contributing many of the central ideas and collecting first-rate interview material. At a later stage the project was strengthened by the presence of C. H. Rolph, who came down to Bethnal Green to collect new material and help the research forward. Nick Reid handled the analysis of the main survey, did most of the final round of intensive interviews, and was a constructive and helpful critic of the various drafts. Michael Young gave his unfailing encouragement and advice throughout, as he has since he started me on the path of social research. Phyllis Willmott supported and helped, in particular with many editorial improvements.

Michael Power, Michael Alderson and their colleagues at the Social Medicine Research Unit of the Medical Research Council (London Hospital) generously made their research data available, carried out some special analyses and commented on drafts. Professor Alan Stuart and Susannah Brown of the Research Techniques Division, London School of Economics, gave statistical advice and arranged for a series of special analyses of our data. Thanks are due to the members of the Institute's Advisory Committee, particularly Euan Cooper-Willis, Geoffrey Gorer, Professor Charles Madge, John Peterson, Stephen Schenk and Professor Peter Townsend; also to Christopher Bennett, Dyke Brown, Geoffrey Dench, David Downes, Leonard Duhl, the late Hannah Gavron, Alan Gibson, George Goetchius, David Hunter, W. G. Runciman, John Sparrow and Jackson Toby. All these commented on drafts or helped in other ways. So did my colleagues at the Institute, of whom Patricia Bourne, Ann Cartwright, Howard Dickinson, Patrick McGeeney and Peter Marris were specially helpful with this study. The interviewers in the main study were Norman Allen, Robin Boyd, Terence Conlon, Duncan Hamilton, Peter Jefferys, Paul Kirsner, Peter Norman, Chris Paige and Dan Varendorff. Maureen Brooke, Barbara Gibson and Jacqueline White did most of the typing.

A number of local officials, youth leaders and teachers helped also; I am sorry that I have to thank them anonymously. Finally, the research depended above all upon the boys of Bethnal Green; I thank them for their co-operation, which was almost always far fuller and more generous than a research worker has any right to expect.

I

THE DISTRICT AND THE BOYS

What sort of place is Bethnal Green to grow up in? Two facts stand out. The first is its 'working-class' character: most local men work for a weekly wage at a manual job, many within a mile or two of their homes, in the docks, in a wholesale market, marshalling yard, factory or workshop. And the same is true of the neighbouring districts of East London; the East End as a whole is largely working-class.[1]

The second fact is equally important. Both the East End in general and Bethnal Green in particular are changing fast. For a century or more these districts symbolized the old working-class way of life at its harshest – unemployment, poverty, overcrowding, slums. This was the background against which the fathers and grandfathers of the young men we interviewed came of age. For the boys themselves the setting is very different, and is all the time becoming more so.

The changing scene

The transformation is dramatically expressed in the buildings, which are being replaced at a speed that surprises the observer, if not the residents awaiting rehousing. Ten years ago, when we first went to Bethnal Green, the characteristic housing was two-storey Victorian cottages, row upon terraced row of them, low-browed and intimate, in patterned short streets with corner shops and pubs. 'Dilapidated but cosy, damp but friendly, in the eyes of most Bethnal Greeners, these cottages *are* the place' was how it seemed in 1957.[2] That is true no longer. Over large tracts the

---

[1] In this book the definition of the 'East End' is the one used in our earlier studies. In terms of the present structure of London government, this is the London Borough of Tower Hamlets and the London Borough of Hackney (with the exception of the former borough of Stoke Newington).

[2] Young, M. and Willmott, P., *Family and Kinship in East London*, p. 22.

bulldozers have done their work, flattening the condemned terraces into rubble, erasing for ever the parlours, the wooden staircases, the stone-floored sculleries and the outside lavatories.

In their place rises the new Bethnal Green, whose symbol is the soaring glass and concrete of the Council flats. More rebuilding has been done locally than in other parts of London: 'A third of all the slum clearance work done by the London County Council since 1945 has taken place in the East End, although this area forms only 6·5 per cent of the County.'[3] The effects are apparent. In 1957 we found that Council property accounted for less than a third of the dwellings in Bethnal Green; by 1964 the proportion was more than a half. The flats are in many styles – point block, slab or cluster block; some massive and ponderous, others delicate and light on podium supports; elsewhere cliffs of glass and curtain-walling dwarf the low promontories of the four-storey maisonnettes. As well as the skyline – still dealing out surprises as one turns an unfamiliar corner or glances over the roofs from the top of a bus in Bethnal Green Road – there is a new variety at ground level. There is, for instance, the paved Market Square off Roman Road where, surrounded by new shops, new flats and a new pub (The Weaver's Arms), the stallholders from Roman Road itself now do a noisy trade. On one housing scheme there is the familiar carpet of railed-off turf between the tall blocks; on another, cobbled foregrounds; on a third, a small hillock, furnished with white fencing and topped by a sculptured mother and child who would barely disgrace the near-by Whitechapel Art Gallery.

The new shops deserve special notice, because they illustrate how Bethnal Green is becoming part of the wider society. Until a few years ago the place never had a Woolworths; now it has a brightly lit new one. The giant new supermarket, a few yards away, offers a range of foods previously unknown to most local housewives – Camembert, mortadello, chop suey, pâté de fois gras. The East End, though not so much Bethnal Green in particular, has always catered for the tastes of its immigrant minorities, but this is something different: it represents an extension of local horizons and of freedom of choice.

The insides of people's homes have changed as well. More households have a separate home of their own. This is partly

[3] L.C.C., *East End Housing*, p. 3.

The District and the Boys

because of the rebuilding programmes; also because the migration
of families to the new towns, housing estates and suburbs has
reduced the population of Bethnal Green – in June 1964, at
46,000, it was three-quarters what it had been fifteen years earlier.
According to successive Census figures the proportion of households sharing a house with others was 61 per cent in 1931, 39 per
cent in 1951, and 26 per cent in 1961.[4] The household fittings
are of a much higher standard: tiled bathrooms, stainless-steel
sink units, built-in cupboards are becoming common. In 1951
less than a quarter of the households had a bathroom, by 1961
nearly half.[5]

Nearly half or only half? The figures show the improvement
and also how far there is to go. Many local families are still without modern housing. Many homes still lack bathrooms, fitted
kitchens and the like. Among the sample of boys, just under
half were living in local authority flats. Most of their homes were
relatively well equipped, though not all were new and some had
no baths, including flats in the London County Council's first
slum clearance scheme – the Boundary Street Estate, built between
1895 and 1900 on the site of the notorious 'Jago' in western
Bethnal Green.[6] A fifth of the boys lived in 'buildings' – the
Victorian and Edwardian blocks where little two and three
roomed flats, nearly always without baths and sometimes without
W.C.'s, were crammed around stone staircases. And as many as
a third were living in the nineteenth-century terraced houses that
remained, most of them poorly equipped and many shared by two
families.

Bryan Wills, aged 15, lived with his parents and younger sister
in a three-bedroomed flat in a new Council block.

To reach the flat means travelling up six storeys in the
aluminium lift that stops at alternate floors – at the other end
of the tiled entrance hall is the lift for floors three, five and
seven. (As a result, Bryan's family does not know the people
immediately above or below.) A ring at the illuminated bell-
push labelled 'Mr. and Mrs. J. B. Wills' and into the thickly
carpeted hall. The kitchen had an electric cooker with eye-

[4] *Census, 1931, 1951, 1961,* London.   [5] Ibid.
[6] For a description of life for adolescent boys in nineteenth-century Bethnal Green,
see Morrison, A., *A Child of the Jago.*

10

level grill, a white enamelled sink unit, a tall refrigerator, a red formica-topped table and four stools upholstered in red and black plastic. The interview took place in the living-room, which had a wide view over the chimney-pots and the tiny workshops in the foreground to more tall blocks and beyond to the River Thames. The room was large and dustless, with an enamel and chrome electric heater filling the fireplace. Loose covers in a broad autumn-leaf print were smoothed carefully over the chairs and sofa, and various ornaments – a miniature ship's wheel enclosing a thermometer, a cruet set labelled 'A Present from Herne Bay', a felt scotch terrier dressed in a tartan kilt – were arranged in a straight line along the mantelpiece. A framed studio photograph of Bryan, taken about three years earlier, stood beneath a table lamp on the television set.

Other homes were more like that of Stephen Archer, aged 17, who lived with his parents in an old block of 'charitable dwellings'. The Archers had two rooms, plus a tiny kitchen–scullery and a W.C.; no bathroom. Stephen slept in the living-room and, as his father was in there watching television, the interview was in the parents' bedroom. Drawn across the window were dull red curtains that had, in places, become detached from their runners. A single unshaded 60-watt bulb provided the only light.

We also went into homes reminiscent of the slums of an earlier era: places where beds and cots were congested together, where there was newspaper on the table, dirty cups and plates, broken furniture and a pervasive smell of urine. But these were now rare. The equipment and furniture in most of the older houses and flats belied their physical condition. The home of Robert Young was one example. It was a two-storey terraced cottage, eighty years old; the Youngs lived on the ground floor and the back room on the half landing, the other two rooms being tenanted by Mrs. Young's uncle and aunt, who 'lived separately' (in other words, they did their own cooking on a gas-stove on the top landing, where they also had a sink). There was an outside W.C. shared by both households. Inside the ground-floor kitchen, Mr. Young had fitted a new sink unit and an Ascot water heater, and there was also a small refrigerator and a washing-machine. The front living-room had a bright mottled carpet – grey with irregular shapes of black, yellow and red. The window was covered in nylon net and impeccably draped with green silk curtains. There were cleanly painted hardboard panels and chromium handles on the door. Inside this sparkling room, it was easy to forget that the house was due for slum clearance, until one noted that the bamboo wallpaper was peeling away at the bottom corners of the damp walls and showed signs of damp staining up to the height of nearly three feet.

Although we saw evidence of poverty in Bethnal Green – and would doubtless have seen more had we been interviewing old people, for example, or widows – the general impression from most homes was of relative prosperity. Bethnal Green has clearly shared in the 'affluence' that has spread among the working classes of Britain in the last decades. In consumption standards, if not in other ways, the lives of local residents are now much more like those of people in other classes and other districts than they ever were in the past.

In many ways, of course, the old Bethnal Green survives. Mothers and their married daughters go shopping together down Bethnal Green Road on Friday afternoon; the old choruses are sung in the pubs on Saturday night; the open-air markets flourish on Sunday morning. People shout cheerful greetings across the street to friends and relatives. There are large family parties and rowdy street-corner quarrels. In some parts the housing is still jumbled up with tailoring factories or furniture workshops. There is also no doubt about the changes. Not only has there been a long-term improvement compared with the old East End; the process of reshaping the district is still going on.

Effects on the boys

The young people of the district are clearly affected by all this. The boys we interviewed, born between 1940 and 1950,[7] were members of the first generation of Bethnal Greeners to grow up without malnutrition and poverty. Some of them were aware of the change. A 17-year-old tailor's presser said:

'You can have a lot more things than they would, the previous generation, televisions and things like that. And a working

[7] This is including those interviewed in the earlier stages of the research as well as the main sample.

man can own a motor-car and go out at week-ends. There wouldn't be any worry about work, because there's plenty of work now, and there wasn't none then, was there? What some people call the good old days were really the bad old days.'

Some could draw upon their own memories to illustrate the change. A 20-year-old plumber's mate remarked:

'Maybe it's just that my own personal family has got on, but I don't think so. People don't seem to be as poor as before. It used to be quite a common thing for children to wear second-hand things. I think I had one new suit, which was something to be proud of, but usually I wore second-hand clothing from Brick Lane. I was about nine then. After that things changed. I don't quite know how; my father didn't change his job or anything like that. Things just seemed to get much better. We started to buy new things.'

A 15-year-old schoolboy was one of those whose family had been rehoused under 'slum clearance'.

'Where we used to live it was real rough, just three rooms upstairs and we shared the toilet and there wasn't any bathroom. When we moved into these flats three years ago it made a big difference. I got a room of my own, for one thing. And Mum having a modern kitchen and there being a modern bathroom and toilet – it was all much better.'

In all sorts of ways, the boys' experiences tell the same story. Compared with earlier adolescent generations in Bethnal Green they enjoy higher standards of life, their horizons are wider.

The boys are certainly wealthier than their fathers were at a comparable age. Abrams states that in the country as a whole '. . . since the 1930's the real earnings of teenagers have risen much faster than those of adults . . .'[8] and most of the boys in our sample who were at work were relatively well-off. All but a handful earned, after income tax and other deductions, £5 a week or more, and a third earned £10 or over. The older boys, of course, usually earned more, as Table I shows.

Among the 17 and 18 year olds nearly all took home £5 or

[8] Abrams, M., *Teenage Consumer Spending in 1959*, Part II, p. 4.

TABLE I

Age and net weekly earnings
(Boys in full-time work)*

	15/16	17/18	19/20
Less than £5 a week	18%	3%	—
£5 or more, but less than £10 a week	80%	70%	21%
£10 or more but less than £15 a week	2%	20%	58%
£15 a week or more	—	7%	21%
Total %	100%	100%	100%
Number	56	70	48

* Excluding three boys whose earnings were not recorded. Boys are similarly excluded from some later tables because the information about them was incomplete.

over, and at 19 and 20 three-quarters got £10 or more. Some of the apprentices earned less than others of the same age; an electrical apprentice of 17 received £4 10s. a week, and an apprentice silversmith of 19, £7 10s. Those who earned more naturally gave their mothers more for their 'keep', but they usually kept the lion's share. Of those who earned under £5, nearly all gave their mother less than £2; of those earning £10 or more, three-quarters gave her under £4. Characteristically a boy aged about 16 would get £6 or £7 of which he would give his mother £2, leaving £4 or £5 for himself, while a 20 year old earning £12 would give his mother £3 or £4, leaving himself £8 or £9.

Among those still at school half aged 14, 15 and 16 got 10s. or over weekly pocket money and, of the six aged 17 or 18, all but one got £1 or more. A third of the schoolboys – particularly among those with less than 10s. weekly pocket money – supplemented their income by working part-time on a newspaper round or in a local workshop, all earning at least 10s. a week and most £1 or more. Thus most boys, and some even of those at school, had fairly large sums to spend on themselves.

This is reflected in the local shops. Alongside the supermarkets, the furniture showrooms and electrical suppliers, are the record shops, with their displays of brightly-coloured LP sleeves and the current 'Top Twenty' lists, and the men's-wear stores, their windows full of the latest in shirts, suits and slacks. The clothing shops, in particular, show an awareness of their teenage customers. Some of the displays emphasize modernity – 'Hippy Hippy Hipsters' on a pair of blue slacks, 'Latest Fly Front' on a shirt. Others stress the international inspiration – 'Wrangler Super Denim . . . Preferred by Champion Cowboys' on a display of jeans; 'Pigalle . . . from France' on a pale grey cardigan; 'Lugano's latest styles from Italy' in a shoe store.

The Bethnal Green boys, most of them, were manifestly contemporary 'teenage consumers'. In music, in television programmes and films, their tastes were close to those of their counterparts elsewhere in Britain. In clothes, shoes and hairstyles they looked almost indistinguishable from boys of similar ages in Plymouth or Wolverhampton, Newcastle or Glasgow, except that the East Enders, being at the heart of the clothing trade, are probably somewhat smarter, trend-setters rather than followers.

Attachments to East London

I remarked earlier that the East End, for all its changes, is still recognizably itself. In the same way most of the boys, despite their affinity with young people elsewhere, were unmistakably East Enders. Though their speech owed something to Hollywood and Leicester Square, its rhythms and diction were usually distinctively Cockney. Nearly all were local boys. Four out of every five had been born in the East End. In terms of Bethnal Green itself, 85 per cent had either been born there or had lived there for ten years or more. 'I've lived here all my life,' said a 16 year old, 'I know my way around here. It's the same with nearly all my mates.'

It does not necessarily follow, however, that they spent much time locally. It is commonly assumed that today's adolescents are less tied to their locality than earlier generations, that modern communications – in particular, motor bikes, scooters and cars – enable them to range far outside their own neighbourhood.

Of the boys in the sample aged 16 or over (those legally eligible to ride a motor bike or scooter), one in ten had a scooter, mostly 16 and 17 year olds, and one in twenty a motor bike, mostly 17 and 18 year olds. One in ten of the boys of 16 or over had a car; these were predominantly older – of those aged 19 or 20, as many as a quarter had one. This means that altogether a quarter of those aged 16 or more had some form of motorized transport of their own, and frequent buses and the Underground offered the others easy access to Central London and other parts of the metropolis. How much did they take advantage of their potential mobility?

There was evidence that some boys travelled quite far afield. One, aged 18, was setting off on a Continental hitch-hiking holiday with a friend the day after we interviewed him. Another had just come back from a holiday in Spain. Then there were those who went by scooter, motor bike, car or train 'to the Coast' – Southend, Margate, Brighton, Hastings or Clacton – at Bank Holidays. Among the motor cyclists, some told us of evening rides in groups along the arterial road towards Southend, to London Airport via the Hammersmith flyover, or out to cafés on the M1 or the A20. There were scooter boys who regularly drove to Epping Forest together. Other boys went fishing in the Lea Valley or at Walton-on-Thames, others camping at Thorpe Bay or Burnham-on-Crouch, climbing in Snowdonia or the Lake District, or – closer to home – dancing at the Tottenham 'Royal' or the West End jazz clubs.

For all the individual mobility, most boys spent much of their time locally. Only one or two attended a school more than about a mile from home. Of those in a job, three-quarters worked within two or three miles – about a quarter in Bethnal Green itself, a quarter elsewhere in the East End, and a quarter in the near-by City of London. The local setting was almost as important outside working hours, at least during the week. The boys were asked where they usually spent their time at evenings and week-ends, and given three possible answers to choose from: 'In and around Bethnal Green', 'Right outside it', and 'About half and half'. Nearly three-quarters said they spent most of their evenings locally and over a third spent most of their week-ends there – this even in midsummer, when the interviewing was done. About one in seven usually went 'right outside' the district in the evenings and a third at week-ends. The diaries suggested that boys who said they were 'right outside Bethnal Green' at week-ends mainly went to the coast or countryside in Essex or Kent, camping, caravanning or fishing, often with their family or with relatives. This seemed particularly true of the younger boys.

In general, whether the boys stayed locally or not was affected by their age; this is shown in Table II.[9]

TABLE II

Age and leisure time in Bethnal Green

Proportion in each age group 'usually in or around' Bethnal Green:	14/15	16–18	19/20
Evenings	87%	71%	54%
Week-ends	53%	33%	24%
Total number	68	128	50

The table indicates that the boys become less tied to their locality as they get older, although even at 19 and 20 as many as half said they usually spent the evenings there.

Where the boys work also matters: those who work locally are more likely to spend their leisure time there too. Of the boys who worked in Bethnal Green, 37 per cent were mostly 'in and around it' at week-ends; for those working elsewhere in the East End or in the City the proportion was 32 per cent; and for those working farther afield 18 per cent. But there was no marked difference, age for age, between those who had cars, motor bikes or scooters and those who relied on public transport.

The boys were also asked in particular when they had last been to the West End. There seemed to be similar variations. Of those aged 14 and 15, a fifth had been during the previous week, compared with a third of those aged 19 or 20. Those who worked in or near the West End had obviously been there more recently; and since boys with non-manual jobs more often worked in Central London, this meant that white-collar workers spent more time in the West End than those with more 'working-class' occupations.

[9] The age-groups in Table II – 14 and 15; 16 to 18; 19 and 20 – are also used in most of the subsequent analyses by age. Our initial analysis suggested that this was usually the most meaningful distinction: most of the 14 and 15 year olds were still at school, and those who were not had only just left; the 19 and 20 year olds were mostly mature young men; and in many respects the 16, 17 and 18 year olds proved to have more in common with each other than their juniors or seniors. In some analyses other age distinctions are used for reasons that are either obvious or stated.

Attitudes to the West End differed as well. There were those
who felt at home there or were gradually finding their way.

'I'm often up West, either after work or at the week-ends.
I like it up there – the pubs and cafés are more lively and you
get more of a mixture of people. My mates and I often have
a meal in a Chinese restaurant in Soho.' (17, *clerk.*)

'Up the West End, it's really an exploration. We watch all
the posh people coming out of their clubs, the way they dress
up makes you giggle. And you see a bloke running after a
cab for one of these posh people, then the posh bloke gets
into the cab as if the other one didn't exist. You learn a lot
just watching.' (16, *grammar schoolboy.*)

To some the West End was as remote as the Antipodes:

'I've never, ever been to the West End. My hobbies are
photography and weight-lighting; you can get all that at
the Club.' (16, *apprentice toolmaker.*)

'I never go to the West End. I reckon the West End is over-
rated. You get up there and you find no one so much as looks
at you. You're dirt, they don't want to know. You're better
off where you belong.' (15, *secondary modern schoolboy.*)

Attitudes to the local community itself differed as well. Many
clearly felt a sense of loyalty and affection towards it.

'Some people, when they find out you live in the East End,
say, "Oh well, you can't help where you live." But I'm
proud of it. There is a great thing attached to being an East
Ender, a great pride in it.' (19, *fitter's mate.*)

'I like Bethnal Green – it's my home town. I know the place
and I know the people. I'd like to go on living here. I've got
all my mates round here. I've got my job here – it's a good
job too.' (17, *upholsterer.*)

These sentiments are similar to those expressed by older residents of the district. A minority of boys made it clear that they
did not share them; they felt no love for Bethnal Green – they
wanted to leave as soon as they could.

'There's not much green in Bethnal Green,' said an 18-year-

old draughtsman. 'You can't see far - all the houses wall
you in. I've always had the urge to break out and stand on
my own two feet. You can't think for yourself here.'

And a 17-year-old shop assistant, working in Oxford Street:

'I want to get as far away as possible from Bethnal Green.
There's no social life in Bethnal Green, no appreciation of
the arts - whenever they put up a statue it's defaced. People
laugh at a statue; they think they won't be able to understand
it, they're afraid of widening their outlook. I'm ambitious.
I suppose you'd call me a social climber. You might think
that's immoral but I do want to get away. Bethnal Green is
untidy, a pigsty.'

We did not ask systematically about attitudes to the district,
but it seemed as if critical views were often expressed by a particular sort of boy. He worked outside the East End in a non-
manual job or, if still a schoolboy, was at grammar school. He
spent more of his leisure time outside the district than in it. His
attitudes and his behaviour were of a piece.

Variations among the boys

One question posed in the introductory chapter was if it would
be possible to distinguish different patterns of response among the
boys. The material on their relationships to the local community
suggests just such a distinction – between those who are broadly
sympathetic to its way of life and its standards, and those who
are more critical of the East End, more 'aspiring'. This distinction
emerges again in later chapters. So too does another, concerned
with attitudes and behaviour not so much towards the local
community as towards the wider society: some boys are, for
example, more anti-school, anti-employers, anti-police than others.
Meanwhile, some impressions of three boys, from those interviewed in the summer of 1964, may help to illustrate the variety.

Kevin James had gone to a secondary modern school and at
17 was working in a manual job. 'School wasn't all that bad,'
he said, 'but I packed it in as soon as I could.' He now works
for a firm of heating and ventilating engineers, as an 'apprentice fitter welder', earning £9 a week; 'I got the job through

my uncle. I like the work – it's quite interesting.' When interviewed he was getting ready to go out 'with some of my mates'; 'we sometimes go down the club or up Victoria Park. Have a bit of a giggle on our scooters, pick up a bird or two if we can.' He has few complaints about his lot: 'I'm out for a gay time, until I get hooked. And I do enjoy life. Get a bit bored sometimes, I suppose, but no real gripes.' He spends his money on his scooter, records and clothes – 'I choose my gear carefully; I like to get the best.' After the interview he waved as he rode off on his scooter, wearing sunglasses.

When interviewed, Arthur Dukes, aged 18, was wearing his grammar-school blazer, white shirt, school tie, grey flannel trousers, black shoes. He likes school, is a prefect there, and is pleased with his progress: 'I can't complain at all: ten "O" levels is no mean achievement.' He is now preparing to take four 'A' levels. His father is a local shopkeeper, but Arthur hopes to go to a university and then to 'some sort of work in science, obviously – I'd like to end up on the business side of a scientific or technical firm.' He says he thinks it important to 'look to the future' – 'If you're just going to live for the moment,' he said severely, 'you can't expect to do well later on.' That is his criticism of most Bethnal Green teenagers – 'Most of them lack intelligence, personality and ambition.'

Jimmy Grove, aged 16, had been to a secondary modern school. 'I hated school,' he said; 'Most teachers stink – they don't really care about you. I didn't learn much at school, and I was always getting the stick – usually for fighting. Anyway it was a crap school I went to. You're supposed to be brainy and go to one of those G.C.E. schools if you get your scholarship when you're 11. I didn't take the scholarship – what do you know about it when you're 11?' He has had five different jobs in the year since he left school, and is at present a labourer in a veneer warehouse, where he earns £8 a week; 'It's just a job,' he says. 'As long as I earn the money, that's the main thing. I couldn't afford to be an apprentice, getting about £4 a week. When you're young, that's the best time of your life, you ought to enjoy yourself.'

Enjoying himself, to Jimmy, mostly means 'going around with the boys'. 'Sometimes there's half a dozen of us, sometimes as many as forty – everybody turns out if there's a real punch-up with another mob. We lark around, go up to the youth club – sometimes we get chucked out. Sometimes we do a job, do a warehouse, nick a load of fags, that sort of thing.' He says: 'I'm very quick-tempered. If I see someone looking at me and I think they're sneering, I say, "Had your bleeding eyeful, mate?" or something like that. That's how fights start.' He does not think much about the future: 'I don't know what I'm going to do. I don't want to work for a living, I know that. And I don't intend to get married – I don't fancy sticking to one girl all the time. Not me, mate.'

This chapter, to conclude, has tried to suggest something of what the district is like and where its adolescent males fit in. As the boys themselves get older, their local community is also changing – improved housing, rising living standards, widening opportunities. All this is close to the common view of how working-class life is being transformed, and the boys, too, seem on the face of it like the popular stereotype of teenage 'affluence'. But behind the familiar exterior their lives are more complicated.

II

THE FRATERNITIES OF THE STREET

The most casual observation in Bethnal Green confirms that, as in other places where adolescence has been studied,[1] the boys are often in each other's company. They stand on street-corners in knots in the early evening, discussing the relative merits of West Ham United and Arsenal one minute, whistling after a pair of girls the next. Younger boys scuffle and race about in the yards of the red-brick blocks of buildings or sit talking on the low walls outside. Older boys speed along Bethnal Green Road three abreast on scooters, or tear through Victoria Park together on motor bikes, wearing silver crash helmets and black leather jackets. An assembly of youths fills a local café, drinking Coca-Cola and playing at the pin-tables to the reverberating music of a giant juke-box. A dozen shout obscenities and push at each other as they leave the youth club at eleven o'clock at night.

These groupings clearly play an important part in adolescence; the purpose of this chapter is to examine them. One question in particular is how far they correspond to the 'gangs' sometimes described.[2] Are they, for instance, large and highly organized, with a clear structure of leadership and authority?

Groups and friends

We asked the boys who they were with 'most' in their 'spare time'. Many said they were in a 'group' – defined as being with

[1] See Thrasher, F. M., *The Gang*; Whyte, W. F., *Street Corner Society*; Hollingshead, A. B., *Elmtown's Youth*; Coleman, J. S., *The Adolescent Society*; Mays, J. B., *Growing Up in the City*; Allcorn, D. H., *The Social Development of Young Men in an English Industrial Suburb*. Also, for a study of pre-adolescent groups in England and Australia, Crane, A. R., 'The Development of Moral Values in Children – Pre-Adolescent Gangs and the Moral Development of Children', in Grinder, R. E., *Studies in Adolescence*, pp. 319–29.

[2] See Fyvel, T. R., *The Insecure Offenders*, pp. 17–18, p. 73, pp. 85–89; Spinley, B.M., *The Deprived and the Privileged*, p. 68.

22

two or more others.[3] Those who gave other answers were asked whether they were sometimes in a group, and the proportions at different ages who said they were are also shown in Table III.

TABLE III

*Age and group membership**

	14/15	*16–18*	*19/20*
Mostly with a group in 'spare time'	57%	44%	32%
Sometimes with a group in 'spare time'	28%	38%	42%
Never with a group in 'spare time'	15%	18%	26%
Total %	100%	100%	100%
Number	68	128	50

* Being 'in a group' was defined as being with two or more others.

Among the younger boys, over half were usually with a group and most of the rest sometimes were. As the boys mature, groups become less dominant. Even among the older boys, however, they are still of some importance; at 19 and 20 a total of three-quarters were with a group at least some of the time.

The boys were also asked if they had a male 'best friend'. About two-thirds said they had. Some of these friends, obviously, were members of the same group. In the sample as a whole, half the boys were sometimes with a group and had a 'best friend'. A third were sometimes with a group but had no 'best friend'. ('They're all my best friends,' said a 14 year old who was usually with four others.) Just over one in ten had a 'best friend' but did not go out with a group – it could be said that these boys belonged to a 'group' of two. The rest – those who had neither a 'best friend' nor a group – amounted to only about one in twenty; the minority was somewhat larger among older boys than younger.

Among those who did belong to a group, some spent the bulk of their free time in the company of their fellows, others changed

[3] Technically, this could have meant any 'group' of people, including their family. (The questions are shown in the interview schedule, in Appendix 2.) It might well have been better if we had been more specific, saying 'a group of people of about your own age' or something like that. In practice, however, the answers to subsequent questions about the groups made it quite clear that this was exactly how the word had been interpreted by the boys.

about more. The younger boys were more often with the same people. A 14 year old, for example, had been with the same three friends every evening in the previous week. They were in a local café together at least part of the time on five evenings and at other times they 'played cricket or larked about'; on one of the other evenings they had been to a cinema in a group and on Saturday night they had 'played records and talked' at one boy's home. A 17 year old spent his evenings during the previous week with the following people:

SUNDAY	Best friend, Fred (also aged 17).
MONDAY	Group of five boys, including Fred.
TUESDAY	Fred and one other boy; the three of them 'picked up' two girls.
WEDNESDAY	Group of five boys (as Monday).
THURSDAY	Stayed in.
FRIDAY	To cinema with Fred; later with same group.
SATURDAY	To a mixed party; Fred and other boys in group all present.

One 19 year old said he belonged to a group of six boys, with whom he had been out one evening in the previous week. One of the other evenings was spent at home, another at football practice (he played for a small local club) and four with his girl-friend.

The structure of the group

Some sort of all-male group had usually been formed when the boys were much younger. A 19-year-old carpenter recounted the history of his group:

'There was a group of four or five of us who always used to go about together. One of them I'd known since before I went to school. We knew each other's mothers very well – I called his mum "Auntie" and he called my mum "Auntie", sort of thing. We used to play together when we were little kids. Then we went to school together and we met other kids at school. It was always just boys – when we were about seven we used to play rounders with the girls in the street, but that's all. There was never any leaders – we decided things together. We used to play football together in the street and go over the park. Then we started going to the pictures together or swimming or playing football with other kids, that sort of thing. When we got to about 12 or 13 we used to lark about – we used to thieve a bit, now and again, but nothing serious. We went out together most nights and we all went to the same youth club when we were about 15. At about 16 or 17 we was all mad on motor bikes. We used to argue about which bike was best – one of the fellows had a Triumph and I had an AJS, and we used to argue about which was the best. But all that's in the past now. They still mostly live around here I see them around, but it's very seldom now I go out with the boys.'

Most other groups, too, were small. More than a third had four or five members, and the great majority six or less.[4] The sizes of the groups were much the same for older boys as younger.

Most boys who talked more fully about their group seemed to have no difficulty in distinguishing its members. They talked about 'our little group', 'me and my three mates', 'the five of us who usually go about together', and so on. The numbers in a particular group did sometimes vary. A 15 year old said, 'There's usually four of us but it sometimes goes up to about fifteen'; and an 18 year old, 'Normally five in the group but it varies from two to twenty or thirty.' Most groups were more stable in their membership: 80 per cent of the boys said that their group was 'more or less always the same crowd of people', 13 per cent said it varied 'a little', only 7 per cent that it varied 'a lot'.

The members of a group were usually about the same age as each other. This was confirmed for those groups about which we collected details in the diaries and longer interviews. Brian Wills, who was just about to leave school and start a job when interviewed, wrote in his diary:

'I went round to one of my mates. There are five of us who

---

[4] These findings agree with those of other studies. Allcorn, D. H., reported that in an industrial suburb in West London the groups consisted 'usually of four or five young men' (op. cit., p. 215) and Downes, D. M., said of adolescent groups in Stepney and Poplar, 'Average group size was four to five . . .' (*The Delinquent Solution*, p. 199). Similarly, the American study of 'Elmtown' found, 'A typical clique is composed of . . . five boys . . .' (Hollingshead, A. B., *Elmtown's Youth*, p. 241).

go about together – Terry and Fred are 16, Stephen, George and myself are 15.'

Jimmy Grove, mentioned in the previous chapter, and his friend Alan talked in a joint interview about the age of their fellow members:

JIMMY   They're all about the same age as what we are. We all more or less went to the same schools – we knew each other then and we've kept together since.

ALAN   Yeah. I don't think there's anyone over 17, is there? They're mostly 16 or 17.

The boys' friends were mostly recruited locally. Of the 156 boys with a particular 'mate', two-thirds said he was someone they had grown up with or had first met at school or as a neighbour. As many as two-thirds of the friends, again, lived within five minutes walk and altogether three-quarters lived inside Bethnal Green. We did not collect systematic information about where friends other than 'best friends' lived, but in the groups we did examine most of the members lived fairly close.

'One of my mates lives a bit nearer than the others, but none of us live too far from each other – we're all within a few minutes of each other.' (16 year old.)

'They all more or less live in the same buildings. One lives round the corner in Cyprus Street but that's all. We all used to go to the same school and we all lived in the same buildings, so we were all mates and that's how we came together.' (18 year old.)

There were exceptions. A grammar schoolboy, aged 18, whose school was in Hackney, belonged to a group of friends some of whom lived in Hackney, others in Bethnal Green. A solicitor's clerk in the City had a 'best friend' at Ilford. But there were no marked general differences, according to either the type of school or the kind of job boys had, in where their friends lived. In other words, as many of the grammar schoolboys as boys at other sorts of school, and as many white-collar workers as those in skilled or unskilled manual jobs, had their 'best friends' living within five minutes walk or elsewhere in Bethnal Green.

Groups or gangs?

We asked if the groups had leaders. Of the boys in groups, over nine-tenths said there was none, 5 per cent said there was one and 1 per cent said two or more.[5] 'No leaders or anything like that,' said a 20 year old whose group was of nine boys, 'That's a load of rot, I reckon.' 'We haven't got a leader,' said a 15 year old with a grin, 'everybody shouts at each other.' Another said, more seriously:

'We all discuss what we want to do and then decide between ourselves. Say on a Friday we decide what we'll do on the Saturday, and so on. If we don't all agree, we just take the majority vote. I mean if three of us say we want to go somewhere and one says he doesn't, well then we'll go and that one just has to decide to come or stay behind.'

Some, as well as denying that their group had leaders, spontaneously said that it was not a gang. A 15 year old belonging to a group of six said: 'There are no real leaders. We're just mates, just a group of boys, not a gang.'

One should not of course necessarily take at their face value the boys' answers to this question. Leadership can be effective although informal. But all the evidence we could collect, including more detailed questioning about some groups, suggested that the general drift of the answers in the main survey was not far off the mark. We did, in the more intensive interviewing, come across one local group which had a recognized 'leader'; this was Jimmy Grove, quoted earlier. Even he protested, 'But it's not like with those American gangsters' mobs.' Jimmy's group was anyway exceptional; it was larger than most – with a membership of nearly twenty – and was the closest thing to a 'gang' or 'mob' that we met in Bethnal Green. In almost all groups, no doubt, some boys have more influence than their fellows, but few have a recognized leader or formal structure of authority. The East End boys' groups are for the most part true 'peer groups': their members are roughly equal in status. In this respect – as in their

---

[5] Cf. Allcorn, D. H., op. cit. 'According to the young men themselves, the peer groups had no recognized leadership and actually opposed individuals who tried to act as leaders' (p. 238) and 'in those peer groups which I studied at first-hand, I was not able to pick out individuals who consistently took the lead . . .' (p. 242).

relative casualness and informality – they are not like the stereo-
typed picture of 'gangs'. Downes came to a similar conclusion,
both from his review of English research on youth and from his
own observation in neighbouring Stepney and Poplar.[6]

What they do

The fact that the boys' groups do not match the model of how
gangs are thought to be organized does not necessarily mean that
they never engage in collective law-breaking. Crime and delinquency are examined later in the book; the point for this chapter
is that, though there plainly is some adolescent law-breaking in
Bethnal Green and though most of it, as elsewhere, is in the
company of others, it does not loom large in the activities of most
groups. This was apparent from the diaries and tape-recorded
interviews; it was the impression of our observation locally; and
it seemed borne out by what the boys themselves reported.

We asked those who were group members what they 'mostly'
did when they were together. The question was an 'open' one,

TABLE IV

Age and 'main' activity of group
(members of groups only)

	14/5	*16–18*	*19/20*
Entertainment and pastimes (cinema, dancing, pubs, jazz clubs)	17%	31%	51%
'Hanging about', 'larking around'	52%	23%	3%
Sport (participant)	17%	15%	22%
Youth club	10%	13%	5%
Motor scooter or motor bike (riding, repairing, discussing)	2%	12%	3%
Other activity	2%	6%	16%
Total %	100%	100%	100%
Number	58	105	37

[6] The relevant part of his review of 'the English experience' is headed the 'non-existent gang' (Downes, D. M., op. cit., pp. 116–23). About groups in Stepney and Poplar, he wrote: 'While these street-corner groups persisted over time, and invari-ably possessed a dominant personality, all the other features commonly attributed to the delinquent 'gangs' were absent, i.e. leadership, role allocation, hierarchical structure, consensus on membership, uniform and name' (ibid., p. 199).

with no set choices offered, but it proved possible to distinguish various principal types of activity, which are analysed by age in Table IV.

Among the broad categories of activity, two types stand out particularly. Nearly a third of the boys, when in the company of their fellows, were 'mainly' enjoying some 'entertainment or pastime'. A similar proportion were more casually occupied, doing what we have classified as 'hanging about' or 'larking around' and what they described in the following terms:

'We stand at the gate and talk, have a lark about.'

'We muck about among ourselves wherever we happen to be.'

'We hang about the block of flats, walk about Bethnal Green, have a laugh.'

'Just walk around and that. We have a giggle together.'

As Table IV shows, these two types of activity – 'entertainment' and 'hanging about' – varied greatly in popularity according to the boys' ages. 'Entertainment' rose from 17 per cent at 14 and 15 (when it was mostly 'go to the pictures') to 51 per cent at 19 and 20. 'Hanging about' fell from 52 per cent at 14 and 15 to 3 per cent at 19 and 20.

The other striking variation with age is over motor bikes and motor scooters, which were the focus of attention for more than one in ten of the 16 to 18 year olds, but for hardly any of those younger or older. 'We work on our scooters or talk about scooters,' said a 16 year old who usually went about with three others. 'We go on the motor bikes out to Johnson's Café on the A20,' said a boy of 18 whose group numbered five. It is around these ages that boys most often own motor bikes or scooters; those younger are not old enough to have them and those older have usually lost interest. Although a fifth of the 19 and 20 year olds had cars, only one of them mentioned a collective interest in these as an 'activity' of his group.

What of the other things the boys did together? Youth clubs and their significance for peer groups are discussed separately in a later chapter, so it is enough merely to report here that the clubs play an important part, particularly, as Table IV suggests, for those in mid-adolescence. The variation with age in what we have categorized as 'other activities' is mainly a reflection of the fact that the boys' interests and patterns of behaviour become more varied, more diverse as they get older: 'activities' mentioned include 'play cards', 'play billiards', 'go to watch stock-car racing' and 'bible study'.

This leaves sport, whose relative popularity does not materially vary with age. Only 'participant' sports were counted under this heading; the boys' answers showed that 'spectator' sports took up much less of their time. The 'sports' mentioned included fishing, camping, swimming, ten-pin bowling and weight-lifting, as well as the more obvious favourites – football and cricket. Some of the play was fairly casual: 'We kick a football about in the yard of the flats' or 'We go to the park and knock about with a cricket bat'. But many boys took their game more seriously, particularly football; for instance, a 15 year old explained that he and his friends had formed, with two or three other local groups, a football team of their own. Others said that they and their friends had done the same. They arranged games with rival teams, finding their potential opponents from advertisements in football magazines or more often by word of mouth. These games, though serious enough, were often makeshift affairs in Victoria Park, piles of clothes serving as goalposts and the touchlines notional; but some teams went to Hackney Marshes and rented a proper football pitch and changing-room. The organizing was done by the boys themselves; it was unconnected with school, work or youth clubs (though, of course, there were local adult-sponsored teams as well).

Wider circles

This chapter has so far confirmed that informal peer groups play a central part in adolescence, and has shown something of how they are organized and what they do. In addition to the small group of peers, as the example of football shows, the boys spend much of their time in the company of other young people.

Age-segregation is strong among those at school, where in general boys do not mix with others in a different form or year. It is less in evidence at work; the age-range of workmates is usually wide, though even so boys of similar age associate more with each other at work, if they can, than with older or younger colleagues. In leisure activities there is some age-segregation. In youth clubs the boys constantly mix with age-mates; and this applies, to some extent at least, to cafés, pubs and dance halls. This can be shown from an examination of the role of cafés, pubs and dancing. The proportion who had visited cafés or pubs during the previous week are shown in Table V.

TABLE V

Age, cafés and pubs

Proportion in each age-group visiting:	14/15	16–18	19/20
Café at least once during previous week	31%	28%	14%
Pub at least once during previous week	16%	42%	70%
Total number	68	128	50

Once again, age is the key: younger boys go to cafés more often, older boys to pubs. Although young people are allowed into pubs once they are 14, they are prohibited from buying or drinking 'intoxicating liquor' until they are 18; it is therefore not surprising that pubs are frequented more by older boys. What is perhaps unexpected is that some even of the 14 and 15 year olds and nearly half the 16 to 18 year olds had been to pubs during the previous week – they presumably looked mature for their age and were therefore unlikely to be challenged by the publican.

Both cafés and pubs can act as social centres for groups of boys. One 14 year old wrote in his diary that, after having been out on his bicycle with his 'best friend': 'At 9 p.m. we arrived back in Bethnal Green and dropped in at Bob's, a little café in Bethnal Green Road. In there we met our other mates Fred and Stuart, who had just been to the pictures.' He went to the same café on four other days in the week, going either with the three others or, more often, alone or with one friend and meeting the others there. We visited the same café ourselves and noted that it was popular with boys of about 14 or 15, especially in the evenings, and that, although they were in pairs or small groups, they also knew many of the other similar-aged customers. We saw the same thing in two or three other local cafés, although of course there are cafés

31

to which boys regularly go and which have a much wider age-range among their customers.

Some pubs, too, attract a wide age-range; others have a predominance of adolescents. A 15 year old wrote in his diary:

> 'I went with my mate Barry to take his dog out for a walk. We walked around and then went in the pub, the City of Paris, for a drink. Barry had mild and I had brown ales. Barry's dog went to the toilet up the curtain, but fortunately nobody noticed. After two drinks, we went home at 10 p.m.'

A 19 year old wrote:

> 'At 8 p.m. I went round to my mate Frank and we went into a pub called the Crown. We met up with another mate there and stayed drinking and playing darts till closing time. Then we walked home.'

But as well as the City of Paris and the Crown (the names, by the way, are pseudonyms), there were some pubs that set out to cater especially for the young. They put on a talent contest, an electric-organ trio or, most often, a guitar group. On Friday, Saturday and Sunday nights in particular, such pubs would be crammed with young people; in a hot atmosphere mingling smells of beer and scent, the boys and girls stand in pairs or groups – a couple of heavily made-up young girls, an ebullient smart-suited band of boys, a grinning, confident mixed-sex circle – shouting to make themselves heard or gyrating to music so loud that it makes the floorboards shake. A 17 year old said of one such pub:

> 'We usually go to the Prince of Wales on a Saturday night. They get good groups there and you get a real good atmosphere. We sometimes go with some of the girls from the club, sometimes just a group of the lads go and we try to pick up a couple of birds.'

There was apparently a similar concentration of young people in most of the jazz clubs to which the boys went, even those in the West End. And the same applied to most of the places where they went dancing. The younger boys danced mainly in youth clubs, the older in commercial clubs or dance halls like the Lyceum in the Strand, the Royal at Tottenham, or Barrie's at Hackney. Though in the larger dance halls, the other dancers often included

The Fraternities of the Street

older people, the young once more predominated. In the sample
of boys themselves, those of 16, 17 and 18 went dancing more
often than the others (Table VI).

TABLE VI
Age and dancing

Proportion who had been dancing during during the previous week:	14/15	16–18	19/20
Twice or more	9%	21%	6%
Once	10%	18%	22%
Not at all	81%	61%	72%
Total %	100%	100%	100%
Number	68	128	50

The boys usually went dancing with their group of closest
friends. Thirty-seven per cent of those who were group members
had been dancing during the week, compared with 9 per cent of
those who did not belong to a group. Again, they met and mixed
with other young people outside the immediate circle. A 17-year-
old apprentice fitter wrote in his diary:

'Tuesday: went to the dance hall with three of my mates. We
chatted to some other fellows who go up there, and we
danced with some girls we knew . . .'

The influence of peers

The peer group in particular and other young people more
generally are, in sociological terminology, important 'reference
groups' for the adolescent boy – he feels identified with them and
shares their attitudes and values.[7] There is sometimes conflict
between the standards of family and those of peers; a 14 year old
wrote in his diary:

'I came home from school and had my tea. My mum knocked
a flowerpot off the window ledge and asked me to sweep it up
for her. I took out the dust-pan and brush and started to clear

[7] See Sherif, M. and Sherif, C. W., *Reference Groups*, p. 164 and p. 180.

up, but then my mate Arthur came along and he said I was a cissy to help my mum, so I stopped. I went with Arthur over the flats where he lives and we met our other mates.'

As is shown later, the boys often share with each other attitudes to stealing and other forms of delinquency that their parents do not hold. They also follow each other, and adolescent fashions generally, in things like dress, hairstyles and tastes in music.

There is another way in which the peer group exerts an important influence. Within it the adolescent boy can enjoy a freedom and equality he cannot find at school, at work or inside his family. This sense of fraternity is often mentioned. 'You can be yourself with your mates,' boys said. They stressed the sense of liberation – 'I like going out with the boys. You can have a laugh'; 'We always have a giggle when we're together.' They sometimes recognized also how this mood could lead to the wildness and 'hooliganism' that are examined later.

'When you're by yourself you're quite tame,' a 16 year old commented. 'When you're with a mob, it's quite different.'

'When you're in a group, you get kind of excited,' said a 17 year old. 'You get carried away. You do things you wouldn't do on your own – smash things up, just for a laugh, or cheek some old man, or fight some other kids.'

Variations in social groupings

I have been talking in most of this chapter as if all the boys had either one male friend or a number, with whom they spent most of their free time. Some led more isolated lives outside work and home.

The explanation for such isolation may lie in temperament or individual psychology. 'I haven't got many friends,' said a 19 year old, who during the previous week had stayed in every evening except one, when he had been to the cinema alone; 'I don't know why, but I just don't like to mix.' 'I don't go out much,' said a 15 year old, 'I'm not much of a crowd type.' At another point he added sadly, 'I like good records like Frank Sinatra, not the sort of "pop" music other boys like. Perhaps that's why I haven't got many friends – I'm not with it.'

Others said they had no friends because they had only recently
moved into the district or because their friends had moved away:
'I live too far away from where I used to live,' said a 14 year old,
'I still travel to the same school every day and I see my friends
there, but in the evenings and at week-ends I'm usually on my
own. I don't really know anybody round here.' 'I did have a best
friend,' said a 19 year old, 'but I haven't seen him for two years
because he's moved out of the buildings. They've been rehoused.'

Boys as isolated as this are a small minority. But it is common for
boys to have less to do with male friends and male peer groups as
they get older. The explanation is not that the boys become less
sociable; it is rather that there is an important change in their
social habits. This is made clear in Table VII, which shows who
the boys were 'mostly with' in their 'spare time', according to their
ages.

TABLE VII

Age and main companions in 'spare time'

'Mostly' with :	14/15	16–18	19/20
A group	57%	44%	32%
One male friend	22%	27%	12%
Girl friend	5%	16%	46%
No one	16%	13%	10%
Total %	100%	100%	100%
Number	68	128	50

As the boys get older, girl friends become more important, at
the expense of male friends and groups. The switch was described
thus by an 18 year old:

'There's a group of about five of us. I go out with the boys
about once or twice a week. I used to go with them all the time
but now I go with a girl.'

The remark implies that the groups of friends to which the
boys belong are predominantly male; this was suggested earlier
and it is broadly true. But the groups are sometimes mixed, and
this too is something that changes, as Table VIII shows. The
proportion of all-male groups falls as the boys get older.

TABLE VIII
Age and the sex of group members
(*Members of groups only*)

	14/15	*16–18*	*19/20*
All boys	76%	70%	54%
Boys and girls	24%	30%	46%
Total %	100%	100%	100%
Number	58	105	37

The pull of male peers is still strong at 19 and 20: even at this age, half the boys who belong to groups belong to exclusively male ones. None the less the trend is obvious. As the boys mature, not only do less of them spend their time with groups at all; of those who do, a growing proportion go out with mixed groups. This is linked to what was reported earlier about the change in what the groups do when they are together – much of the dancing, drinking and cinema-going is clearly with the other sex.

This chapter has confirmed that the male peer group is a crucial social unit in the lives of the adolescent boys. There are variations – some belong to a large group, others a small, a minority have just one 'mate', and even less have none. But the characteristic pattern is to go about with one male friend or, more often, a small company of them. For most boys, though, this is only a phase.

III

GIRLS, SEX AND MARRIAGE

This chapter traces out the phases through which most boys pass in their relationships with girls. At first, feminine company hardly figures at all. This is the common pattern until 12 or 13, and sometimes persists until 15. A quarter of the boys aged 14 and 15 in our sample said they had 'little to do with girls'; most of them belonged to the male peer groups that formed the subject of the previous chapter. They 'played "he" together round the buildings', 'larked about', went to the cinema together, met and talked in the local café, played football in their street or in Victoria Park. Though such boys are of course aware of girls and most are certainly 'interested' in them, this is not expressed much in their day-to-day behaviour.

The first awkward advances are usually made from the safe ranks of the boys' group. Two diary extracts:

'In the evening the four of us went over Victoria Park looking for birds. We tried to pick up some girls who were sitting on a bench by the lake, but they wouldn't talk to us.' (14 year old.)

'7.30 p.m. Went to the Regal with three of my mates. We sat behind some birds and tried to start talking to them. They kept on giggling and telling us to shut up.
'10.30 p.m. When we came out we walked along with them and mucked about. We went to where they lived. We said we might see them at the Regal again next Friday night.' (15 year old.)

Of course, 'picking up' girls is not confined to the younger boys; it is a recognized method of approach right through adolescence. In describing what they did in the company of their 'mates', a number of boys mentioned this – 'We hang around and try to pick up a few girls' (16 year old); 'We drink and look out for a couple of girls' (18 year old). A 16 year old wrote in his diary:

'Sunday. 6 p.m.   Went and called for Arthur and Barry and we all went down to Trafalgar Square. We picked up some birds and took them into St. James's Park. Lovely grub!
'10.30 p.m.   Took the birds home and then came back home by tube . . .
'Tuesday. 7 p.m.   Went for a walk with Arthur and Barry, but there were no birds about because it was raining. So we came back to the flats and talked on the stairs until 10.'

And a 19 year old:

'Friday. 8 p.m.   Went round to my mate Steve and we went round to call for Pete, had a few drinks in the Green Man and went up the West End at 11 p.m. We went to the Flamingo. We got talking to three girls there, had a few dances with them and Steve went off with one of the girls. Pete and I took the other two girls for a cup of coffee in a place called the Contact, had a chat and then left at about 2.30 a.m. and got a taxi home.'

But 'picking up' – though it may continue – does not remain, for most boys, the main source of feminine contacts. Most of them, in one way and another, get to know girls and mix with them. As the previous chapter showed, there is, outside the group of close friends, a wider circle of acquaintances, and as boys get older this is likely to include girls as well. The circle is usually a local one, and its female members, at least up to 16 or so, often local girls the boys have met at school or as neighbours. A 15-year-old grammar schoolboy belonged to a group of six boys living in the same block of flats (although not all went to the same school); the boys were friendly with some of the girls living there. He wrote in his diary:

'After school I went home and waited outside the flats for Colin, June and Linda to come back from their school. I particularly wanted to see June, first because I like her, and second, because I always take the mickey out of her school uniform (she has to wear white socks). Colin came home from school first and we both waited for June and Linda. When they came, of course we took the mickey. We talked to them for half an hour and then we all went in for tea. At 6.30 p.m. I went out again and called for Colin and Mick and we met up with our four other mates who live near by. The girls came out too and we were with them, talking and larking about around the flats, until 8.30 p.m. Colin went round the back with Carol but not for long – she ran out after he tried to give her a "French kiss". After 8.30 the girls went in and we went up Colin's home to look at TV. At 11 p.m. we all went home, and I wrote my diary. Then I went to bed and started thinking about June. She is an angel, about the best girl I've ever met. I don't trust Mick – he is the Don Juan in our group. But I don't think June likes him.'

Sometimes the girls are members of the same youth club or go to the same dance hall or dancing club. A 15 year old reported:

'We were over the fair in Victoria Park. At about 8.30 one of my mates said, "Let's all go up the Blue Beat Club in Mare Street." When we got there we found they had two good groups playing. We danced with some girls we knew – we usually see them up there.'

At about 15 or 16, mixed teenage parties become common. Six of the thirty diarists described parties on Saturday or Sunday night during their week. One was a boy of 14, whose party was an all-male affair. The other boys who reported parties were aged 15, 16, 17 (two) and 18, and the pattern they described seemed much the same – girls, records, dancing and beer or cider to drink. Although newcomers are sometimes brought along by other guests, the girls at such parties are usually drawn from the familiar circle. Here is the account by the 16 year old, a van-boy:

'On Saturday afternoon Jill came round and asked me to go to a party at her house that evening – her parents had gone to her aunt's for the week-end. She told me to ask some of my friends and said she'd ask some of hers. I went round to Robert and Frank, and told them to ask our other mates. . . . When I got there at 7 p.m. the party had started. Me and my mates went over the off-licence and bought some beer and cider – we all put 5s. each. We had all the top records;

39

we danced a lot and I got a little drunk. I went upstairs with Jill and we did a bit of snogging on the bed.'

That is one way in which boys and girls begin to pair off. Other boys start by taking a girl home from the dance or the youth club, or arrange to take her out alone – to the cinema or for a walk in the Park. The girl may have been 'picked up' one night and 'dated' by the boy who partnered her then, or she may be a member of the existing circle of acquaintances. However it happens, most boys have started taking girls out alone by about 16 or 17.

The effects on peer groups

The previous chapter remarked upon two changes as the boys get older. First, the older groups more often include girls as well as boys – the proportion of groups including girls was less than a quarter at 14 and 15, nearly half at 19 and 20. Second, older boys are less likely to belong to groups at all. In other words, the peer group may broaden to include girls or it may break up altogether.

The shift from all-male to mixed-sex groups is one reflection of the general enlargement of the boy's social world. Mixed groups are usually larger than those made up of boys alone: two-thirds of the former had six or more members, compared with less than a third of the latter. There seemed, however, to be two distinct sorts of 'mixed group'. One type was smaller and was made up of two or three couples, older and with stable partnerships, who had joined together to go dancing, to the cinema or to jazz clubs. The other, larger groups which were more common had been formed by extending or amalgamating one-sex groups to include girls from what I have called the 'wider circle of acquaintances'.

Within these 'amalgamated' peer groups, the boys' own set sometimes survived as a distinct sub-group. Charlie Stephens, an 18-year-old apprentice electrician, provides an example. He said that he belonged to a mixed group of 'about a dozen'. One of the girls, Carol, was his own girl; 'I'm courting steady,' he said at one point. His week's diary showed that he had spent some of the time with Carol alone – he had spent Sunday evening at her home, 'watching television, listening to the gram and necking on the settee' and had taken her to the cinema on Friday. On four other evenings he had taken her home at the end, but most of the time had been spent in the company of some or all of the group. One evening Charlie took Carol to a dance and met the others there; another evening he took her to a party at a friend's home; on the third he went to a dancing club 'with five of my mates and found that Carol was there dancing with her friends'; and on the fourth 'we all got in the van with the girls and drove out to Epping Forest for a drink'. On the remaining evening he, 'Went out with the boys. We had a few drinks and skylarked around a bit. I really enjoy a night like this, out with my mates.'

What has happened to Charlie Stephens and his 'mates' is clear. The constant companions of a year or two earlier are now fellow members of a wider boys-and-girls set. The boys spend less time together; their solidarity as a group of 'mates' has been weakened. They stay together at least some of the time, but now usually with their girls as well.

Not all male groups change in this way. If the group is not widened to include girls, the acquisition of a girl friend by one of its members may threaten the group's unity, indeed existence. The groups do not necessarily break up completely: one in seven of the engaged boys still belonged to an all-male group, as did nearly half of those with a 'regular girl'; but this was compared with two-thirds among the rest.

When one of their number starts going out with a girl this inevitably poses problems.[1] Obviously the boys are interested in girls – they clearly talk about girls and sex a good deal of the time they are together. On the other hand, they value the group's solidarity; for most boys, as I have said, the male group is the crucial 'primary group' in early adolescence, and feelings of friendship and loyalty die hard. As a result many, at least to begin with, are wary of 'going steady' with a girl. The cynical 'male' view at this stage is that you go with a girl for what you can get sexually, and above all you avoid becoming entangled. This attitude was expressed thus in a tape-recorded conversation between two boys aged 16.

RON   Three-quarters of us don't go out with girls; we'd
         sooner go out with boys and have a giggle. It's more

[1] Allcorn, D. H., found the same in his West London study: *The Social Development of Young Men in an English Industrial Suburb*, pp. 273–4.

41

excitement. A girl will do you for one night, but you get over it. Some boys nowadays they take a bird home and they think 'I like her, I'll go with her again and again,' but I don't think that's no life.

JACK   Well, it depends if you're that sort of bloke. If you go with a bird and you like her enough, you keep her, don't you?

RON   I'll put it this way, supposing you go for a walk through the park and you see a couple of nice-looking birds, and you can get what you want, sort of thing, and you leave them, you've got none of the expense of carting a bird out? Right?

Right, maybe. What usually happens, though, is that the boy's attitude changes.

'The three of us always used to go round together. Now we don't so much, now that Arthur and myself have got girls. George is jealous. I mean, *he's* trying to get a steady girl now because the thing has caught on. Before, we all used to say, "We won't go steady," but now it's all the rage. I used to laugh at it as well. But now – well, it's fabulous.' (19 year old.)

Others similarly find that they are becoming more attached, more involved. The unity of the group – and its pattern of behaviour – is disrupted. 'Five of us used to always be together,' said a 17 year old, 'Now one of the lads has started courting. He comes with us sometimes but he's with his girl three or four nights a week. It's all breaking up.' 'I used to go out all the time with a group of mates,' said a 20 year old. 'That was before I started courting. I don't go with them now.'

The boys may have some regrets about the change. As an 18 year old put it, 'My pet like is going out for a night with the fellows. I'm afraid I don't get a chance to do it so much, now I'm courting rather strong.' But he does not propose to give up his girl; 'We're practically engaged. I intend to marry her.' Another – a 17 year old – was perfectly clear what was at issue: he said, 'I don't want to get caught with a girl. I still like going out with the boys.'

From courtship to marriage

The boys' first encounters with girls are unlikely to turn into anything lasting or to offer much of a threat to the peer group. Later partnerships may be taken more seriously – the girl is then regarded as 'my girl friend', and others recognize that the pair are 'going out together'. Even so, the attachments may still be relatively temporary. Among the boys of about 18 and under, we found that having a 'regular girl' did not always mean quite as stable a relationship as it might suggest. When a boy wrote up his diary, only a week or two after saying in an interview that he had a 'regular girl', it sometimes turned out that she had apparently disappeared from his life. Perhaps some boys had invented the liaison for prestige. What seems more likely, from what they told us when we asked about the discrepancy, is that 'girl friends' come and go fairly rapidly at this age. A girl whom a boy described as his 'girl friend' might only remain in that relationship for two or three weeks. A 17 year old said he had taken out 'dozens of girls' since he was about 15; 'One lasted several months but with the others it was only a week or two, if that.' The boys explained how such relationships ended. 'I packed her in'; 'We got fed up with each other'; 'She went off with my mate.'

At some stage, more 'serious' liaisons are formed. It is obviously difficult to pin an age to this transition: some boys of 15 had been going with the same girl for 18 months, and some of 19 and 20 were insistent that, though they took girls out, they were 'not going to get hooked yet'. But the general trend is clear; it is apparent in Table IX, which sums up the developments discussed in this chapter, by showing the answers of boys at different ages when asked how much they had to do with girls.

At 14 and 15, a quarter of the boys say they have 'little to do with girls'; from 16 onwards the proportion is down to under one in ten. Taking girls out 'sometimes' is most popular around 16, 17 and 18. As the boys get older they become involved in more lasting relationships – the proportion with a 'regular girl' goes up and by the age of 19 or 20 more than a quarter of the boys are engaged. One of the boys in our sample was already married.[2]

Inevitably the sheer time spent in the company of girls increases

[2] The sample almost certainly under-represents married young men. See pp. 182-4, Appendix I.

TABLE IX

Age and relationship with girls

	14/15	*16–18*	*19/20*
'Have little to do with girls'	26%	9%	6%
'See girls around'	32%	24%	14%
'Take girls out sometimes'	24%	41%	24%
'Have regular girl friend'	18%	21%	26%
Engaged	—	5%	28%
Married	—	—	2%
Total %	100%	100%	100%
Number	68	128	50

as the boys mature. Among the thirty who wrote detailed diaries for us, the proportion who were with a girl on four or more evenings in the week rose from one in ten at 14 and 15 to nearly three-quarters at 19 and 20. The diaries illustrate what happens in the more stable relationships.

'Sunday evening   I had my tea, washed and left for my girl-friend's house, in Bow. When I arrived her mother let me in and told me to take a seat in the living-room. Christine (my girl) and I watched "Sunday Night at the London Palladium". Afterwards we went for a walk until about 10.30 p.m. when I took her home and said "Good night", for about 20 minutes before leaving . . .'

'Friday evening   I went to call for Christine. I took her to the Mile End Odeon. I think they were two good films – to tell the truth, I didn't pay much attention to them. After the films I took Christine down Chinatown, and we had chow mein, which is very nice. I saw her home and, after saying my good nights, left for my own home. I got into bed at 11.45 p.m. . . .'

'Saturday evening   After tea I went round Christine's house and watched the television. I was tired out and fell asleep while we were smooching on the bed-settee.' (18 year old.)

'Thursday evening   About 7.30 I put on a suit and went to

my girl's house in Shoreditch. I took her out for a drink. We had a chat about what to do over the week-end and decided to go to the pictures on Saturday and over Regent's Park Sunday if it's nice. We left the pub when it shut, got to her house at about 11.30. I left at about midnight.' (20 year old.)

As I have already reported, boys who had earlier joked with their 'mates' about 'going for what you can get' and had resisted 'being caught' or 'settling down' with a girl found their attitudes changing. They said in interviews, 'I've found the right girl for me' (18 year old) or 'I love the girl' (20 year old). Another 20 year old said:

'I found, before I met this girl, that I could get away with anything. I used to mess the girls about, not turn up for dates and all that. Now this girl, I'm a bit under her thumb. It's very nice being under her thumb. Now I live for the days I go out with her – Monday, Wednesday, Saturday and Sunday. The way things are going I can't see myself giving her up. We'll get engaged.'

Some of the boys had passed this stage and were engaged already or making the plans for their marriage.

'Sunday. 2 p.m. Went round on my motor bike to my fiancée, who lives in the flats near Victoria Park. We were going to go for a ride but it started raining, so we stayed in playing records until 6 o'clock. Then we had tea, the usual Sunday salad, with her family.
'7 p.m. We rode round to Jack and June, a married couple who are friends of ours and live in Bow. Jack collects the same sort of records as I do – folk-music and blues. We played records and talked. While my fiancée and June were fixing something to eat, Jack and I went round to the off-licence to get some cider and cigarettes. We then had a meal and talked some more.
'10.30 p.m. We left and I took my fiancée home. I then went home, covered up my motor bike and went to bed.' (18 year old.)

During the week, he had spent every evening but one with her, either at her home, visiting friends or going for a motor bike ride. The remaining evening he worked on his motor bike and then 'decided to have an early night'.

Two other boys, both 19, were busy with wedding arrangements:

'Tuesday evening   After watching television I took the girl home at 10.30. We discussed our wedding which is on 10th August . . .

'Friday evening   I went round to Sheila's house to sort out some wedding arrangements with her father and mother . . .'

'Monday evening   After I had picked my girl up at her office in the City, we caught the 253 bus to Bethnal Green Town Hall – we went to the photographer's shop opposite to book up a photographer for the wedding. They showed us different wedding photos and asked what kind of photos we wanted done . . .

'Wednesday evening   After I had my tea I went round to my girl-friend's and picked her up – we went to see about a hall for the wedding reception. Afterwards we went round to see my Uncle Jack, who lives off Roman Road. He asked how much we intended spending on beer and we said about £50, and he asked how much on spirits and we said about £60. He said if he was going to be barman, like he was at our engagement party, he suggests holding back the spirits at the beginning . . .'

If we could look ahead a few years, we would find most of the other boys doing the same things – calling in at the photographer's, booking the hall, making arrangements for the wedding party. In 1961, according to the Census, more than a third of the men in Bethnal Green aged 20 to 24 were married, and nearly three-quarters of those aged 25 to 29.[3] We asked the 245 unmarried boys in our main sample (that is, excluding the one already married) whether they expected to get married. Seven per cent said 'No' and 2 per cent that they did not know; the remaining 91 per cent said 'Yes'. Most expected to marry young; of those who thought they would get married, 66 per cent thought it would be before they were 25, 27 per cent between 25 and 30,

[3] *Census 1961, London*, Table VI, p. 10.

only 5 per cent over 30 (2 per cent said they did not know when).

More than a quarter of those who expected to marry gave as their 'reason' that it was just 'natural' or 'inevitable'.

'Everybody seems to sooner or later. All my brothers and sisters are married. It seems the most natural thing to do. You have your fling, then settle down.' (17 year old.)

'There's not much else to do after you stop being a teenager. You've got to have a change some time – I more or less just go out drinking now. I don't want to go on doing that.' (19 year old.)

A quarter of the boys laid the emphasis on love; the proportion was understandably higher – more than half – among those already engaged, who were answering in terms of a specific partner, although some younger boys also gave this answer.

'I should think it will be because I love the girl.' (15 year old.)

'I'm in love. When someone means enough to you, you want to spend all your life with them, not just nights.' (19 year old.)

About one in seven said they would need companionship and a similar proportion that they would like children.

'I want to have a family – because I like children.' (17 year old.)

'I wouldn't like to live alone all my life. I'd want someone to come home to after work, companionship in my old age.' (19 year old.)

The remainder – just over one in ten of the boys who expected to marry – gave reasons that could not be classified under any of these four headings. Some were facetious. 'It won't be for love,' said a 14 year old, 'Sex is more like it.' And a boy of 20: 'I might get someone into trouble.'

Similarly, some of the minority who did not expect to marry were cynical about marriage.

'I'd like my freedom, instead of worrying about a wife and kids.' (15 year old.)

'When you get married you've got to tag along with one girl. I don't fancy that.' (16 year old.)

Most of those who express such views will no doubt change their minds later. But there will still be some who remain, as one 18 year old described himself, 'not the marrying kind'. A fifth of the 19 and 20 year olds said they either 'had little to do with girls' or just 'saw them around'; they explained 'I just don't bother with girls' or 'I don't like girls all that much'. 'I've never taken a girl out,' said a 19 year old, 'I don't think about girls.' Some will never marry, like the 'born bachelors' mentioned by Hoggart[4] or the single working men who 'never bother with women' described by Zweig.[5] They are a minority, though. Most boys both expect to marry and think it right to do so.[6] As one boy of 16 summed it up, 'You expect to get married. You can't be a teenager all your life.'

Sexual experience

The sexual element in the boys' relationships with girls has so far been implicit rather than explicit. Sexual drives, excitements and frustrations are, however, so much a part of adolescence that they must be brought into the account. The treatment can only be sketchy, because we discussed sex just with some of the boys who came to the Institute for tape-recorded interviews. Their answers certainly cannot be regarded as representative; of the twenty or so who talked about sex, all were not equally communicative, and they formed no sort of sample. But they provide enough information to support a plausible chronological account of what commonly happens, parallel with the more general one presented so far in this chapter.

First the boys suggested that masturbation was common, if not universal.[7]

'Some people with a big mouth say, "I do this and that with

---

[4] Hoggart, R., *The Uses of Literacy*, pp. 83–84.
[5] Zweig, F., *The British Worker*, p. 68.
[6] This has been found in other studies. See Jephcott, P., *Rising Twenty*, pp. 70–71; Allcorn, D. H., op. cit., p. 279; Veness, T., *School Leavers*, p. 26.
[7] Kinsey's data suggest that in the United States by the age of 20 virtually all boys are masturbating. (Kinsey, A. C., Pomery, W. B. and Martin, C. E., *Sexual Behaviour in the Human Male*, p. 500).

my girl". But they go home and masturbate, the same as everybody else.' (18 year old.)

'I suppose all boys do it. I know all my mates do. We talk about it sometimes, have a joke about it. I think you do get some boys who think, "I'm not going to tell anyone in case they think I'm dirty, wanking myself off". But me and my mates, we tell everybody we wank off.' (17 year old.)

They had usually started at 12, 13 or 14.[8]

'When I was 13, my friends at school asked me if I'd ever had a wank. I didn't know what they were talking about. Then I walked into the toilets one day and there were two geezers in there doing it. I watched them and then one night I tried it myself. Then I started doing it pretty regular.' (16 year old.)

'I started at 14. When I first discovered it I went really mad over it. Then after a while it turned me off a bit. There were boys at school who used to do it underneath the desk. Glassy looking and going it like made, they were. That always sickened me somehow.' (19 year old.)

Apart from early games of 'doctors' or 'mothers and fathers', the first sexual explorations with girls had often been at about 14 or 15. The interest that many boys took in girls at this age was predominantly sexual, rather than romantic. If they 'picked up' a girl in Victoria Park or London Fields, they would often try to move on from kissing to sexual play; as they put it, they 'titted a girl up' or 'had a bit of lumber', 'went up her skirt' or 'touched her up'. One 16 year old described two of his early sexual experiences of this kind.

'When I was about 14 I walked a girl home for the first time, but I didn't really do anything. I kissed her and cuddled her and had a bit of lumber. Some time after that I was out with my mate and we picked up a couple of girls. We took them round to his house because his mother and father were away for the night. We had the lights out and I started getting to work on my girl: I started rubbing my hand up and down her ribs, getting nearer and nearer to her tits, and all of a

[8] Kinsey, again, reports that 12, 13 or 14 are the most common ages among American boys of a comparable educational level to most Bethnal Greeners (ibid., p. 500).

sudden I got my hand on her tit and I thought well, that's all
right. So I thought I'd try for her quim. I started rubbing
away at it on the outside and she didn't seem to mind. Then
all of a sudden my mate jumps up and switches on the light.
I pulled my hand away and she pulls her skirt down quick
and that was it. He wasn't getting anywhere himself, and his
girl said to my one, "Coming home, Jeannie?" and off they
went. That was the end of that.'

Some boys had approached girls in a different way. A 19 year
old explained:

'When I was 14 there was hardly any sex life at all. It was all
kiss and cuddle and just talking – it was a great experience just
to talk to a girl, to see how a girl thinks.'

We obviously do not know how many had started sexual play
or intercourse by different ages. Those we talked to suggested
that by 18 something like a third or half the local boys would
have had intercourse.[9] There were variations not only in the age
at which they began but also in the type of relationship and the
circumstances. It seemed that when boys had experienced sexual
intercourse relatively early – at 15 or 16 – it had often been with
someone 'picked up' or met casually.

'I've been all the way with girls twice, both times in the last
six months or so. The first time was over London Fields and
the second was up an alley over Hackney Wick. The first
time I wasn't expecting nothing. I picked this girl up and
was taking her home and we stopped in London Fields on the
way. We started kissing and I started feeling her up and that
led on to it.' (16 year old.)

'I didn't really know the girl. We'd all had quite a lot to drink
and it turned into an orgy – the parents of the chap who gave
the party were away for the week-end. I got on the bed with
this bird and got it in. I got the impression everybody was
doing it. One girl cried afterwards.' (17 year old, first experience of intercourse a year earlier.)

[9] Schofield, M., *The Sexual Behaviour of Young People*, a survey based on interviews
with a national sample of boys and girls aged 15 to 19, suggests that a quarter of
boys have had intercourse by 17 and a third by 18 (p. 33).

The boys suggested that this more promiscuous sexual intercourse was usually with a minority of girls who, in their words, were 'easy lays', 'old slags' or 'bangers'.[10]

'I could see straight away she was a right banger,' said a 17 year old of one girl. 'A banger's a goer – a girl who'll do anything with anyone.'

'You can always get a bit if you want it, with the girls with the big mouths. It gets around that they're that sort of girl. But that sort of thing turns you off after a while – you realize that if you can get it, so can anyone else.' (18 year old.)

If a boy's initiation into sex is with such a girl he may feel guilty afterwards – or at least pretend to.

'I did it once, but it wasn't a good thing to do. I was there, so we had it, that was all. One girl took eight of us over the park, on the grass over the park.' (16 year old.)

'Some girls are forced into it with a crowd of boys, and then the word gets round and everyone tries. I did it myself once like that, six months ago, over Hackney Marshes. I knew she was like that, but I didn't like her.' (17 year old.)

The other sort of boy, if he had experienced intercourse at all, had started later; he was more likely to begin with a 'steady' girl friend.

'The only girl I've been all the way with is my girl, the one I'm going with now, and that's only in the last three months or so. We do it in the front room late at night, when I've seen her home and her parents are upstairs in bed.' (18 year old.)

When the relationship is relatively stable – when the couple are engaged or nearly so – it is often regarded as quite 'respectable' to become sexual partners.

'I've been going out with the same girl for two years. We're engaged now. We'd never done anything except kissing and

[10] Schofield's study supports this. He says: 'There is a hint . . . of a small pocket of less cautious girls who engage in more casual relationships' (ibid., p. 92), and he also remarks that girls who start having intercourse at a relatively early age are more likely to have it with a 'casual partner' (p. 72).

petting until a couple of months ago, when her mum and dad went away for the week-end. We got up to some really heavy petting, and we just couldn't hold it back any more. I think it's all right to do it – to have intercourse – if you really intend to get married. Just don't take it too far, is what I think – don't knock the daylights out of it.' (19 year old.)

Many boys seemed to think that this was generally recognized. As one put it, 'It's done so much, it's just a natural thing – it's all right if they're engaged.'[11] Not all agreed; among those with a fiancée were some who believed, in the words of a 19 year old, in 'saving it up until we get married'.

This discussion about sexual behaviour can now be linked to what was said earlier about the development of the boys' relationships with girls generally. The conclusion is broadly the same. Though there are inevitably variations in sexual experience, particularly at the younger ages, all but a minority are moving on the familiar path. As they do so their attitude may change. A 20 year old said, 'When I was younger I was all for sex. I'd pick up any bird and get all I could. Now that I've met the girl, all that's out.' Sex is still important, of course, but now it is more and more likely to be associated with love and with the idea of marriage. It is channelled into something approaching a husband–wife relationship. In this sense, the boys have begun to 'settle down'.

---

[11] Schofield reports: 'Many of the teenagers marry the only person with whom they have had sexual intercourse' (ibid., p. 167).

IV

FAMILY AND KINSHIP

Earlier study has shown that family and kinship loom large in the day-to-day lives of many people in the East End, as in similar working-class areas. How much do they matter in adolescence? The question needs to be answered in two parts – first, for the 'immediate family' of parents and unmarried brothers and sisters; and second, for the wider circle of relatives.

Most of the boys in our sample were living at home with their parents. Apart from the young man who was married, 80 per cent lived with both parents and most of the rest (16 per cent) with either their mother or father.[1] Two per cent lived with other relatives and another 2 per cent with foster-parents or other non-relatives. Fewer of the older boys were living with both parents – 62 per cent of the 19 and 20 year olds, compared with 84 per cent of those younger. But this was because parents had died or separated, not because the boy himself had left the parental home. The boys expected to go on staying at home; there was little demand for residential independence.

> 'You should stay with your parents till you marry,' said a 17-year-old furniture salesman. 'All the other fellows I know are living at home and expect to stay there. Apart from anything else, you owe it to your parents – from their point of view it's a waste of time if you just pack up and leave them when you leave school. Anyway, most teenagers can't cook for themselves.'

[1] Ten per cent of the sample were with their mother, 4 per cent with mother and stepfather; 1 per cent with their father, 1 per cent with father and stepmother. Death was more often the cause of 'broken homes' than divorce or separation. Of the fifty boys with neither parent at home or only one, twenty-five said that their father had died, three their mother; nine said that their parents were divorced, three that they had separated; seven were living apart from their parents for other reasons and three did not know what had happened to them.

Because most boys lived with their parents and expected to stay on until they married, it does not necessarily follow that they spent much time at home. We asked how many times they had 'stayed in for the evening' during the previous week. This is obviously a somewhat vague question. But the general sense was clear enough to the boys, as the diaries and lengthier interviews showed – they said they were 'in for the evening' if the bulk of their time that evening was spent at home.

More than a third (36 per cent) had been 'out' every evening in the previous week and a similar proportion (35 per cent) all but one or two evenings; only 3 per cent had been 'in' every evening. On the average, each boy had been out five evenings. Younger boys were out as often as older. The fact that these interviews were done in the summer should be borne in mind; at other times of the year the home may have more appeal. But all our information (including some interviews that were done at other times of the year) suggests that in other seasons as well most of the boys' leisure time was spent outside the home.[2]

Home sometimes seemed to be little more than a hotel, somewhere to wash, eat and sleep.

'4 p.m.   Came out of school. Went round the flats, fooled around with my mates.
'5.15 p.m.   Went home for tea.
'6.30 p.m.   Went round the flats again and called for my mates.
'10.15 p.m.   Came home, had a cup of coffee and went to bed.' (14 year old.)

'I left work at 5.30, came home, washed and changed, and had my tea. At 6.30 my girl friend came round and we went for a walk. After I had seen her home I went home to bed at 11.15.' (17 year old.)

But the link with home was usually less tenuous than these examples suggest. First, there was television; some evenings reported as spent outside the home included a spell of watching television inside it.

'After school went home, had tea, watched TV for a while,

[2] Mays found the same in his study in a working-class district of Liverpool: 'Over the age of 12 boys do not seem to spend much time in the home except when they are sick.' (Mays, J. B., *Growing Up in the City*, p. 91).

then got ready to go out. When ready went round my friend
Terry's. We called for our girls and took them over the
park. I got home about 10.30, then watched TV for about
30 minutes. Went to bed at 11.10.' (14 year old.)

'5.30 Came home from work and had tea of steak and
beans with boiled potatoes. Watched television for about an
hour.
'7.00 Went round for Stephen to go up the club . . .
'10.45 Got home and had a wash, then went to bed.' (16
year old.)

This was a common pattern. Although only 3 per cent of the
boys had stayed in every evening during the week before the
interview, 27 per cent had watched television every evening. The
diaries showed that the bulk of this viewing was done in their
own homes. Younger boys, though they reported no more
evenings at home than their older fellows, had watched television
more: the proportions who had watched every evening in the
previous week were 46 per cent at 14 and 15, 23 per cent at 16,
17 and 18, 12 per cent at 19 and 20.

Also, boys sometimes spent the whole evening at home; nearly
two-thirds had stayed in for at least one evening during the week
before the interview. For some, this was a deliberate break from
the rest of the week. An 18 year old who had been out every other
evening in the week reported in his diary:

'Arrived home at 5.30, had a wash and my tea and played
records till 7.30. I had decided to have an evening in. I sat
back and watched TV and then washed my hair. After that
I had a cup of coffee and had an early night.'

A 20 year old, who spent most evenings out with his girl,
wrote:

'After tea I watched telly until 8 p.m. Not seeing Pat tonight
as she was going to go to her aunt's with her parents. My
dad is decorating the front room so I gave him a hand in
putting the paper on the walls. We had done one wall and a
half by about 10.30, so we was well pleased. About 11, I
felt a bit tired so I stopped and went to bed.'

The evenings that some boys spent at home were, by co ntrast with people who came in. Younger boys were visited by fellow members of their peer group, who would come to listen to records, play cards, talk or watch television.

'At 7.45 three of my mates came round to my home and we played records. My mother made coffee for us and they went home about 11 p.m.' (14 year old.)

With older boys the visits were more often from a girl friend or fiancée.

'9.30 p.m.   My girl friend came round and we listened to records and watched television.
'10.30 p.m.   Took her home and got back about 11.20 p.m.' (18 year old.)

This kind of entertaining in the boy's home was, however, relatively rare; more commonly, male peers or 'steady' girl friends called in briefly at the beginning or end of the evening. All this, like the example of television, rather qualifies the general impression of a sharp division between the home and the boy's life outside it, but it does not alter the main conclusion that most boys are mainly out.

Outside the home their companions are seldom members of their immediate family. The diaries included a few examples, mentioned later in the chapter, of younger boys accompanying their parents on visits to relatives. Otherwise they hardly went out together. Apparently this represents a change compared with earlier childhood. In a study by Musgrove 460 boys aged 9 to 15 living in the Midlands were asked whom they would like to have with them 'on an outing'; the proportion choosing their parents as companions fell from nearly two-thirds at the age of 9 to one in forty aged 15.[3] A Bethnal Green boy of 16 gave his own reason for such a change; he may have been particularly aware of the problem because his mother, being a widow, missed his company more than most parents.

'We used to go out together, my mum and me, but we don't now. It's no enjoyment for me to go out with her. I can't pick up any girls, I can't have a giggle, I can't swear. I told her last week. I said, "No, I don't fancy going out with you,

[3] Musgrove, F., *Youth and the Social Order*, p. 93.

Mum." Then all of a sudden she started bringing up my girl. "Oh, you want to go out with your girl," she said. "You don't care about your mother," and this, that and the other. I don't know what that's got to do with it.'

The boys seldom go out with their brothers or sisters either. Nearly three-quarters of them had at least one brother or sister at home: 31 per cent had one, 30 per cent two or three and 10 per cent four or more. These siblings did not figure as close companions and only occasionally played any part outside the home. One boy's diary told how he had met his brother unexpectedly in the West End on Saturday night: 'Met my younger brother in Leicester Square; he relieved me of half a crown, and told me about a party he was going to. Said I might go too.' Another, aged 17, described how his elder brother 'asked me to play cricket for his club'; their team won and after the game 'we all went to the local pub and bought drinks for each other. After the pub closed, my brother and I came home together.' But these were almost unique examples.

Relationships within the family

More important than the contacts are the emotional relationships within the family – how well do they get on with each other?

First, brothers and sisters. We did not collect systematic information on the boys' feelings about their siblings, but there were certainly examples of conflict. One boy of 17 had a sister of 18.

> 'We're always quarrelling. She tries to make trouble with my mate. Every time he comes round she goes to the door. "Sorry, Frank," she says, "he ain't in." I ran out one day. I said, "I am in, you liar," and she went all red. I got my own back though; there was a real row over it. When one of her mates came round, I said, "She ain't in. She's gone round with some other bunch of girls," I said, like that. My sister went mad.'

Another, aged 15, wrote in his diary:

> 'Saturday. 7.30 p.m.   I got into an argument with my elder brother about who would stay in and look after our younger brother while our parents went to a family reunion. I said

that he never did any baby-sitting and anyway I had a party to go to at Fred's flat.
'8.30 p.m. I won the hour-long argument and went round the flats to the party.'

There are sometimes changes in the relationships: brothers who are enemies at one stage may become friendly later.

'I've got an older brother and a younger sister. I used to fight with my brother nearly every night. We used to quarrel over every little thing. He used to hit me. Now we get on all right. He's even agreed to let me borrow his scooter, something I never thought he'd do.' (16 year old.)

He was now at odds with his younger sister.

'When she was little I used to like her. Now she seems to have got some nasty ways. Mind you I suppose it's my fault a lot of the time; I'm always picking on her. But she's nasty. If I say something to her, she'll say "So what." I'll say "I'll hit you in a minute," and she'll say "Go on then." If I just pretend to hit her, she will start crying and call my dad, and he'll come running in.'

There were also illustrations of the familiar ambivalence of siblings towards each other; quarrelling is mixed with loyalty.

'I'm always fighting with my younger sister. She seems a bit spoilt, a bit don't care. My younger brother's a pest. I've thought of laying into him sometimes but, well, it's up to Mum and Dad. My eldest sister is still a kid but she's got more sense than the younger one. If anyone asked me which one I preferred, I'd say the eldest one. But if anybody said anything about either of them I'd be up in arms equally as much for one as for the other – or for my brother.' (19 year old.)

Parents appeared in diaries more frequently than either brothers or sisters.

'Dad and I talked about my work and he said did I think I would like it?' wrote a 16 year old who had just started work as a clerk. 'He told me about his job as a banana ripener. The different temperatures the rooms had to be, and the various grades of bananas. The spiders there used to be in the bunches.

If there happened to be a spider they had not seen before they would put on a glove and put a jar over it in case it was dangerous – then they would call in an expert from the zoo. Dad had to give the job up for health reasons.'

'Arrived home at 5.45, had a wash and a meal. Did not go out this evening. Stayed in with my mother, had a talk with her, and played some records – my rhythm and blues and her classical records. Then I did a little repair job on one of the cupboard shelves. My father came in at 10.30 – he had been working late – and we had a snack and a cup of tea.' (18 year old.)

When asked how they got on with their parents, some asserted they got on well with both.

'I always tell mine where I'm going, don't wait for them to ask. If I miss the last bus on a Saturday night I have to walk, get in about one o'clock. They don't complain.' (17 year old.)

'If a boy has a home he's cared for. There are untold dangers in going on his own. He might hit bad times or do things that were unlawful. My parents usually want to know where I've been and I tell them. I've never been out later than 11 o'clock except at parties and weddings and at Christmas. They are very understanding.' (18 year old.)

Others seemed to respect their parents and have fairly smooth relationships with them, but still felt there was something of a gulf.

'My mother's very good. She thinks the world of her family, she'd do anything for us. She's a very hard worker. As for my father, I think the world of him. He's always done right by his family. He's worked hard for us, he's kept four of us. Mind you, he's ignorant. He can hardly write his own name. I talk to him about work and things like that. But I don't argue with him. Blimey, he's my dad. You can't say "Shut up Dad and sit down", can you, out of respect? But he doesn't really know what's going on, to us kids or to any other kids.' (19 year old.)

Some boys described conflicts with parents.

'My parents are old-fashioned. They don't like jazz. They imagine I'm still at school, still dependent, things like that. They still ask me where I'm going of an evening and I resent that. When I buy a record they don't agree with that; I think it's your money and you're entitled to do as you like with it.' (18 year old.)

'I reckon my parents don't understand *anything* I do. My mother doesn't seem to like my clothes, and my dad, he thinks it's silly to go dancing. I don't tell them my ideas any more. I talk to them, but not about anything important.' (15 year old.)

Fathers were more often singled out for criticism.

'About a year ago I used to ask if I could go out to a club I'd joined and my dad would say "No, it's too far to go of a night". I used to hate him for that. And some nights they used to go out and leave me staying in. I used to hate them for that too. I think it was my father more. My mother used to understand a bit and she'd say "Go out then", but my father used to step in and say "He ain't going nowhere". The past couple of months I've been arguing about going out more, particularly since I've started work. One night, if I argued, they'd make me stay in, but the next I'd go out, and now I go out nearly every night and they don't say nothing.' (16 year old.)

'They don't understand me at all. My father's the worst. I just don't talk to him now; we don't get on at all. Sometimes he tries to start trouble with me. I might have a cup of tea and drink it and my mother'll say "Take out your cup," and I'll say "I'll take it out in a minute". Suddenly he chips in and says, "Take it out now." He's trying to make a big thing of it, sort of thing. I've changed in the last year or two. Now I ignore him; I don't take any notice. More or less, I go my own way and they go theirs.' (18 year old.)

Fathers were sometimes described as rather remote figures of authority.

'My old man doesn't start on me for any reason of his own. It's generally the little report Mum gives him at the end of the day – "Oh, he didn't get up this morning, he didn't do this, he didn't do that." When the old man starts rowing me, I sometimes lose my temper and he clouts me round the ear. I don't try to hit him back – if I did I guarantee I'd be flat out in ten seconds, because he don't stand for anything in his way. I just go into my bedroom and hit something when I get into a fume. Once I shattered a table lamp in a temper. I went into my bedroom and swung it round; it went crash, it belted into the wall. My dad came rushing in and saw the bulb busted and the table lamp in about three bits where I'd hit it. I said, "I knocked it over by mistake." It was all lying in bits on the floor, you know. He said to me, "Yeah, I know you did".' (16 year old.)

Some said explicitly that mothers were more sympathetic. A 19 year old remarked:

'I get on better with my mother than my old man. She told me the facts of life straight through when I left school. I'd bring my children up the same way that she brought me up. I call her old Doll. I have done since I was 14. My father's not so intelligent as her. She always spots it if I'm bothered with anything.'

Are there any detectable patters in these different feelings about parents? The boys' answers to a question about how well they thought their parents 'understood' them are shown in Tables X and XI.

These tables point to two important conclusions. The first is

TABLE X

Age and attitude to mother

Mother 'understands' :	*14/15*	*16–18*	*19/20*
'Very well'	52%	42%	61%
'Fairly well' or 'Quite well'	45%	44%	32%
'Not too well' or 'Not much at all'	3%	14%	7%
Total %	100%	100%	100%
Number	62	121	41

Family and Kinship

TABLE XI

Age and attitude to father

Father 'understands' :	14/15	16–18	19/20
'Very well'	43%	36%	34%
'Fairly well' or 'Quite well'	46%	46%	47%
'Not too well' or 'Not much at all'	11%	18%	19%
Total %	100%	100%	100%
Number	56	108	32

that, as the remarks already quoted suggest, fathers are indeed regarded as 'less understanding' than mothers.[4] The second is that there seems to be a cycle in relationships with mothers: more boys aged 16 to 18 say they are at odds with her than do those younger or older, and the proportion who say she understands 'very well' rises to 61 per cent at 19 and 20. The clear implication is that in mid-adolescence some boys experience a difficult period in their relationships with their mother, but have often passed through it by the age of 19 or 20.

The apparent absence of any similar variation with fathers presents something of a puzzle. A possible explanation is that, as fathers are often more remote anyway, adolescence does not present such a problem of emotional adjustment to them. Or possibly, in psychological terms, any serious emotional difficulties with fathers have usually been resolved in early childhood, at the so-called Oedipal stage,[5] when the son has to learn to come to terms with his rival for the mother's affection; on this view adolescence, with the shift towards girls and marriage, demands that a boy makes some sort of emotional break and then re-adjustment with his mother (who is a 'rival' to girl friends), in a way that he obviously does not need to with his father. Alternatively, it is possible that there *is* a similar cycle in the boys'

[4] This is in line with the findings of other studies. Musgrove found both boys and girls from 11 to 15 more critical of their fathers than their mothers (ibid., p. 99 and p. 103) and Andry found that fathers were more criticized by boys in both a 'delinquent' and a 'control' sample (Andry, R. G., *Delinquency and Parental Pathology*, pp. 52–53).
[5] See for instance Freud, S., *Two Short Accounts of Psycho-Analysis*, pp. 77–78 and pp. 126–7.

dealings with their fathers, but that it starts too early and finishes too late to show up clearly with a sample aged between 14 and 20.

A close look at the older boys who were engaged – and were, in this sense, more 'mature' – suggests that this last explanation may be at least partly right. Such boys more often spoke approvingly of their fathers, though the numbers are too small to establish whether the difference is just due to chance. Certainly most of the engaged boys who told us about their lives in some detail seemed to be pretty well reconciled to their fathers as well as mothers. They described Sunday tea when their fiancée was at home with the family or evening outings when the parents and the young couple joined company for drinks at the local pub. This lends some support to the idea that the cyclical pattern may apply to fathers as well as mothers. If this were so, it would mean that boys often become rather estranged from both their parents in adolescence only to rejoin the fold, in their new, adult role, as they move closer to becoming husbands and parents themselves. They would say with Mark Twain: 'When I was 16 my old man was so stupid I could hardly stand to have him around; but when I got to be 21 I was surprised to see how much he had learned in the meantime.'[6]

The place of relatives

Now to the wider family circle. The first thing to see is whether the boys have relatives in Bethnal Green. Since the earlier local studies showed that older people had relatives in the district, one would expect the boys to have them too. It is true that the steady emigration from the East End had effected some changes.

'Only the grandparents live in Bethnal Green now – that's my mum's mum and dad. Most of the other relatives have gone out to the housing estate at Aveley. In the past five years about 14 relatives have gone there.'

'Most of our relatives have moved out now – mostly down the line to new estates. We've still got aunts and uncles and cousins living round here, though.'

Despite the shifts of population, 71 per cent of the boys in the

[6] Quoted in Bierstedt, R., *The Social Order*, p. 212.

Family and Kinship

sample had one or more relatives in Bethnal Green. The boys who had lived longest in the district most often had relatives there, as Table XII shows.

TABLE XII

Length of residence and relatives in Bethnal Green

	Born in Bethnal Green	In Bethnal Green ten years or more	In Bethnal Green less than ten years
No relatives	18%	38%	58%
Uncles, aunts	63%	46%	31%
Cousins	54%	35%	20%
Grandparents	44%	27%	14%
Married brothers, married sisters	18%	10%	8%
Nephews, nieces	10%	3%	6%
Other relatives	3%	2%	3%
Total number	147	63	36

As is clear from the table, many of the boys had more than one relative living locally, and some had many. A boy of 19 said, 'My grandparents on my father's side live in the Green, and my uncles and aunts and cousins are all here as well.' A 17 year old said he had in Bethnal Green both grandparents on his mother's side, three uncles, four aunts and eleven cousins; 'They all,' he added, 'live within five minutes walk of here.' A motor mechanic of 18 said he had many relatives near by and explained:

'When we go on holiday we go to a holiday camp on Canvey Island – my brothers, their wives, Mum and Dad, my Uncle Joe and his wife, Aunt Flo, and her husband who live in Hackney Road, Aunt Jean who lived in Cambridge Heath Road, and Aunt Margaret from Bishop's Way. There are only twenty-two of us this year. We're going to Dymchurch near Folkestone. We're going in a big Dormobile and we'll have four chalets and a caravan.'

Though this was exceptional, the boys with relatives living in the district usually saw quite a lot of them. Of those with relatives in Bethnal Green, 55 per cent had seen one or more in the previous twenty-four hours and altogether 88 per cent at some time in the previous week. But relatives living farther away were often seen as well. An 18 year old said:

'I've got an aunt over the road. I see her a lot, nearly every day in the street. She comes over here quite often, and I pop over there for a cup of tea. I've got an uncle at Leyton, I see him at football, and another uncle who lives with my grandmother at Ilford. I go over to see them about once a month at Ilford with my parents and about once a fortnight they come here.'

Taking *all* the boys in the sample, not just those with relatives in Bethnal Green, 43 per cent had seen one or more in the previous twenty-four hours and 79 per cent at some time in the previous week.

Married brothers and sisters, though not the most numerous relatives, are particularly important because they have usually left the household fairly recently. A 14 year old went out with his married brother and the brother's wife, as his diary for Sunday told.

'I got up and had sausage, egg, bacon and tomatoes for breakfast and read the *Sunday Mirror*. Then my brother Wally knocked at the door. He asked me if I wanted to go fishing with him and June, my sister-in-law. I quickly got my boots on and went with them in their van. We got to Broxbourne at about 12.30 and Wally and me started fishing and June starting getting the dinner with a calor gas cooker. We had sausage, egg and bacon again, after that a cup of hot orange and a piece of swiss roll. Then it started to rain. It poured down and we all got soaked, so we made for home. When we got back they came in and Mum made us a hot cup of tea. Then Wally and June went off home.'

A boy of 19 said of his married sister:

'She's 21 and she got married about eighteen months ago. They live over in Poplar now. They started off living with his mother and then when the baby was born they got the chance of a flat in Poplar. She comes over home at least two nights in the week and I'm usually in then and see her. She comes on Saturdays as well.'

Apart from married brothers and sisters, three sets of relatives in particular stand out – grandmothers, uncles and male cousins. Grandparents, particularly grandmothers, and particularly the mother's mother, play a major role in the childhood of most Bethnal Green boys and girls.[7] By adolescence, though less in evidence, the grandmother is still frequently mentioned, particularly when she lives locally and is alone or infirm.

> 'Saturday. 9.10 a.m. Went over to my nan's (maternal grandmother) house and cleaned her windows and got her errands . . .
>
> 11.40 a.m. Bought a small bottle of brandy in Tanner's the wine shop for my nan as she has a bad heart.
>
> 11.55 a.m. Went and got my nan's coat out of the cleaners and took it round to her with the brandy.' (14 year old.)

In Bethnal Green, as in many of the societies studied by anthropologists,[8] there is often a specially close relationship between young children and their grandparents. As adults who are frequently at hand, but who do not need to exercise authority as parents do, grandparents can give children another model of adult behaviour. It seems from the present study that, with boys of about 14 or 15, a similar function is performed by uncles.[9] The strains over authority within the immediate family make it difficult for adolescent boys and their fathers to be at ease. Yet most boys of this age enjoy the companionship of an adult male they can respect and feel relaxed with. Grandfathers will no longer do as models; boys prefer someone closer to their own age, more in touch with their own lives. An uncle can offer a relationship something like that between father and son but without the inhibitions. The Sunday morning of a 15 year old gives an example:

---

[7] See *Family and Kinship in East London*, pp. 40–43.
[8] See Radcliffe-Brown, A. R., 'Introduction' to *African Systems of Kinship and Marriage*, p. 28.
[9] In Western kinship systems, an uncle can be in four possible relationships – father's brother, father's sister's husband, mother's brother, and mother's sister's husband. The boys who told us about their uncles in diaries or interviews did not say which sort of uncle they were. We asked twenty boys at a local youth club, most of them 14 and 15, which uncles they saw most often, as we did twenty-eight boys of 14 and 15 at a local secondary school. Though not properly-selected samples, both groups suggested that father's sister's husbands were seen least. Altogether about one boy in twenty said he saw this sort of uncle 'most often', against between a quarter and a third who saw the other kinds most.

'Today I got up at eight o'clock and went swimming with my uncle. We got to the York Hall baths at nine. There were not many people in there. We fooled around and had a couple of races; I lost both. We came out at 10.30 and I came home.'

And a 14 year old, again on Sunday:

10.10 a.m. My uncle came over and told me he had been down Brick Lane and bought some bait, and would I like to go fishing over Victoria Park for a few hours.
10.30 a.m. Fishing tackle ready. I went off to the park with my uncle. We fished till 1.30. I caught twelve roach and threw them back. Then went home for my dinner.'

Other boys reported: 'My uncle often takes me out for a drive in his car' (14 year old); 'I see a lot of my uncle. He comes round our house every Saturday and Sunday morning, and he talks to me about all sorts of things' (15 year old).

The apparent bond between male cousins may have a somewhat similar explanation as the tie with uncles: if uncles are, as it were, 'substitute fathers', cousins are perhaps 'substitute brothers' – boys who are like brothers but without a brother's rivalry. Cousins of the same age are specially friendly. They appear in two roles. If they live at a distance, there may be a special link with them, inside the circle of kinship, just because when uncles and aunts visit or are visited the boys of similar age have more in common with each other than with members of older or younger generations. A 14 year old, who went with his parents to visit an uncle and aunt at Ilford, wrote:

'We had tea with them. After that I went for a walk with my cousin, aged 15. We walked over the park. When we came back we played table tennis in his bedroom. I was sorry to go.'

Another boy, aged 15, had relatives staying at his home for the week-end. These included a cousin of the same age. On Friday night the two cousins 'went to the Chicken Bar to get chicken and chips for supper'. On Saturday afternoon, together with some other local boys, they played football, and on Saturday evening:

'My cousin and I took the dog out for a walk at 10.15. We stayed out quite a long while looking for girls.'

Cousins who live in the same district may be more constant companions. When they are of similar age they may well be members of the same peer group. Descriptions of leisure activities with a circle of 'mates' often included specific reference to cousins.

'At 5.30 p.m.,' wrote a 16 year old, 'I went round to one of my mates and we went on to call for the others. There are five of us altogether; two of them are cousins of mine. We usually go about together.'

A 19 year old described a Sunday spent building a garden hut for a married friend living in West Ham; those who did the job were 'Fred, my mate who is a private builder, my cousin Albert and his mate.'

Age and kinship

There is no marked general change in the boys' frequency of contact with relatives as they get older. Closer examination suggests, however, two contrary trends. Older boys, it seems, go out with uncles less and are also less likely to accompany parents on visits to kin. On the other hand, among the older boys, those who were engaged or had a 'steady' girl reported that they quite often called, with the girl, on their relatives or hers.

'7.30 p.m. Went round to call for Sandra, my girl.
'8 p.m. Left Sandra's house and went with her over to my uncle's at Hackney.
'9 p.m. We went out for a drink with my uncle and aunt. After that, took Sandra home.' (17 year old.)

'6 p.m. Started out for the girl's home, arriving about 6.30. We'd decided to go and visit her aunt and uncle.
'7.30 p.m. Arrived at her uncle and aunt's. We sat down and watched television. Then, after a chat and a cup of tea, we left.' (18 year old.)

'8.30 p.m. My fiancée came round. We went to see my nan, who lives in the same flats as me. We always have a good laugh when we go to see her, and my girl loves hearing her talk about the people she meets in the market every day.' (19 year old.)

Though the numbers are small, there are clear differences in kinship contacts between the older boys with 'regular' girl friends or fiancées and those without. Among the 19 and 20 year olds with girls nearly nine out of ten had seen a relative during the previous week; among those without the proportion was less than two-thirds. As the boys move towards marriage and a family of their own, they take up with relatives once more. Now they visit them in their own right, not just as members of their parents' household.[10]

The parents and other members of the immediate family are themselves also affected, even more than the outside relatives, by the boy's shift towards marriage. I suggested earlier in the chapter that as boys developed stable partnerships they both became more reconciled to their immediate family and, along with their girl, spent more time within the family circle. It is now clear that these changes are part of a general re-ordering of kinship relationships.

These changes actually affect the girl's family more than the boy's. A distinctive feature of kinship in districts like Bethnal Green is that it is organized around the wife's 'family of origin' rather than the husband's. Couples tend to live near the wife's parental home and see more of her parents, particularly her mother; in short, the husband is drawn into his wife's 'extended family'.[11] This future pattern is reflected in what happens before marriage.

'When we came out of the pictures we went up Sylvia's house and her mother made us coffee. We talked to her parents about what we were going to do later in the week and about our friends.' (18 year old.)

'I had my tea, washed and left for the girl-friend's house. When I arrived her mother let me in and told me to take a seat in the living-room. We watched television for most of the evening.' (19 year old.)

[10] Allcorn, D. H., noted the same thing in his study. (*The Social Development of Young Men in an English Industrial Suburb*, p. 281).
[11] See *Family and Kinship in East London*, Chapters II, III and IV.

'About half past seven I went round my fiancée's flat, and sat down with her mum and dad and had a talk with them. We watched television for a while and then all went out for a drink.' (20 year old.)

These examples were part of a more general pattern. Of the thirty boys who wrote diaries for us, sixteen said they had a 'regular girl' or fiancée. Three of these boys – two aged 14, one 15 – recorded no joint visits during the week to either their home or their girl's. We counted all the visits with girls to one home or the other that were mentioned by the remaining thirteen, who were all older: they had made a total of thirty-four visits, twenty-seven to the girl's home, seven to the boy's. We also noted, for each of the thirteen boys, whose home they went to most often: three went, as far as we could judge, to their own home and their girl's about equally; all the remaining ten went more often to the girls.

The numbers are small, but they seem to suggest a preference for the girl's home. This would fit in with the main conclusion of the chapter: as the boys get older, the familiar dispositions of the local sub-culture begin to take shape.

V

SCHOOL

Earlier chapters have described the informal groupings around which the boys' lives are organized – the peer group, the courting couple, the family. This and the three following chapters take a different view: they begin with the institutional framework of the wider society and examine how the boys get on.

School is the first large-scale highly-organized institution with which the child has any continuing contact. From the age of five onwards, a large part of his daily life is spent in what is to him a huge building, with its flat asphalted playground, stone staircases, long corridors and high-ceilinged classrooms. Run bureaucratically, with a formal structure of authority, with 'morning assembly' and dinner queues and bells marking off the day, it is a strange and very different world from that of Mum and Gran and the corner shop.

By the age of 14 the educational system has become familiar, and the boys have moved on from infants' to juniors' and then to secondary school. Like everything else, secondary education was changing in East London while our research was in progress. Although the London County Council (now the Inner London Education Authority) had embarked on comprehensive secondary education in 1947, the process of reorganization was still going on twenty years later. Some of the older boys in the sample had attended schools that had since ceased to exist – they had been turned into primary schools or amalgamated, campus-style, with new blocks of buildings. Some younger boys had gone to sparkling new schools of glass and steel – a large boys' school in Stepney, for instance, or a mixed one in Shoreditch, and, in Bethnal Green itself, a new church school or a 'reorganized' school which, with a crop of new buildings, concentrates on training in technical subjects like carpentry and bricklaying. Our research cannot provide any evidence on how much of an improvement all this really amounts to, but architecturally, at any rate, it certainly looks an immense advance.

The secondary schools in mid-1964 were of four main types. First, there were the grammar schools – one, Parmiters' School, in Bethnal Green and half a dozen in near-by districts. These were, typically, historic institutions founded by City Guilds or Companies – like Parmiters' itself or the Coopers' Company's School – or by private benefactors – like Owen's School in Islington and the Davenant Foundation School in Stepney. All the grammar schools attended by local boys were either 'direct grant' or 'voluntary-aided' schools: they had a large measure of independence from the local education authority. Such schools emphasized their long traditions; their walls were hung with heraldic shields bearing Latin mottoes, portraits of former headmasters, or Rolls of Honour listing boys who had won scholarships to Oxford colleges or places in other universities. The aim of these schools is to provide an education for boys with the ability and aptitude for 'academic' study; the curriculum is geared to G.C.E. 'O' level and 'A' level. About one in seven of the 246 boys in our sample were present or former pupils of grammar schools.[1]

The second main category of local schools could be called the 'comprehensive' type. These were not fully comprehensive,[2] because they lacked the more successful pupils from the primary schools, who were 'creamed off' by the grammar schools. But some local secondary schools were more 'comprehensive' than others, in that they provided a wider range of curricula, including 'academic' courses up to G.C.E. 'A' level (in other words, up to the age of 18 or 19) as well as commercial or technical courses. I have classified as a 'comprehensive' school any local school which, though not a grammar school, offered a range of academic courses up to G.C.E. 'A' level. These were either former 'Central' schools like Morpeth School in Bethnal Green itself or South Hackney School a mile to the north, or new schools like those in Shoreditch and Stepney already referred to. Just over a quarter of the boys

[1] Here, as elsewhere in this chapter, the information about boys who were still at school relates to their school when interviewed, and, about those who had left school, to the last school they had attended.

[2] The Ministry of Education Circular in 1947 defined a comprehensive school as 'one which is intended to cater for all the secondary education of all the children in a given area. . . .' (Circular No. 144, 16 June 1947.)

in the sample had been to, or were at, schools of this 'comprehensive' kind.

The third main school was the secondary modern, which provided for more than half the boys in the sample. Some of these schools offered courses up to G.C.E. 'O' level; some ran special technical courses, often with a vocational bias; others gave what was described as a 'general education'.

These three kinds of school catered for the great majority. A small minority – about one in twenty – were present or former pupils of 'special' schools of various kinds. These included schools for physically handicapped or 'educationally sub-normal' boys. None of the schools was actually in Bethnal Green; they were either boarding-schools, outside London altogether, or more often day schools in other local districts.

Just under half the boys went to mixed-sex schools; nine out of ten of those who went to 'comprehensive' schools were at mixed ones, as were a third of the boys at secondary modern schools. All but one of the grammar schools boys, and all but one of those at 'special schools', were at schools for boys only.

Differences in opportunity

The grammar, secondary modern and 'comprehensive' schools clearly differ in the educational opportunities they offer their pupils. (The numbers at 'special schools' are much too small to justify even an attempt to draw conclusions.) These differences are brought out in Table XIII, which shows the examinations that boys had either passed or expected to take. More boys at grammar schools took examinations, though over a quarter of them took none and half took only G.C.E. 'O' level. Over a third of the pupils at 'comprehensive' schools took examinations, mainly G.C.E. 'O' level; only a handful of pupils at secondary modern school took any examinations.

Grammar schoolboys also received a longer education than the 'comprehensive' schoolboys, and the latter longer than secondary modern. Among the seventeen boys aged 16 or over and still at school, nearly half were at grammar school, a third at a 'comprehensive', and less than a quarter at a secondary modern. The six boys aged 17 or 18 and still at school were all at grammar schools. Among the boys who had already left school, a third of

TABLE XIII

Type of school and examinations passed or to be taken
(Boys who had left school, as well as those at school)

	Grammar	*'Comprehensive'*	*Secondary Modern*
No examinations passed or to be taken	29%	62%	88%
G.C.E. 'O' level only passed or to be taken	50%	29%	8%
G.C.E. 'O' and 'A' level passed or to be taken	21%	3%	—
Other examinations passed or to be taken (e.g. Certificate of Secondary Education, Royal Society of Arts Examination)	—	6%	4%
Total %	100%	100%	100%
Number	34	66	134

the grammar school pupils had left at 15, compared with two-thirds from 'comprehensives' and over nine-tenths from secondary modern schools. The longer schooling and the G.C.E.s apparently often have their reward. When they had left school (to anticipate the next chapter) more of the ex-grammar schoolboys and, to a smaller extent, more of the ex-'comprehensive' had white-collar or skilled jobs than the ex-secondary modern.

There is nothing unexpected in these findings. After all, middle-class parents presumably care so much about their children's secondary education largely because they believe that grammar schools open the way to better career opportunities. In the country as a whole, the higher the occupational class of the parent, the bigger the child's chances of going to a grammar school.[3] Even in a fairly homogeneous community like Bethnal Green, the occupational class of the fathers is reflected in the type of school the boys go to. This is shown in Table XIV.

Which school a boy went to had been determined in practice by what had hapened in his last year at primary school. Those

[3] See *The Demand for Places in Higher Education* (Appendix One of the Robbins Report), p. 49.

TABLE XIV

Father's occupation and type of boy's school
(Boys who had left school, as well as those at school)

Boy's school	Non-manual	Skilled manual	Semi-skilled and unskilled manual
Grammar	25%	14%	9%
'Comprehensive'	22%	30%	27%
Secondary Modern	51%	50%	63%
Other	2%	6%	1%
Total %	100%	100%	100%
Number	41	127	68

who went to grammar schools had been selected by the 'eleven-plus' examination, since abolished in inner London in favour of a 'profile' for each child based on his full record of primary education.[4] Those who went to 'comprehensive' schools did so either because they were 'selected' through the eleven-plus or on a headmaster's recommendation or because they happened to live within the 'catchment area' of such a school. Apart from the few who were thought to need special education, the rest of the boys went, as a matter of course, to the local secondary modern.

As Table XV shows, parental background has an influence upon the kind of school that a boy goes to. Parental encouragement and anxiety were evident over the eleven-plus.[5] The son of a foreman explained:

'Everybody in the family hoped I'd go to grammar school, and I got around to thinking it was something marvellous. I've got a cousin Janet, she's a month younger than me. Her father is my dad's brother and he's another foreman at the same printing works. Of course, both of us growing up together, both sets of parents were always comparing us. It

---

[4] This method, which on the face of it seems 'fairer', may in practice be more biased against children from working-class homes than the much criticized eleven-plus. A study in Hertfordshire in 1952 and 1954 showed that the proportion of working-class children getting grammar school places fell after the local education authority 'abolished the eleven-plus' in favour of teachers' assessments. (Floud, J. and Halsey, A. H., 'Intelligence Tests, Social Class and Selection for Secondary Schools.')

[5] The motives underlying educational ambitions for children are discussed by Jackson, B. and Marsden, D., *Education and the Working Class*, pp. 51–79.

was always "Your cousin Janet can do it, so can you". I knew I had to pass.'

The parents who were concerned about the eleven-plus included some who had themselves 'passed the scholarship' but had been unable to take up a grammar school place.

'My father had been pretty well up in school when he was a kid,' said one boy, 'and he passed the exam, but he couldn't go because of the uniform and all that. It was the same with my mother. They couldn't afford it in those days and they wanted me to.'

In other homes, it had all been taken more casually. It is true that, later in life, a few of the boys who went to secondary modern schools were somewhat bitter, like Jimmy Grove and two of his friends.

RON   I wish I'd learnt different languages at school. Then if I went abroad I'd know how to speak the language.

JIMMY   You can learn about foreign languages in some schools, but you haven't got the intelligence to go to one of them. None of us went to those high schools, grammar schools – whatever they call them.

ALAN   When you're in the junior school you're supposed to be able to choose out of three sorts of school. But you can't really.

RON   No, you can only go to crap schools.

JIMMY   They reckon you ain't got the brains for it, see. Did I pass the eleven-plus, did you pass the eleven-plus?

ALAN   They judge you at primary school. If you're no good at primary school they say, 'Right, you'll never be any good.' They don't give you a chance.

But, though this was the mood of some boys, it had not apparently been the dominant note at the time of selection.

'I didn't give it a thought,' said one boy. 'From my junior school you usually went on to the secondary modern round the corner, and that was that.'

'The eleven-plus – the school never put me in for it,' said another. 'I didn't really know about it.'

Sometimes the boy's attitude had been changed by the results of the examination. One had been surprised to hear that he had passed.

'I didn't know anything about the results – they give it to you in an envelope – but of course when the papers came through to say that I had passed I was a bit happy, so was my dad and the old woman. After the Easter holidays my dad took me up there. All the boys who were going to the school stood in the hall and as the headmaster called out their names they went into the different classrooms. At the end I was the only one left standing there. My old man went up to the headmaster and they were talking about it. It turned out that they had got the names mixed up; there was another boy in my class at the primary school called "Lamb" and my name's "Land". He was the one who had passed but they'd sent him to the other school and me to this one. It was all a mistake. It was a right let-down.'

Although he had been 'a bit happy' about the result at the time and 'let down' when the mistake was discovered, he had since come to think – or so he said – that he was better off at the school he did go to: 'If I'd gone there I wouldn't have known nobody. Another thing that would have put me off is all the homework. And they're not so strict at the school I went to.'[6]

Another boy, about whom there was no mistake, had also not expected to 'pass'. He had not been particularly encouraged or pressed at home. 'Before, I thought I had no brains at all,' he said. 'My mother thought I was just a tearaway who could never go to anything but a secondary school; now I seemed to have found a new talent.' He remembered the excitement of the new uniform: 'It looked marvellous to me – two eagles' heads and bits of blue and gold.' And he had enjoyed the challenge of the new subjects: 'The first term was wonderful. The masters? Lovely! Algebra, trigonometry – all new stuff, marvellous!' Others had felt much the same about going to their new school.

'In the first year you were a cut above everybody else. You

[6] Compare with an earlier study of working-class girls: 'The children know how important it is that they should pass this examination, and they are very jealous of the secondary (now grammar) school girls, though when they fail they disguise their bitterness by saying that they did not really want to go . . . because of the homework and because the teachers are so strict' (Jephcott, P., *Girls Growing Up*, p. 51).

were proud of going to a grammar school. You went to a *grammar* school; you didn't just go to a secondary modern. You thought, "I'm a clever bloke."' (17, *ex-grammar.*)

Once channelled into their respective schools, what did they make of the experience? An obvious point, but one that in fairness to the better local schools should be made at the outset, is that schools of the same 'type' are not necessarily alike in quality. Though pupils of the same school often disagreed in their judgement on it, there were some consistent contrasts in the comments on, for instance, one local secondary modern school as compared with another. Some stood out as better than average, others as worse. Another qualification to be borne in mind is that, since little more than a quarter of the boys were still at school when interviewed, the account is largely retrospective.

The school course

We asked the boys about the 'usefulness' of their lessons. There were no striking differences between types of school, but there was a contrast between those still at school and those who had left (Table XV). Boys who had left school, judging their education against their life and work outside the classroom, were more critical.

TABLE XV

Attendance at school and 'usefulness' of lessons

Lessons :	Still at school	Left school
'Very useful'	33%	22%
'Quite useful'	60%	58%
'Not much use' or 'No use at all'	7%	20%
Total %	100%	100%
Number	69	177

As Table XV shows, over half the boys, both at school and at work, said their lessons were 'quite useful'. The general tone, however, was less complacent than this may suggest; most of the boys who said 'quite useful' did have complaints –

'Some of the subjects are a waste of time'; 'A lot of it was pointless.'

Despite the similarities in the proportions who were approving or critical of the various types of school, the comments varied markedly. The grammar schoolboys who spoke enthusiastically, for instance, often specifically mentioned the value of the G.C.E., as well as of their education more generally:

'You get a chance to ask questions at school and to find out things that would take an awful lot of time to find out for yourself. I assume I've got some intelligence, and the school can help you to use it – I got seven "O" levels, and I'm now preparing for my "A" levels. I think the school has given me a broader outlook on life as well – more of an appreciation of different things. And because of having a higher education, I can talk to all sorts of people.' (17, *grammar*.)

Present and former boys from 'comprehensive' schools more frequently mentioned the vocational usefulness of their courses.

'I'm getting on all right at school. I want to be a draughtsman, and what we're doing at school is useful – it's all technical.' (15, *'comprehensive'*.)

Some also mentioned more general benefits. An 18 year old, formerly at a mixed 'comprehensive' school, said:

'For printing, which is what I went into, the technical lessons were very useful. The English helped me too – the way I speak – and, apart from the actual lessons, I learnt concentrating, which is useful.'

The secondary modern boys who felt their education useful to them usually made more modest claims for it. Some, like those from 'comprehensive' schools, did talk about the value of technical courses – 'I want to be a tool-maker and they're teaching me how to make tools' (14 year old); 'The lessons were quite useful to me because in my job I have to do technical drawing and I need quite a lot of maths' (16 year old). More expressive of the general view taken by ex-secondary modern boys was the remark of one, now aged 20, who said, 'The lessons were useful for the type of brain we had – only basic English and basic arithmetic.'

The criticisms, too, were related to the type of school. The grammar schoolboys often complained of what they saw as the academic remoteness of their course.

'It's far too general,' said a 16 year old. 'It doesn't really equip you to find a job. All you can do with it is to be a teacher, and who wants to be a teacher? Boys who go to grammar school and don't go on to be teachers or to university can really only be clerks – I think in the modern world they'd do better to get some sort of technical training that would equip them for a technical job. The grammar school won't give you that. If you go on through a grammar school course you may be very educated, you may be able to read all sorts of languages, but what good does that do you when you come to get a real practical job?'

Grammar school critics often mentioned, in particular, subjects they regarded as dead or out of date. 'What use is Latin to me?' said one boy. And another – 'I'll never be a Frenchman as long as I live, what's the use of me learning French?' Yet another – 'I'm not interested in reading Shakespeare or anybody like that; I'm just not interested because they're out of date. I haven't got much time for tradition or the past.'

The 'comprehensive' and secondary modern critics also felt that much of their course was remote from life. But the complaint was not so much that the subjects were part of an out of date or irrelevant culture, though this was sometimes said. It was more often that the school simply provided no practical training. The secondary modern boys, particularly, complained that the lessons were of no use in their job.

'Most boys at my school, their attitude was this isn't going to help me when I leave school so I won't bother. The school didn't give you enough scope on trades – it was nothing to do with your job later on. Maths, history – all that crap; anyway half the time I didn't know what they were talking about, to tell you the truth.' (19, *ex-secondary modern*.)

'My favourite subject was arithmetic, which is fucking useless to me now. (18, *ex-secondary modern*.)

It is easy to say that these boys were missing the point, that their education was not intended to be narrowly vocational but to deepen their understanding and broaden their interests. If their own testimony has any weight, however, it seems as if the teaching of non-vocational subjects often failed to connect with their own interests or arouse their enthusiasm. A number remarked, for instance, that although they were interested in music the school did not encourage.

'We used to have music, but the way it was taught it never interested me. It was all classical music and that sort of thing. And when you wanted to learn the guitar or the clarinet, all they would teach you was the recorder. You couldn't get on with the things you wanted to do.' (16, *ex-secondary modern*.)

Another former secondary modern pupil, aged 16, said about history:

'History was horrible; it drove you up the wall. He'd write something on the wall and you just had to take it down in your books. Fucking Napoleon and all that crap. You couldn't make a noise and then he'd start talking and then he'd be writing and he'd be nagging away about it and you'd have to write it all down. And it's very hard in a subject like that, because you know nothing of what people say and quotations and all that sort of junk. And we didn't know nothing about it – fucking Napoleon and some battle. We'd say, "We ain't got no interest in this," and he'd say, "Then you've got to find interest; it may come in useful to you." So I said, "I ain't leaving the country," and he said, "Don't you ever read the papers? Perhaps it will help you to read what's in there." Yes, he said all that junk would help you read the papers.'

A common theme among former and present secondary modern boys was that, in general, the school curriculum was dull or uninteresting.

'It's dreary, it's a drag. I'd like to get out to work and earn some money.' (15, *secondary modern*.)

'It was the same thing every day – dead boring, dead dull. I didn't pay much attention. It's just a laugh, really, because they never learned us nothing. Mostly it was a waste of time.

81

School

I didn't go to school all that much, to tell you the truth. At one time I stayed away a bit too much, and the teacher said, "You'll have to shoot in a bit more often."' (17, *ex-secondary modern*.)

The teachers

Asked how many of the teachers they 'liked' at their past or present school, most boys answered favourably. A fifth said 'all' and two-fifths 'most'; another fifth said 'about half' and the remaining fifth 'a few'. There were no marked differences between types of school, nor between those still at school and those who had left. Some boys were warm in their praise:

'They're a pretty fair lot of blokes. Most of them are very helpful.' (17, *grammar*.)

'They were good teachers, not stuck up. They understood you and treated you as equal.' (17, *ex-'comprehensive'*.)

'A decent lot. They always gave you a fair chance.' (15, *ex-secondary modern*.)

Such general admiration was, however, rare. Many boys, reasonably enough, distinguished between teachers. 'Some all right, some lousy,' said an ex-secondary modern boy. 'Some of them can be terrible,' said a 14 year old at a 'comprehensive', 'but a lot of them are very good.' Most other boys showed little real enthusiasm. Though they might say they liked 'most' or even 'all' of their teachers, they often added, coolly: 'They're not too bad' or 'They're all right'.

Among the most critical – the fifth who said they liked 'few' teachers – the main complaint was that the staff were distant. 'You can't class them as people,' a 15-year-old secondary modern boy put it, 'You can only class them as someone in charge of you.' It was sometimes said that they lacked interest or patience.

'Most of them weren't much good at teaching and didn't take much interest. A couple of the young ones from college or trainees were good. The rest just didn't understand anybody – they were just not interested in what I felt or what anyone else felt. You couldn't ask any questions with our mathematics bloke, for instance. He shouted at you for not listening, and if you said you did listen and you didn't understand, then he lost his temper. I never once found out how to do H.C.F. and L.C.M. I don't know even now what the letters mean.' (16, *ex-secondary modern*.)

'Some of the teachers got on my wick. They didn't have no patience. If they thought you couldn't learn they just turned their back on you, for the rest of your schooldays they just jumped on you if you couldn't answer a question. If you couldn't catch on quickly, they just clopped you round the earhole.' (16, *ex-'comprehensive'*.)

They were often seen, too, as socially different. In particular, it was suggested that most of them travelled in daily from the suburbs ('They mostly lived quite a way out,' said one boy, 'at London Airport and Braintree and places like that'); in consequence, they were thought to be out of touch with the East End and with working-class life.

'A schoolteacher knows his own subject but he's not a man of the world. He doesn't seem to be a working man, he's at school himself. He's not really a working man – he doesn't come home with his hands dirty like your father probably does. You see, in this part of the world – it's not a professional part of the world, and a professional man doesn't really seem like one of us. You don't really accept him.' (17, *ex-grammar*.)

'Some of them seemed to think the school a bit beneath them. They seemed to think they were being more or less degraded by being sent to a school down here. One of them told me to get back in the gutter where I belonged.' (18, *ex-secondary modern*.)

Another boy said he remembered only two masters – one of them a supply teacher – whom he thought of as coming from 'round here'. It made a great deal of difference: 'You could understand them more; they got through to you.' Others singled out particular teachers for praise on similar grounds; an ex-grammar schoolboy said there was only one teacher he had really respected.

'I was hopeless at French, but he used to persevere a lot and say, "Well, try," and although it was obvious I was hopeless I never used to get bad reports. He treated you decently. And you noticed little things about him. On sports day, or at football, he'd always kick the ball back to you if it went his way; the other teachers would just wait to let you go up to it. Or, if he was late for a bus, he would belt after it like a greyhound. The other teachers, if they missed a bus, they'd walk up to the bus-stop and wait for the next one. Well, you look up to a man like that. You say, "Well, he's one of your own, he's one of us." I mean you can imagine your father belting after a bus like that, if he's late. His class was about the only class the boys didn't mess about in. It just shows, if a teacher's respected, you don't mess about.'

An ex-secondary modern schoolboy of 15 had also liked one teacher specially:

'My last teacher, you could talk to him. Some of the others had no time for you. But with this one we used to have giggles; he seemed to be the same sort of class as us; he wasn't stuck up. He was born in an area like this and he talked like myself. He was a right Herbert. Whereas the others, any little thing you slipped up on, they'd give you a right rucking, the ladies especially – they talked posh, real English. Everything pronounced right, with a la-di-da accent. They probably went to high school themselves, where a lot of people do talk like that.'

As with the lessons, the criticism was essentially that the teachers, or some of them, failed to make contact with the boys. It seems likely that this accounts not only for much of the open hostility of the few, but also for the relative apathy among boys not overtly critical. The teachers, for their part, face a double difficulty. They are adults, trying to control and teach boys in large numbers, at a stage when peer loyalties are strongest and adult authority most open to challenge. And most teachers, whatever their social origins, are further separated from the boys by differences of class and culture.

The school régime

We wanted to see how far the boys were sympathetic to school in a wider sense than has been discussed so far. In an attempt to get at this, we asked what they thought of their school 'rules': how far did they think them 'reasonable'? Our assumption was that boys who were pro-school, in a general sense, would approve of all or most of the rules, and that those who were anti-school would be more critical.

On this index, most boys – over two-thirds – were broadly sympathetic. The common view was a reasonable one; it certainly did not suggest any great bitterness towards the school.

> 'If you find a rule's sensible you can turn round and say, "Well, I'll obey it"; but if it's not, you say, "Well, where did they get that idea from? What's the idea of that one?" It's like this thing of running through the passages; it's obviously dangerous to run in passages, and therefore it's a good idea to have a rule that you shouldn't do that.' (17, *ex-grammar*.)

Many were still more approving.

> 'All the rules have got good reasons, else the school wouldn't make them. In playtime, for instance, you're not supposed to go out of the playground – that's because you might get knocked over. And the rules about not playing with scientific equipment without permission – they are to stop you getting hurt as well.' (14, *secondary modern*.)

> 'They are all good rules at my school – otherwise they wouldn't have been made. But they aren't pushed too far or too hard. That's sensible.' (15, *'comprehensive'*.)

Others were less sanguine. Nearly a third regarded only 'about half' or 'a few' of their school rules as reasonable (one boy said that none were). They objected to being made to wear uniform or have their hair cut; to being punished for 'waiting on the staircase before the bell rang' or failing to call a teacher 'Sir'. And though, once again, there were no substantial differences in the proportions who complained at different types of school, there did seem to be differences in emphasis, particularly among boys who went beyond the discussion of specific 'rules' to talk more generally.

Among the secondary modern boys who were most anti-school, there were two themes. One was that school and teachers oppressed them.

> 'I didn't like things being forced down my throat. They tried to stop you wearing jeans and tell you what sort of shoes to wear.' (18, *ex-secondary modern.*)

> 'I didn't get on at all at school – I didn't take no interest in it. It used to get on my nerves all the time. They seemed to be getting on at you the whole time. They treated you like little kids.' (16, *ex-secondary modern.*)

A second note, echoing what secondary modern boys had said about their lessons, was that they felt the school could offer them little. 'I didn't really take much interest in school,' said a 17 year old, 'it was just something you had to do.' Jimmy Grove said, 'You can't expect to get much out of school if you go to crap schools like we did.' A study in Sheffield, based upon interviews with 200 boys and girls at secondary modern schools, noted the same lack of interest and enthusiasm.[7]

With the boys from the grammar school, the suggestion was that the school was constantly demanding. Most grammar school boys came to terms with this, more or less successfully. A minority reacted strongly.

> 'The school was always trying to turn you into something you were not. The idea was to make you into a collar and tie type, and I didn't like that.' (17, *ex-grammar.*)

> 'They kept on at you all the time. They wanted you to stay on after school in all sorts of activities. They wanted you to join the drama club and the badminton and the cricket and the table tennis and the School Association. I told them to go to hell. Nine to quarter to four was enough for me – once I'd finished school I was off home. It was bad enough having to do all the homework.' (17, *ex-grammar.*)

> 'School had a grip on your entire life. I mean, school wasn't finished when you came home. There was always the home-work, and then, when you'd done that, you'd think to your-self, "Is it all right? What's the mark going to be like?"

[7] Carter, M. P., *Home, School and Work*, p. 70.

You'd never finished with it. At a grammar school you're tied to school all the time. Every minute of the day. That's why I hated it – because it had such a hold on your life. You'd get home on Friday night, a case full of books and papers, and you'd think, "Well, I've got to allocate three hours Friday night, and then a couple of hours Saturday afternoon, and if I don't do any Saturday afternoon, I'll have to do it all day Sunday." And you knew if you didn't get it done straightaway – and you never could get it all done on a Friday – it wouldn't get done, and then you'd think, "Oh, bugger it, at least I'll have Saturday off, and I'll do it on Sunday." And it's nagging at you all the time – homework, homework, homework. It preyed on you, you could never really get away from it. And you get to school and you think, "Well, I've done my best," and then it comes back – three out of ten or something like that. "Useless", "Write all this out again", "Why haven't you done better?", "You've got a good brain, you're damn lazy, bone idle." There's no encouragement, they stamp on you all the time – "Shocking", "Horrible lazy lout", "Why don't you do better?" It used to get me down; I got in a shocking state when I was about 13. After that I got over it and I thought, "Bugger it, they can go and jump in the lake as far as I'm concerned; I'm not going to try any more – if I get nought out of ten then I get nought out of ten. That's it!" After that, any work I did I was bullied into.' (18, *ex-grammar*.)

'"You've got to get the G.C.E." Every week they said that. "You've got to get the G.C.E." Our maths master, every single lesson we got a lecture on something like that – "To get on in this world you must have your G.C.E." If you didn't have your G.C.E. you were no good. The G.C.E. was God Almighty.' (17, *ex-grammar*.)

School and community

Just because the grammar school demands more from its pupils, it is more likely to come into conflict with the values of the local community. The earlier research in Bethnal Green, like that in similar working-class areas, does not suggest any great interest by most parents in their children's education,[8] though attitudes are probably changing.

Homework was one source of contention. A 17 year old who had left grammar school at 15 said:

'My parents took no interest in my school. They didn't like me doing homework at all; they thought you shouldn't be doing it in your own time. I used to take up a whole table every night with homework. They thought there was a time for work and a time for play. You got no encouragement. They'd look at the report at the end of the term and that was about it. They didn't seem to realize what education meant.'

Another boy said that his parents' attitude had changed as he got older.

'In the beginning it was "Do your homework"; at the end "Have you done your homework?" to which I would answer yes whether I had done it or not. For the first two years it was a straightforward order. After that, I don't know whether my parents got fed up with asking me, but they started changing round. Probably trying to treat me like an adult before my time. Of course, in the East End they do leave you to go your own way at a much earlier age than they would in what you might call a higher-class suburb. Because they know life's been harder in the East End – or it has been, before the war – and they think that if you're thrown on your own devices early enough, you'll do better. I won't say that they're not interested, or that they won't help you if they can, but they do say to themselves, "Well, it's his life. Let him get on with it."'

Thus some families did not give much encouragement to their grammar-school sons, and others were actively discouraging. There were sometimes also conflicts with friends who lived near by and who had not gone to grammar school. To judge from what the boys said, feelings were rather less intense than they sometimes were in the East End before the war.[9] There was still some strain.

[8] See Young, M., *Innovation and Research in Education*, Chapter IV.
[9] See the discussion of social mobility via the grammar school in *Family and Kinship in East London*, where the ex-grammar school girls were those who had left school in the five years up to 1939 (pp. 144–8).

'If you've got friends who go to secondary modern school and you go to a grammar school, there's not so much hostility, but you do feel slightly apart from them. They sort of regard you as a separate person from them, you never quite get into their clan. I found out; you went with them but you never felt a part of them. They never sought you out, they never came knocking at your door, calling for you as much as they did for one another. They were chaps you knew because they were in the street, and you went to primary school together. The hostility only comes if you upset them and they sort of throw it in your face. You know – "You go to grammar school, you're stuck up, toffee-nosed. You think you're better than we are."' (17, *ex-grammar*.)

'They just didn't seem to understand. They didn't look down on you, or call you a snob or anything for going to grammar school, but if they came and knocked on the door and said, "Coming out? We're going to talk a walk over the park" or something like that, and you said, "No, I've got a load of homework to do," they would say, "Oh, sod the homework, come out." I used to say, "I can't, I just can't, I've got to do my homework." They said, "No, you don't have to do it, can't you leave it?" They don't understand.' (19, *ex-grammar*.)

According to another boy, the difficulties intensified after about the age of 15.

'The boys who didn't go to grammar school weren't particularly against you because they didn't go. But you found a big change as soon as they left school at the age of 15. You'd still got another couple of years to do and they'd started going to work, and from then on there was a difference. They went to work, they made their way in the world, and you were still at school and they thought of you as a kind of low life. They almost regarded you as a cissy. Possibly the reason for that is that deep down they resented the fact that you still went to school because you had the brain capacity and they hadn't.' (18, *ex-grammar*.)

Another boy, still at grammar school, complained in his diary about the problems of being a sixth-former. He began by describing the conversation in the prefects' room one morning.

'The topic was the usual one – "A" level. We talk about money – how much better off we will be than the rest of the teenage morons. It's not that we hate them that much, but it's just a pillar for us to lean on. Oh for the apathy of the rest of the East End. I wonder what it feels like to sit and stagnate in front of the telly every night without having to worry about exams or homework.' (18, *grammar*.)

It is clear that, in a working-class community like this, at least some grammar school boys feel cut off. The school and its values are not in tune with the local way of life. Sometimes the strain may lead boys to become 'early leavers'.[10] Of the boys in our sample who had left grammar school, nearly a third had left at 15, and altogether nine out of ten had left before they were 17. One boy, who had left at 15 a few months before he was interviewed, explained his reasons.

'Loads of times my parents used to say, "You're doing no good at school. Why don't you leave?" I always used to say, "What? End up doing a labouring job?" But after a while I got cheesed off with it. It was all very well studying for those G.C.E.s that they kept on about all the time, but I couldn't see what use things like Latin and English Literature were ever going to be to me. And I got fed up with being ordered about all the time at school. I decided to turn it in.'

Not that the critics of the grammar school are by any means all early leavers. Some stay on at school, though still under strain. They may stay on to do their 'A' levels, while feeling in an uncomfortable in-between world – at school when others of their age are at work, sometimes in conflict with the values of their parents, committed to ends which seem alien to their local community.[11]

[10] See *Early Leaving*, pp. 34–39, for a discussion of the influence of the home.
[11] The problems of working-class pupils at grammar schools are discussed more fully in Hoggart, R., *The Uses of Literacy*, pp. 295–7, and Jackson, B., and Marsden, D., op. cit., pp. 93–135.

The influence of peers

Family and neighbourhood may come into conflict with the educational system. So, too, may the peer group – and this applies as much in secondary modern as in grammar or 'comprehensive' schools.

It is obvious enough that within the formal structure of the school the boys are linked to each other in a multiplicity of peer groups. According to one boy, this was the main attraction of school: 'I like school all right. You see your friends there every day.' The part that friends play can be illustrated from diaries.

'9.15   Left for school. The reason I go so late is that I detest having to go to Assembly; every day it's the same old thing about things you're supposed to do and not do.

'9.30   I was in the classroom when the others came in from Assembly. I have three particular friends in my form – Mac, Ian and Steve. The teacher wasn't there so we sat around on the desks playing cards. Then he turned up and we started a double lesson of English. When the work started it was accompanied by obscene comments.

'11.00   During the break, Perkins came up to Ian and I, and asked if we were betting on the big race. . . . Steve and Mac came up and asked if either of us, meaning Ian or myself, had a fag. None of us had any, so we whipped up the price of a packet of fags and went round the corner and got ten Embassy . . .

'4.00   The bell went and the four of us went home together. I went into the cake shop and bought a cake for each of us.' (16, *'comprehensive'*.)

'9 a.m.   Started out for school. On the way I called for my mate Andy L. and we went together . . .

'10.55 a.m.   The milk bell went and me and my friend John B. gave out the milk cartons.

'11 a.m.   Me and three of my mates went into the toilets for a smoke . . .

'12.30 a.m.   Went up the fish and chip shop with Andy. We had our dinner there and then went over the park for a walk . . .

'3 p.m.   Had a fight in break with a boy called Stephen D.
I got a busted mouth and I got the cane for fighting . . .
'4 p.m.   School ended and I went up the café with my
friends.' (14, *secondary modern*.)

These relationships among the boys themselves, as teachers
have no doubt long recognized, can sometimes operate as
'counter systems' inside the school, working against its values.
From all three main types of school, there were extreme examples.

Secondary Modern: 'There was seven of us. If there was anything wrong we would do it. You know, the silly things you
used to do when you was at school, causing a commotion –
well if it was a student teacher, he nearly cried. We just kept
on shouting and shouting and he couldn't make himself
heard; he sent one boy to go and get the cane, he came back
and said he couldn't find it. Then he went out of the room,
and when he came back his books were flying around.'

'Comprehensive': 'There were a group of us stuck together.
We just sat about each day, messing about and doing half-
witted things. You only had to find a weak teacher and that
was it.'

Grammar: 'When I used to go to the junior school, I was keen
to learn. You know what I mean? I was dead keen; I used to
get up dead early to go there. As soon as I came to this
school the atmosphere got me down. There was the discipline
and all the teachers getting on to our little clique. There were
nine of us. We were the main butt for them; we bore the
brunt of their attack. Every lesson became a battle; either the
teacher went down or we did.'

As well as affiliations of this kind there are also antipathies,
those who are anti-school being rather contemptuous of those
among their fellow-pupils who accept the school's standards most
fully and fit in with them.

'The teachers had their favourites. There was a real sod at
school but the teachers made him a pet. It seemed to be the
spoilt kids they always made pets of. We were all scruffy
kids and it was the ones who had better clothes and better
houses who got on best at school. I always hated them –

the well-looked-after boys whose fathers had shops.' (17, *ex-grammar.*)

'There was always a minority of goody-goodies – the people who liked homework and were good at everything and were always top of the class. I felt that say the top four in the class never got on quite so well with the rest.' (19, *ex-grammar.*)

Prefects were sometimes seen in the same way – as potential allies who had deserted to the enemy. An 18 year old, a former secondary modern school boy, said: 'I wasn't a prefect and I didn't want to be. We used to sauce them, we used to think that because they were prefects they were teacher's pets, crawlers trying to get round the teachers so that they could get away with things. They were the top-class boys, the ones who knew every-thing. I never did like any of them.'

For their part, some of those who became prefects were fairly closely identified with the school and its values. An 18 year old at a grammar school wrote in his diary:

'Tuesday. 9 a.m.   After registration I took house prayers as House Captain. It's a job I really enjoy. I enjoy it because you have a chance to make an example to the young kids – the hard nuts of the Fourth and Fifth. I find it a rewarding experience.'

The *misfits*

All in all, the evidence of this chapter does not suggest either severe antagonism to school or strong affection for it. Some boys, at all types of school, clearly did like it very much. Most, judging by their comments, simply accepted it. School was just a part of life, something they did not feel strongly about one way or the other. A former grammar school boy, aged 17, put it like this:

'It wasn't too bad. It was certainly useful. I didn't like the homework because it interferes with your social life. But I got on all right – I wasn't an angel and I wasn't the sort who got caned. Some subjects I liked, some I didn't.'

Boys at the other kinds of school said much the same. 'It's OK; there's nothing wrong with it,' remarked a 14 year old at a 'comprehensive' school, 'You've got to know something when you go out to work.' An 18 year old, formerly at a secondary modern, said:

> 'School was all right. I more or less just plodded on. I done fair – I got on adequate for what I wanted to know. The last year was the best; it was nice to know you didn't have to stay another year.'

It is against this background that the criticisms have to be assessed.

On each of our indices – lessons, teachers, 'rules' – something between a fifth and a third of the boys were critical. Those who complained on one score did not necessarily cavil on another: some, for instance, thought their lessons 'no use at all', but approved of 'most' of their teachers. There was, however, a correlation between all three indices.[12] All types of school have similar proportions of critics. But the reactions against the school seem to take different forms in different types of school, particularly grammar as against secondary modern. It is not possible to offer any generalizations about 'comprehensive' schools; for boys in 'higher' or 'lower' streams they seem somewhat like grammar and secondary modern schools respectively.

The grammar school seems to impose strain upon some pupils because of its whole-hearted pursuit of what might be called 'middle-class' success. It demands not only politeness, cleanliness, 'good manners', but also the virtues of character associated with the 'Protestant ethic' – ambition, drive, the will to work hard and to defer pleasures until they have been earned. As earlier research has also shown, some of the difficulties of boys who come into conflict with the grammar school arise from the clash between

[12] We carried out a series of correlations (a 'correlation matrix') for the 177 boys who had left school (the reason for excluding those still at school is given in a footnote on p. 211, Appendix 4). The purpose of this analysis was to see what facts or attitudes were associated with others: for instance, were the boys who criticized the lessons also more likely than others to complain about the teachers or the rules? If the correlation between two items were complete – in other words, if each boy gave an identical answer to both questions – the 'correlation coefficient' for that pair would be 1·000. With this sample of 177 boys, a figure of more than ·147 or less than —·147 means there is less than one chance in 20 that the correlation (positive or negative) is due to chance. The analysis showed that there was such a correlation between the answers to all three questions about school: between attitudes to lessons and to teachers it was ·307, between those to lessons and rules ·230, and between those to teachers and rules ·254.

these values and those of the local community and the peer group.

There is something of the same conflict in the other sorts of school as well. In a sense, all schools are dedicated to the 'Protestant ethic'; all try 'to turn you into something you are not'; all are out of sympathy with the working-class community. 'Teachers represent middle-class attitudes and enforce middle-class values and manners.'[13] But, presumably because the staff of the secondary modern schools themselves expect less from their pupils, they press them less and this particular note of discord is more muted. The main complaint against the secondary modern school was that it was dull and uninteresting, sometimes that it was a 'crap school', inferior to others. And this, it will be remembered, is the secondary education of the majority of local boys.

After school

The sense that they might have got more out of their secondary education was certainly expressed later, by secondary modern boys in particular. Those who had left school were asked what they had felt about leaving 'at the time'. In all types of school, about four-fifths said they were glad. They were also asked if they had changed their minds since, and on this the proportions varied – just over one in ten of the boys who had been at grammar or 'comprehensive' schools said they were now sorry they had left school when they did, compared with over a quarter of the ex-secondary modern boys. Similarly, the boys in semi-skilled and unskilled jobs – again, overwhelmingly former secondary modern pupils, and the less successful among them – more often said that they had changed their minds about leaving school. Sometimes they blamed the school, sometimes themselves.

'I wish I'd got somewhere while I was at school. I can see my mistake now, but I didn't know what school meant at the time. I didn't realize about G.C.E.s and all that – I can see now that you're much better off if you can stay at school a bit longer and get G.C.E.s. But at my school there was only about one person in fifty who did G.C.E. My girl went to a better school and she's got nine G.C.E.s. I've decided I've

[13] Warner, W. L., Havighurst, R. J., and Loeb, M. B., *Who Shall be Educated?*, p. 106.

got to give her up because I'm really just a drag on her. I'm holding her back, if you know what I mean.' (17, *ex-secondary modern.*)

'They didn't tell us anything at school about G.C.E. being a big help in getting a job. Nobody bothered to explain about it. It's no use crying over spilt milk, but I wish now that I had had a better education – I realize now that I would have liked to have gone to a grammar school if I could.' (18, *ex-secondary modern.*)

Few of the boys who fail at school make up for it afterwards through further education. Of the 177 who had left school, not one was a full-time student at London University or at a technical college or other institution of further Education. About one in five of those who had left school, however, was in some kind of part-time further education. Of these, three-quarters were on day-release courses (a majority of them attending evening classes as well) and a quarter evening classes alone. More than half of these part-time students were going to technical colleges, a fifth to Day Colleges, about a tenth to Junior Commercial and Technical Colleges, and the rest to a variety of other kinds of institution including art schools, commercial colleges and the like.

There was a high wastage from local further education institutions. A quarter of the boys who had left school had been to day or evening classes at some time in the past, but had since stopped going. Since the ages of the boys who were in further education were much the same as those who were not, it looks very much as if the people who had been engaged in further education earlier and given up had done so not because they had finished their course but for other reasons. The local technical colleges confirmed this. One reason for giving up was that the boy had changed his job.

'The first job I had when I left school, I was working for a firm that used to send all their boys off to these day-release classes. I didn't mind it – it was time off work and it was better than going to school. But when I turned that job in, the governor where I'm working now doesn't do that. It more or less went with the job before, and when I changed the job I stopped going.' (18, *ex-secondary modern.*)

'When I was at school I thought I wanted to go in for electrical engineering, and the first job I got was in that. I used to go to evening classes with that job, but after a while I got fed up with it. I had a friend who was working in the firm I'm with now as a cabinet assembler – he was earning more money than me and it seemed a good little job, so I decided to give up electrical engineering. There's no real night school to do with the job I'm in now.' (17, *ex-'comprehensive'*.)

The main reason for giving up evening, as distinct from day-release, courses was that attending was too difficult or the demands of work too heavy. 'It was a long way to go,' said one boy, 'I had to go right over to Poplar three nights a week.' Another said, 'You had to go nearly every night. You didn't get any time to yourself.' And, as might be expected, the same reasons were given by boys who had never attended evening classes.

'I think that when you're young you ought to enjoy yourself. It's all very well these people going off to night school three and four nights a week, but where's their fun? You may say I'd get a better job later on. Perhaps I would. But I think you ought to enjoy yourself while you've got the chance.' (17, *ex-secondary modern*.)

A few other boys said they did not have the necessary qualifications or did not know where to go.

'I'm working as a store-keeper now, but I don't want to do that for the rest of my life. I'd like to be a commercial artist if I was any good at it; I always used to be good at art when I was at school, but I never bothered with it then. I always used to play about during the lessons and get chucked out. If I could I'd like to go to night school and do commercial art, because then I might get into a job in that line. But I don't really know where you're supposed to go. I don't know whether any of the art schools would take me. I haven't got G.C.E.s or anything like that.' (18, *ex-secondary modern*.)

'I think I've really missed my chance. If I'd known about it at school I might have been able to go on to night school. I

don't know whether I'm right, but I don't think I'd stand a
chance of getting in as I am at the moment. You've got to
have some sort of grounding in education to be able to
benefit from night school.' (17, *ex-secondary modern.*)

In general, the boys attending evening and day classes were
not those who had done badly at secondary school. There was no
indication that boys who were critical of school were more likely
than the others to be in further education – if anything, the
opposite was true. Boys who had gone to grammar and 'comprehensive' schools were more often attending day and evening
classes than those who had gone to secondary modern schools –
about a third of the former were evening or day students, compared with just over a tenth of the latter. Similarly, it was overwhelmingly the boys in non-manual and skilled manual jobs who
were going on with their education, as is shown in Table XVI.
What is more, those going to evening or day classes were predominantly boys who were already in jobs as apprentices or
trainees – a third of these boys were in further education, compared with less than a tenth of the other boys at work.

TABLE XVI
Boy's occupation and attendance at day or evening classes

	Non-manual	Skilled manual	Semi-skilled and unskilled manual
Attending day or evening classes	20%	26%	5%
Not attending, but has attended in past	38%	19%	19%
Never attended	42%	55%	76%
Total %	100%	100%	100%
Number	45	95	37

All this suggests that further education was closely linked to
the boys' jobs and to their former schooling. On the whole, the
boys who had not done well at school and regretted the fact were
unlikely to make up for it in some sort of further education. This

seems particularly unfortunate, since it is clear, from those who were going to day or evening classes, that they found the régime more congenial than that of school. The thirty-six boys engaged in further education were asked how they thought the 'atmosphere' of their college compared with that at school. A tenth of them said that there was no marked difference; none compared further education unfavourably with school; the remaining nine-tenths said that it was much better – the main reason being that it was 'freer'.

'It's much freer and happier there and the relationship with the teacher is better. They treat you like grown-up people and they impose discipline from respect. They can make it more interesting by telling you why you're learning a subject you think is going to help you.'

'It's completely different from school. You call the teachers by their first names, and there's no "Yes, Sir, No, Sir". They treat you like men. They treat you with more respect, so you act right yourself. I've learnt more in three months at evening classes than I learned in three years at school.'

Part of this difference is presumably a reflection of their own self-selection – the boys who go to evening classes are volunteers, who can see the point of what they are doing. Even when this is allowed for, it seems as if the more 'adult' atmosphere – so much in contrast with the kind of thing about which some complained at secondary school – would prove congenial not only to those already attending further education courses but to many others as well.

This chapter, to sum up, has tried to show the interaction between the boys and the educational system. The boys themselves react in different ways, and the schools differ in how they work and in the strains they generate. All the schools seem, in greater or lesser degree, out of tune with the local community. Some press too hard; others offer too little. On the whole, the failures of secondary schooling are not made good in further education. Though the general tone from the boys is uncomplaining, the conclusion must surely be that the contact between them and the system is less fruitful than it could be.

VI

WORK

'Got up at 6 o'clock, after being called about five times by
my elder brother, got washed and dressed, had a cup of tea
and went to work. When I got to work I got my delivery
sheets – there were nine pubs to do over Enfield way, and I
went with my usual driver. We had to load up the lorry first
of all and then unload when we got to the different pubs.
We also have to pick up their empties, which is all com-
mission to us – we get paid threepence on a barrel; this may
not sound a lot but you earn quite a bit. My basic wage is
£11 9s., but I earn between £15 and £21 a week, and you
don't sneer at that. One of the pubs we went to had got
cellars older than anyone can remember. It still has the old
wine vaults; the public house has been rebuilt, but the cellar
has been unchanged. It's now very musty and the floors are
slippery as the damp forms slime on the old flat-stones, so
it's still a good place to keep beer in – it stays cool all the time.
With one of the pubs we went to the publican seemed rather
moany. With people like that you have to be ready to give
quick answers to all their complaints. It gets maddening at
times, as if you say the wrong thing they phone the Transport
Office about you. The only way you can get back at them is to
say you will report them for dirty cellars. Some of the stillons
are disgusting – a stillon is what we have to place the beer
on, and if they're not clean the keg slides and could easily
trap your fingers. We got back to the depot at about 3.45 and
as the day was hot the free beer at the depot was very welcome. It's not as strong as the beer at a pub, but when you're
thirsty it tastes all right. After that I went home.' (18, *brewery
dray boy, ex-secondary modern.*)

'9.00   Signed in at the office, which is just off High Holborn.

I say "Good morning" to Arthur, who is a year older than me and is the other junior clerk there. I also have a talk with the girls in the office – the typists. There are about eight girls as well as Arthur and me working in one big office. My first job is to change the date on the franking machine – that's the machine that does the stamping for the post. Next I file away all the carbon copies and confirmation copies, and then do the post book – that's how much we pay and all that. Various other duties around the office, including taking some office memoranda round to people in other departments.

'10.30   Coffee break. Glad to stop for a drink today because it is so hot. Have a bit of a talk and a laugh with some of the girls, paying special attention to Sandra, who's about the same age as me and is one of the girls I've got my eye on there.

'11.00   Had to take some urgent papers out to another office. I had to go by taxi, which I quite enjoyed, but it was nice to get out of the office and into the open air.

'11.45   Back at the office again, I got on with the job of filling in various invoices.

'12.30   One of the girls, Carol, showed me how to operate the switchboard, and I took it over for half an hour while she went to lunch and before the other girl, Linda, came back and took over from me.

'1.10   As I was going out for my lunch, found that Sandra was going out at the same time. I asked her if she would come to lunch with me at the restaurant in the next street. We had fillet of plaice and chips and fruit salad. It cost me ten shillings, but it was worth it.

'2.15   Got back from lunch. More work on invoices, and then I had to take an urgent parcel down to Waterloo station.

'3.30   Tea break. Talked to Arthur and the typists. I kept looking at Sandra, hoping that she'd give me a special look – my next step is to ask her if I can take her out one evening, dancing or to the cinema. But she didn't look in my direction at all, just laughed and joked with the other girls.

'4.00   Started to do some photo-statting.

'4.30   I had finished the photo-statting and Mr. Brooks came in; he's the head of the department we are in. I don't like him – he sort of slides along the ground and if he sees something wrong, he'll say it in a nasty joke. This time he came up and saw that I had forgotten to turn off the photo-stat and cover it. So he came up with a big grin and said, "I do hope you've covered up the photo-stat and turned it off." You can't trust him – he's smiling one minute and then he's sort of got his hooks in your throat the next. I tried to ignore him and got on with my work.

'5.00   Went round to collect the post. My job is to seal and frank the letters.

'5.30   The typists packed up and went home, leaving the letters I hadn't already collected. I collected them up, sealed them and franked them, and then took all the letters to the Post Office at about quarter to six. On the way out I met Jack – he's a friend of mine who used to go to the same grammar school as me and who works for the same firm, but in a different part of the building. I sometimes see him when I go home – not always, because he usually leaves at 5.30 when the rest of the staff do. But this evening he had stayed behind to finish, and we met as we were both going out of the building. We walked along to Chancery Lane station and went home together on the tube.' (16, *office boy, ex-grammar.*)

The diary extracts describe a working day in two contrasted jobs. Of the 177 boys who had left school, none were in the Registrar General's top social class ('Professional') and only eight in the second highest ('Intermediate'), with jobs like insurance claims broker, commercial artist, trainee manager and 'cub' reporter on a newspaper. Thirty-seven boys were in non-manual jobs of a more 'routine' kind, mainly clerks and shop assistants, draughtsmen and betting-shop 'settlers'. The remaining three-quarters were in manual occupations, skilled workers outnumbering semi-skilled and unskilled by more than two to one. Skilled jobs included butcher, compositor, motor mechanic, upholsterer; examples of the less skilled were building labourer, fish porter, storekeeper and van boy. Although there were of course some boys with very different jobs from their fathers, the proportions in non-manual, skilled and less skilled work were broadly similar in both generations.

All the boys were asked whether they were 'an apprentice' or 'trainee'. Almost exactly half said they were. This seemed such a large proportion that we decided that some of them must have been describing as an apprenticeship or traineeship a less formal arrangement for learning their job. To check on this, we compared the boys' occupations as they had described them with the Ministry of Labour's list of National Joint Recruitment and Training Schemes. Some jobs were not in the official list – for example, trainee manager, crane driver, shop fitter, silversmith and store-keeper. But most were, and as many as two boys out of every five of those at work were in jobs for which there were recognized apprenticeship or traineeship schemes. The jobs were pre-dominantly skilled manual, but there were some apprentices and trainees in non-manual occupations and some in so-called semi-skilled jobs.[1]

A fifth worked in Bethnal Green itself, and altogether half inside the East End. The proportions who worked locally varied with the type of job (Table XVII).

TABLE XVII

Boy's occupation and workplace

	Non-manual	Skilled manual	Semi-skilled and unskilled manual
Bethnal Green	9%	28%	19%
Elsewhere in the East End	20%	32%	30%
City or Central London*	65%	32%	41%
Elsewhere	6%	8%	10%
Total %	100%	100%	100%
Number	45	95	37

* The definition of 'Central London' is given in the interviewer's instructions, Appendix 2, p. 199.

The boys in Westminster or the West End or the City of London often worked for large organizations – big commercial or industrial firms, government departments or nationalized

[1] Here, as elsewhere in this book, occupations have been classified according to the Registrar General's *Classification of Occupations, 1960*.

industries. Some were with bodies like the BBC, large insurance companies or daily newspapers, organizations with a complicated hierarchy of power, large airy offices or workshops, staff canteens, specialized wages departments. For those who worked in the East End, particularly Bethnal Green itself, it was different; the firms were often small, sometimes with only three or four employees. An 18 year old worked as a cabinet maker in a firm five minutes away from his home, where there were six others. A 17-year-old cabinet assembler explained: 'There are only four of us there – the governor, two men and me. It's a really old place, where we work, it's almost coming down. The factory inspector's been up here and we've got to have the lot put in – a sink, fire escape, ventilators. But I don't mind working in an old place, because I earn good money and I get on with the other people. It's friendly when it's a little firm like that.'

Other firms may not be so small. Still, the industry of the East End is largely run in small units. The characteristic local industry is not at all like the giant factories that line the arterial roads. There are some new industrial buildings in Bethnal Green, but they are the exception rather than the rule. In one back street eight tailors work, almost elbow to elbow in the converted bedroom of what used to be a terraced cottage. To the whirr of wood-saws men are making furniture in a tiny workshop off a jumbled alley that looks almost as Charles Dickens might have described it. From another workshop in an otherwise residential street the veneered sideboards pile out onto the pavement.

The connection between the kind of education the boys have and the kind of job they get when they leave school was mentioned briefly in the previous chapter. Grammar school boys more often get non-manual jobs than 'comprehensive', and 'comprehensive' more often than secondary modern. Conversely, a quarter of the secondary modern boys were in semi-skilled or unskilled jobs, against a tenth from the other two types of school.

The ways in which education influences occupation are fairly obvious. Ex-grammar school boys more often enter white-collar jobs because they have the G.C.E.s the employers demand, and because the school, their parents and they themselves have come to think such a job appropriate. Boys with some form of technical training, whether in 'comprehensive' or secondary modern school, are able to use this in getting an apprenticeship or trainee-

ship for a skilled job. Those who have not done well at school
and have no qualifications or skills to offer, though they may
sometimes find their way into a job with prospects, are more
likely to end up in an unskilled job.

Getting a job

In theory, the youth employment service is available to help
school leavers find suitable work. In fact, although more of the
boys in the sample had got their first job through the Youth
Employment Officer than any other single source, they were not
a majority. This is shown in Table XVIII, which also indicates
how boys got their present job if it was not the same as their
first.

TABLE XVIII
Source of first and of present job

	First Job	Present Job (if not first)
Youth employment service	39%	14%
Employment exchange	2%	6%
Advertisement	12%	15%
Relative or friend	32%	47%
Other source	15%	18%
Total %	100%	100%
Number	177	101

The table shows that, with the first job, informal contacts
through relatives and friends were about as important as the
youth employment service.[2] But when the boys came to change
their jobs – and over half of them had been in more than one since
leaving school – then the 'youth employment', as the boys called
it, was less important, the influence of family and friends more.
It could be argued that this drop is not surprising, since the youth
employment service is only available until 18. But when the

[2] The figure of 'first placements' by the youth employment service – 39 per cent –
is close to that in England as a whole – 37 per cent (*The Work of the Youth Employment Service, 1959–1962*, p. 9).

influence of the employment exchange is taken into account as well, it is striking how small a contribution is made by official agencies.

One boy was particularly grateful to the youth employment service.

'When I left school I worked in an office as a draughtsman. I was there for three months – I'd been trained for that job at school. But I can't stand being locked in. So I went up to the youth employment, and they got me this job – working as a street paviour. Most of my friends are office workers, and when they found out it caused quite a joke. They called me a labourer, a road-digger, a plain common labourer. But I've never regretted it. I think the important thing is to get the job you prefer, and I prefer working outdoors. I wish I'd gone to the youth employment before.' (19, *street mason and paviour working for Borough Council.*)

Many more, however, spoke in the opposite sense.

'When I left school I didn't have any idea about the sort of jobs I could do. All I thought was engineering? No. Print? No. Carpentry? No. That's the only three things I thought of. My father had been in engineering but that didn't appeal to to me very much so I didn't know what to do. Since then I've had about a dozen jobs. I've been in insulating, planning and building. I'd never heard of insulation – never thought of it as a job until I went down to the youth employment. When I went down there they didn't give me much hope; they said, "You either take this job" – that was working for an insulating firm – "or you find your own." I took it but I didn't stay there very long.' (17, *building labourer.*)

'I've had eight jobs since I left school, that's eight jobs in 18 months. I never had any jobs from the youth employment. Well, they do their best I suppose, but I just didn't fancy what they said, and a bloke down there acted as if he was your governor or something already.' (17, *building contractor's clerk.*)

The local community – relatives or friends – proved more satisfactory. Of the boys who got their first job through the youth employment officer, 30 per cent were still in it. The proportion for those who got their first job by other means was 52 per cent, and amongst those who got it through relatives in particular 64 per cent.[3]

Many examples were given of how relatives and friends had helped.

'I heard about this job from a mate of mine who used to go to the same school as me. He left school before I did and started work there. He said that they were quite good employers – good pay and prospects and all that. When I decided to leave school at the end of last term, I was talking to him about it, and he said, "They've got a vacancy for a junior at our firm. Would you like me to mention you to the governor?" Well, I agreed, and he spoke up for me and I went up to see them, and I got the job.' (16, *insurance clerk*.)

'I was a painter's mate and I wasn't cut out for it – I didn't like the job. After I'd been there about three months I decided to chuck it in and give a week's notice. I was looking for a job so I went round to my Uncle Charlie. I knew that he wanted a boy to work at his firm about three months earlier. So I went round to him one night when he was round my nan's, and I said, "Charlie, is that job still going?" He said, "No, but the boy they've got at the moment is a bit of a nutter, he's not cut out for that kind of work, and I don't mind sacking the other boy and giving you the job." So that's what he done. He sacked the other boy and gave him a week's notice and found him another job somewhere else. And I started working round there instead – I get on well there – there's only my uncle and the other governor and three more people there besides me.' (17, *plastic injection moulder*.)

Fourteen boys – 8 per cent of those at work – were in the same occupation as their father or working for the same employer. One was a clerk in a warehouse where his father worked as a storeman. A father and son were both compositors. Another father was a plumber and the son his mate. Other pairs, for example, were in

[3] Carter similarly found the turnover higher with jobs secured through the Youth Employment Service. (Carter, M. P., *Home, School and Work*, p. 169.)

upholstery, shoe manufacture and Billingsgate fish market. Another boy worked in Covent Garden, like both his father and brother.

> 'I'm a porter in what they call an empties warehouse in Covent Garden. We keep all the empties – they come in every day for the market and then go out at night. We start at six o'clock in the morning and finishing time is supposed to be three o'clock, but we always stop at half past two. My dad's been there fourteen or fifteen years and my brother seven or eight years. They've got a list down, a waiting list for jobs, and my dad put my name down on it. That's how I got the job – through both of them working there.' (18, *market porter*.)

Satisfaction at work

Once at work, how content were the boys with their jobs? We put some specific questions about attitudes to work; whether the boys were satisfied or dissatisfied with their job in general, with the pay and with the prospects, and what sort of work they first 'expected' and, second would 'choose' to be doing in future.

The answers to the first three questions, as far as they go, suggest a fairly high degree of 'satisfaction'. About four-fifths of the boys said that they were 'satisfied' with their job generally; just over two-thirds with the pay; nearly three-quarters with the prospects. Most of the rest said they were 'dissatisfied'; on prospects, two boys gave 'in-between' answers – 'so-so', 'difficult to say' – and one did so on his job generally. So the level of contentment was apparently high. In talking about the future – we asked them about the prospects ten years ahead – half said not only that they expected to be doing the same kind of work but also that they would 'choose' to.[4]

There were no marked differences in their answers on most of these questions in terms of the kind of job they had, the district they worked in, whether they were apprentices or not, or the kind of school they had gone to. One exception was that the

---

[4] Carter found in Sheffield that 60 per cent of boys and girls both 'expected' and 'wanted' the same jobs. (Carter, M. P., ibid., p. 134.)

Work

'higher' the status of the job, the more likely were the boys to describe themselves as 'satisfied' with their prospects; 80 per cent of the boys in non-manual said that they were 'satisfied', compared with 73 per cent in skilled manual work and 62 per cent in semi-skilled or unskilled. As with attitudes to school, there was some variation between the answers on different indices. Opinions of the job in general were correlated with those on pay ($\cdot$187) and still more on prospects ($\cdot$375).[5]

It is obvious that to ask the boys whether they were 'satisfied' – with pay, prospects or their job generally – could provide only a crude measure of their attitudes. In fact, most were neither completely 'satisfied' nor 'dissatisfied'; they generally liked some aspects of their job but not others. It is clear, too, that boys can 'like' their job in different ways. Some meant that they got satisfaction from exercising their skill, others that they found the job tolerable or that they liked the other people there. Some laid more emphasis on their present feelings about their work, others on its prospects for their future. In all this there seemed a different emphasis between boys in different types of occupation.

Among some boys in skilled jobs, the skill itself gave pleasure.

'Arrived at the firm at 7.55. Sat down at my bench and started repairing a pair of Georgian candlesticks which were made in the year 1759 by James Gould. First I took the bottom off and then ran the rosin out of them. Then I burnt them out and pickled them – pickle consisting of eight parts water and one part sulphuric acid. I left them in the pickle for about fifteen minutes and then rinsed them under water and dried them out. Then with a colet hammer I tapped the bruises out of them and burnished them. Then, using easyflow flux and easyflow solder, I filled in the holes and pickled them again to remove the flux. I went to dinner at one o'clock in the café across the road, and returned to work at 1.30 p.m. Then I got the candlesticks out of the pickle again and filed them up, filled them with rosin and sent them down for sanding and polishing ready for plating. My last job was to sort out some elephant feet ready for the next day – we make all sorts of things out of them, such as umbrella stands,

[5] A footnote on p. 94 explains how to interpret these figures, which are the 'correlation coefficients' between pairs of items.

decanters, waste-paper bins. At 4.50 p.m. I had a wash and I left work at five o'clock. (19, *silversmith.*)

'Most of the people at the school I went to had an ambition to be bank clerks, doctors and things like that. But printing always fascinated me right from the beginning, and I made up my mind to go into it six months before I finished at school. It's very interesting – you're doing different things all the time, and one day a week I go down to the London College of Printing to learn more about the theoretical side of it. There's one machine in our firm that I'm really looking forward to working on when I get the chance. There are only two of them in the country, and most of the time people are coming in and looking at it. It's a kind of show-piece, four-colour work – you know, really good-class work.' (18, *printer, ex-grammar.*)

'I like the butchery trade very much. It gets you full of grease and it makes you smell a bit when you come home, but it's a good life – open air, you're in the shop and you meet people, it's really interesting, never monotonous. The most important thing about a job is getting to the top – mastering the whole lot. In this particular job it's not just cutting meat – you've got to take the veins out, you've got to know where the veins are.' (19, *kosher butcher.*)

There were other boys who said they were happy in their work, and who, though they did not expressly say so, gave the impression of enjoying the work itself as well as other aspects of the job. One was a 17-year-old fitter's mate who worked in a converted railway arch in Bethnal Green, now a garage.

'I'm happy there, I have a laugh. Everybody likes everybody else. I'll stay there as long as I can, as long as they'll have me. The only promotion I would want is to become a fitter; I'd be happy as a fitter. I'm underneath cars for about four out of every eight hours – putting in new clutches, axles, giving it a clean-up. Sometimes you lose your temper, but there's nothing you can do. And you get cheesed off having to wash so much when you get home from work. Some of my mates don't have to wash till next morning, but I have to take my boots off and get washed all over because of the grease.

But I don't mind being dirty, as long as the money's there – the money's all right in this job. Sometimes when a job won't give way I lose my temper; and I walk away for five minutes and have a smoke. It's worse in the winter, the snow coming in your face, you're under a lorry, and you really just want to give up. Sometimes you get called out at night on a breakdown. In winter you can hardly feel your fingers; you think about the people in an office, it's so cold you wish you were in there. But if I had my time again, well, I'd do the same again.'

Others had jobs that seemed, on the face of it, hard and tedious. Yet many of them, too, said, without much enthusiasm, that they 'liked' the work. It is obvious that their attitudes were partly determined by what they thought it was reasonable to expect from a job. They might say that they 'liked' their work, that they were happy with it and 'satisfied'; at the same time, when they talked about it, they sometimes said things which showed that their attitude was much more one of 'not particularly minding'. A 17-year-old box-maker said about his job:

'I'm satisfied with my job – real satisfied with it as a matter of fact. I'm happy there most of the time, though of course sometimes I get fed up. Let me give an example: I've got a job I'm doing now, I've got to do sixty boxes, they're about a foot by a foot, I've got to cover each side. I get bored with a job like that. What I try to do is to cut it down and do thirty and then do another job and go back to it. Then it's all right. But if I have to do it straight off, then I do get bored with it, very bored.'

When the same boy was asked whether he ever 'watched the clock' he said:

'I do, but it's only because I'm tired. In the morning, I'm usually all right, but round about three o'clock, I start feeling tired, particularly if I've had a late night the night before. After about three o'clock I'm waiting to get home – I'm looking at my watch. I can't say that I'm clock-watching or waiting for dinner time because sometimes I've worked right through my dinner hour – I worked till five past one or ten past one, I'm so caught up with what I'm doing that I haven't noticed. But of course I'm glad when dinner-time comes, like anybody else. I like to get away from it for a bit, and then go back again. But it's not that I hate my work or anything like that, I mean, you've got to work to earn your living, haven't you. But I quite like it. I've got a good governor and I've got good mates, and the pay's all right. Yes, I'm real satisfied with my job.'

Some did complain more, like the 18-year-old ledger clerk who said, 'I'm bored with the job. I'm looking for another but I don't know what I want to be.' A warehouseman of 17 said:

'There's not much difference in the days at work. It's nearly all routine. I'm getting a bit fed up with it, and I'll probably leave after the holidays. It's not the job I want – I want a trainee rep's job, but I can't get it.'

Another complaint, particularly among those in semi-skilled or unskilled jobs, was of the authority exercised over them. One boy of 16 working for a small local factory said:

'The governor of my place is horrible. You do something and he rucks you if you take more than ten minutes for a quarter of an hour's job. You've only got two pairs of hands, but some people think that when they are high up they can do anything. They're like madmen. They say, "Arthur, get on with this, get on with that."'

Two kinds of people were particularly singled out for criticism – the foreman and the 'crawlers'.

'Take a geezer in our firm. He's just took over the job as foreman, and you can see the change in him. He don't trust nobody and he's always arguing now. He was with us against the foreman before, when we was always messing about against the foreman and all that, but now he's took over the job he don't trust nobody. You can see the change in him in three months.'

'Most people who work their way up are crawlers. At my place the governor's only got to say the word and they jump for it.'

These remarks, however, have to be set against those of boys who said they liked their charge-hand or foreman, those who said they had a 'good governor', those who seemed not at all resentful about their seniors at work.

Future prospects

Divisions of opinion were equally sharp over future prospects. The minority of boys in training for professional jobs were cheerful about their future. A 17-year-old architectural assistant who was taking 'A' levels at evening classes said, 'As soon as you get at least five G.C.E.s – that's three "O"s and two "A"s – you can become a probationer for the R.I.B.A. and the R.I.C.S. You can go on to become a qualified architect or surveyor. You see, there's every opportunity in my job. An architect is what I hope to be.' An 18-year-old trainee manager (the son of a clerk) said, 'The prospects are good. I'll become manager when I'm 21 and from then on the sky's the limit.'

Among some in clerical jobs there seemed a similar optimism. A 17-year-old shipping clerk, an ex-grammar school boy, said: 'I'm happy in this job. I'll stay here as long as they'll have me. The prospects are good because there are so many branches of the firm under different names that whenever there's any vacancy it's always filled from within. Whenever any job becomes vacant, everybody moves up a place. My idea of promotion is, well, say when I'm 23 I might become assistant manager of the shipping and forwarding department – that's a small department of the office I'm now in. And then I might become manager.' A clerk working for the BBC, a former secondary modern school boy now aged 18, was also hopeful: 'If I don't like what I'm doing I can always move over to another section. All the vacancies in the Corporation are put up on a board, and you can put in for anything. What I'd quite like to do is to go over to the cameras at some time, but in fact any job is open to me inside the BBC, except Director General.'

A few of the boys training for skilled manual jobs also seemed to think in terms of advancement up a promotional ladder. A 17-year-old engineering apprentice said, 'When you complete your apprenticeship you become an assistant engineer and then you can go on to become engineer and later executive engineer. After that, if you do well, you can go on to one of the top engineering positions.' A mirror silverer aged 17 said:

'I'm in a trade and there are prospects in my job. I can go on from silverer to charge-hand, from charge-hand to foreman, and from foreman to management.'

When asked what he expected to be in ten years' time, he said 'the manager of a glass firm.'

Most of the people in, or training for, skilled jobs had more modest expectations. An ex-grammar school boy aged 19, who was working as a photo-engraver, said that he 'loved' the work and added: 'There are no real prospects but the money is good later on. I don't really want prospects, except to carry on in the same sort of job. This is what I expect to do in ten years' time and it's what I would choose to do anyway.' A plumber's mate aged 17 said that he would become a plumber when he had finished his training: 'Then I'll have a trade behind me. That's the main thing.' An 18 year old training to become a clicker (who cuts out the leather for shoe manufacture) said: 'I'll go on to become a fully qualified clicker. I'll earn quite good money. It's a good trade. I could become a foreman but I don't want to.'

There was sometimes a similar contentment among boys with less skilled jobs. A 17-year-old van boy, for instance, said that he could go on to become a van driver – 'That's what I want to be.' A 20 year old explained, 'I'm a fish porter and that's what I expect to go on being. It's not really a promotion job at all. I suppose I could go on to be a salesman, but I'd rather have no worries. As it is, when I get home from work I'm finished. I prefer it like that.'

Again, in almost all types of job, some were less content. An 18-year-old clerk said, 'The prospects are almost negligible. Our firm is a very large firm, you know, and unless you've got a university degree you can't get anywhere.' A 19-year-old engineering apprentice remarked, 'There's a limit to how far you can go in the kind of work I'm in. It's interesting, but I'd rather do something requiring more from me, something occupying all of my interest. As it stands I haven't the chance of getting on to that sort of work because I haven't the qualifications, and I'm not likely to get them. If I had the money I would like to be a full-time student, and go on to be a design draughtsman or something like that.'

Prospects for the unskilled

More complaints about the lack of opportunities came from the boys with unskilled or semi-skilled jobs, as was noted earlier in the chapter.

'I get a fair wage for what I do, but I'd like to better myself. There are really no prospects in my job. I'd rather be a trades-man – I don't like to sort of wait on other people. In ten years time? I'd definitely like to have a trade in my hands by that time – or at least a semi-skilled trade. I think I'd like to be a carpenter or a joiner.' (18, *building labourer.*)

'It's not what I want – there are no prospects at all. I'll be doing the same job and earning the same amount of money when I'm about 30.' (17, *warehouseman.*)

Dissatisfaction was reflected in how often boys changed their jobs. In general, they did not change jobs much – nearly half (44 per cent) of those at work were still in the job they had first taken when they left school. But there were some who had a much less stable work-history and it is not surprising that they were more often in semi-skilled or unskilled work than skilled or non-manual, as Table XIX shows.

TABLE XIX

Boy's occupation and number of jobs since school

Number of jobs	Non-manual	Skilled manual	Semi-skilled and unskilled manual
One only	49%	46%	30%
Two, three or four	36%	37%	35%
Five or more	15%	17%	35%
Total %	100%	100%	100%
Number	45	95	37

Less that a third of the semi-skilled and unskilled boys had remained in their first job, compared with nearly half of the others. Conversely, more than a third of them – compared with a sixth of the others – had been in five jobs or more. The explana-tion for this difference is not simply that boys in less skilled occupations had generally left school earlier and therefore had less time to change jobs; among boys who had been at work for the same number of years, those in unskilled and semi-skilled jobs had consistently changed more often.

What this changing about can mean was described by a 17 year old who had held six jobs since leaving school at 15.

'When I left school I went down to the youth employment and told them I wanted to go in for a mechanic or something like that. They said I didn't stand a chance, and I've more or less done unskilled jobs ever since then. I've been looking for something better, but I can't seem to find anything. You get in a job and you know it's not for you. You dislike it and you're unhappy, and you try to find another job, but when you get to that you find it's just a labourer again. If you're not a tradesman you have to do any job that comes along, and when you're a labourer you just go to work and you're the underdog. You don't know any job, so you got to do what someone else says. Sometimes it really gets you down to be told and told and told all the time. And then you look for something else and you find you're back at the same sort of thing all over again.'

A 20 year old recounted his experience.

'I stayed in my first job as a clothing salesman in a shop for about six weeks. I thought there'd be younger people there I could work with. They were all about 40 – middle-aged – I felt out of place. So I went into the Post Office until I was 17½, and then I worked as a builder's labourer. Then I had some other jobs after that – the last job I had before this was at a builders' merchants – I didn't like the foreman, he had no patience, not only with me but with the customers too. I always used to get the needle about that. I packed it in. Now I'm at a radio and TV warehouse. I don't know whether I'll stay there – I think the most important thing about any job is comradeship. In my last year at school I didn't have a clue what I wanted to do. I didn't take up any apprenticeship because I had the impression that once you've done that you're stuck to that job for the rest of your life, and I didn't want to get tied up.'

Why had such boys not followed so many of their schoolmates into jobs where they could learn a skilled trade? The reason may have been that their school records were so poor that they would not have been accepted. Some gave a different explanation – either, like the boy just quoted, arguing that they had not been willing to surrender their freedom, or suggesting that they or their parents could not afford it.

'If you go in for an apprenticeship, you only earn about £5 a week until you're 21, and yet that's the best time of your life, isn't it, when you're young? I mean, I know people who're doing apprenticeships and they go to night classes every night, or they have to sit at home because they haven't got any money. I know your future's all right and all that, but you're not enjoying yourself, are you?' (17, *assembler*.)

'My family haven't got anything, and therefore I've got to have a job that suits the family, to keep them sort of thing as well as me. I mean, most boys who take these apprentice-ships, their fathers have got a bit of money behind them. If they haven't got enough money to go out with at the end of the week, the father says, "Here you are, son, you go out and have a good time." Fellows like that, it's all laid on for them.' (18, *labourer*.)

These remarks often contained an element of envy and regret. Whatever their reason for not entering apprenticeships, the fact remains that these boys did lack a 'trade', did often drift from one job to another, did account for most of the rebelliousness and resentment about work.

There are some obvious parallels here with the previous chapter. At school, as at work, the boys could be broadly divided into those who were content, those who were moderately so, and those who rebelled. But how far do attitudes to school and work coincide? Are the 'rebels' at school also those at work? If job-changing is taken as an index, it seems that there is an association. Table XX compares the boys' attitudes to 'rules' at school with the number of jobs they had.

Of the boys who were critical of the school régime, less than a third were in the job they had when they left, against more than half of those most sympathetic to the school. Similarly, nearly a

Work

TABLE XX

*Attitude to rules at former school
and number of jobs since school*

Number of jobs	School rules regarded as 'reasonable'		
	'*All*'	'*Most*'	'*About half*', '*a few*' or '*none*'
One only	53%	42%	31%
Two, three or four	35%	41%	35%
Five or more	12%	17%	34%
Total %	100%	100%	100%
Number	68	57	52

third of the former, against just over a tenth of the latter, had been in five or more jobs. This is not simply a reflection of the relative instability of boys in unskilled and semi-skilled occupations: there was the same relationship between attitudes to school and number of jobs amongst non-manual and skilled manual workers. The correlation analysis described earlier also showed that the boys' views on their jobs generally were correlated not only with the number of jobs (·167) but also with their opinions of the school lessons (·218) and the teachers (·222), and those on employment prospects with their opinion of the lessons (·159).

The influence of age

So far the discussion of attitudes to work has ignored age. The question is whether the boys' views change as they get older. Table XXI shows the proportion 'dissatisfied' at different ages with their job generally, with the pay and the prospects. The age groupings are different from those used elsewhere, the 15 and 16 year olds being combined; this is partly because the absence of all the boys of 14 and many of 15 justifies some sort of rearrangement, but also because preliminary analysis suggested that, on these issues, there were differences between the 17 and 18 year olds and younger boys.

All three indices tell much the same story. Relatively few boys of 15 and 16 were 'dissatisfied' and relatively few, again, of 19

Work

TABLE XXI
Age and 'dissatisfaction' at work

	15/16	*17/18*	*19/20*
'Dissatisfied' with job 'generally'	12%	27%	16%
'Dissatisfied' with pay	21%	44%	24%
'Dissatisfied' with prospects	14%	34%	24%
Total number	56	71	50

and 20 (though this is less marked with 'prospects'). In general, the most 'discontented' age is 17 and 18. The same conclusion was suggested by a closer examination of the few boys who were 'dissatisfied' on all three counts. There were only nine of them; eight of the nine were aged 17 or 18.

Why this cycle? It seems that, when boys first leave school, there is a 'honeymoon' phase. The boys who had not long left school revelled in their new independence: 'You have more freedom'; 'You're treated as an adult at work, not like a child'; 'It's mainly the money. You can stand on your own feet – don't have to keep running to Mum every time you want a couple of bob.' Later, the job is more likely to pall and excitement about 'independence' gives way to resentment at adult authority.[6] But as the boys mature they apparently become more content with their lot. It may be that as they move into adulthood they are increasingly accorded adult status by their workmates. It may simply be part of a more general 'settling down' associated with courtship and the approach to marriage. It is worth noting, by the way, that the figures suggest rather less 'acceptance' over 'prospects'; presumably boys still in dead-end jobs at 19 and 20 have more reason to be anxious.

There are three main conclusions from this chapter. The first is that most boys are – perhaps surprisingly – content with their work, though 'contentment' means different things in different

---

[6] A recent study of 'unattached' boys and girls noted the change: 'Age was an important factor affecting the extent to which the attitudes and problems had become crystallized. Many of the symptoms were already visible with the younger groups, but the problems really began to express themselves by about the age of 16 or 17 when the novelty of the first job had worn off, work was becoming boring, and the question of adult authority had become particularly acute.' (Morse, M., *The Unattached*, pp. 76–77.)

sorts of job. The second is that there is a distinct chronological cycle, a movement in the direction of greater dissatisfaction and then back again towards reconciliation. Thirdly, age is not the only variable that matters: certain sorts of boy, in particular, are discontented with their job and resentful about it. They are predominantly in unskilled work (though by no means all in such jobs are unhappy); they change jobs often; they resent the authority of their superiors; and many of them are the same boys who disliked their schooling. These are not the only boys with employment dissatisfactions, but they do present special problems.

VII

YOUTH CLUBS

Bethnal Green is relatively well-endowed with youth clubs.[1] Historically, the East End was the kind of 'deprived' area that attracted the attention of social workers. The university settlements started in East London, and Bethnal Green still has five of them; although not all have youth clubs catering for boys aged 14 to 20, all do some kind of youth work. In the middle of 1964 there were altogether about a score of clubs in Bethnal Green, including one local authority 'Recreational Institute' and a local authority 'Youth Centre' (both based on local schools).[2] Something less than a third of the clubs were linked to local churches (with attendance at church usually a condition of membership) and the rest were 'open'. All but three were 'mixed' clubs, for girls as well as boys. There were also two 'pre-Service' organizations – a Cadet Corps and an Air Training Corps – three Boys' Brigade Companies and eleven Boy Scout Groups. Of course not all the boys who were members of youth clubs went to one in their own borough and some of the local clubs drew their members from farther afield. But this brief inventory – nearly forty organizations to meet the needs of about 2,000 boys aged 14 to 20 – gives an idea of the scope and variety of local provision.

The biggest and probably the best known youth club in Bethnal Green is housed in a tall, rambling building, looking out on a carefully-tended public garden. The building is not only a youth club; it is one of the local settlements and is used by a variety of other organizations, but on most evenings the place is dominated by young people. The visitor goes in through swing doors and up a wide stone staircase to the vast canteen and common room

---

[1] Unfortunately, no figures are available on the youth service provision in different areas, but there is little doubt that the East End has more clubs per head than most other districts.

[2] In London the 'Recreational Institutes' were gradually being closed down in favour of 'Youth Centres'.

which is the hub of the building and which contains, behind steel and glass partitions, the club leaders' office. A few youngsters may be watching the large-screen television set high on the wall, others may be sitting around the small tables drinking tea or minerals. There are 'activities' going on in a score of other rooms – upstairs in the gym it may be boxing or the girls' judo class. In one of the handicraft rooms a group is painting still lifes under the encouraging guidance of an instructor. In yet another room neatly-suited boys are playing billiards with professional aplomb, in another the game is table tennis. One room is set aside exclusively for the girls.

From nine o'clock, half the immense room in which table tennis is played is given over to what, for many of the youngsters, is the important business of the evening – dancing to records or a hired group. As time goes on this corner of the club becomes more and more crowded, the cigarette smoke thicker. Only a minority dance and there are as many pairs of girls amongst them as mixed couples. The crowd of spectators spills up the steps into the canteen, the boys and girls standing in knots, talking, tapping their feet, twisting their bodies in time with the music. Most of the groups are exclusively of boys or of girls, though there are one or two mixed circles and there is some communication, mostly jocular, between the boys of one group and the girls of another.

Half a mile away is another, smaller club. It is housed in a low modern building, less spacious than the first. The canteen is smaller and open only for a limited period each evening. There is the familiar table-tennis room and the handicrafts room, where a group of boys are building a boat. Downstairs in the hall a game of five-a-side football is in progress; the boys are playing so aggressively that the club leader finds it hard to hold them to the rules, and there is also some boisterousness amongst the spectators. In another room, next to the canteen, the record player is blaring out the latest hits; but in this club hardly anybody dances – a pair of diminutive girls try self-consciously and half-heartedly under the gaze of clusters of cigarette-smoking boys, while the other girls gather similarly into one corner. Here the members are younger than in the other club; hardly any of them are more than 16. Girls and boys seem to have little to do with each other, their contacts being mainly confined to an occasional wisecrack for the benefit of friends and the push or squeeze which provokes a high-pitched squeal.

These are just two of the clubs attended by local boys. At the time of interview two-fifths of the sample were members of a recognized club or youth organization. The great majority of these – more than four-fifths – currently belonged to only one. As might be expected, the 'open' youth clubs were the most popular. Of the boys who belonged to anything, only about one in twenty belonged to the Scouts or Boys' Brigade, a slightly larger proportion to the Cadets or A.T.C., and rather more than one in ten to Church youth clubs. About a quarter belonged to the local authority Recreational Institute or Youth Centre; the rest – well over half – belonged to the familiar kind of 'open' or 'general' club.

The age of club members

Thus, of a sample of the boys in Bethnal Green for whom the youth service is intended, two in five were members when they were interviewed, most of them members of youth clubs rather than other organizations. But this neglects age; its influence is shown in Table XXII. The boys are again grouped together in a different way from most earlier tables, because the pattern turned out to be so different with youth club membership.

TABLE XXII
Age and membership of youth clubs and organizations

	14	*15*	*16/17*	*18/19*	*20*
Belonging to at least one youth club or organization	32%	49%	53%	33%	15%
Total number	31	37	90	61	27

There is a peak age for belonging to clubs – at around 15, 16 and 17. At 14 about a third of the boys belong, at 15, 16 and 17 about half, at 18 and 19 again a third, and at 20 about one in seven.

We asked boys about clubs they had belonged to in the past as well as those they belonged to when interviewed, and their answers confirmed these findings. About two-thirds of those aged 19 and 20 who had formerly belonged to clubs had left them three or more years earlier – in other words when they were 17 or younger; similarly, more than two-thirds of those aged 17 and 18 had left their clubs one year or more earlier. If membership of past and present clubs is combined, the overwhelming majority of boys turn out to have belonged to some club by the time they are about 17. The proportions who either still belonged or had belonged to one or more youth organization were four out of five at 14 and 15 and nine out of ten from 16 to 20. Sometimes so called 'junior clubs' and other organizations catering for youngsters under 14 were among those to which boys had formerly belonged, but they only amounted to a handful of all those mentioned. In other words, the great majority either now belonged to or had belonged to an organization catering for young people between 14 and 20.

This puts the figures for club membership quoted earlier in a different light. It seems that nine out of every ten local boys, by the time they are 16 or 17, have belonged to at least one youth club or organization. In the sample as a whole just over one in ten had not belonged to a club; about a third had belonged to only one, just over a quarter to two, and just over a quarter to three or more. Apparently most of them really did belong; they were not merely fleeting members who stayed for a week or two and then left. Of the boys aged 18, 19 and 20 who had formerly belonged, for example, well over half had done so for more than two years and only 6 per cent for less than six months.

These facts seem important in the light of much of the current debate about the youth service. In that debate it is usually assumed that the service fails to connect with the lives of the majority of those for whom it is intended.[3] Even though, as noted earlier, the proportions who join are higher than elsewhere in Bethnal Green because the opportunities are greater, the problem might look very different in other districts as well if past membership were taken into account along with present, and the ebb and flow between 14 and 20 borne in mind.

---

[3] The Albemarle Report said, 'A particular weakness in the Youth Service, for which all our witnesses have shown concern, is its failure to reach so many of the young people today.' (*The Youth Service in England and Wales*, p. 12.)

Membership and functions

Most boys attend clubs that are close at hand. More than four-fifths of those who belonged to clubs were members of ones inside Bethnal Green itself, and nearly all the rest of clubs elsewhere in the East End. Only four boys, of the 100 who currently belonged to a club, attended one outside the East End altogether. Although some join clubs at the other end of Bethnal Green from their homes, most membership is localized. The boy who wrote in his diary that on Monday evening he 'came home, had some tea, got changed and went to my local youth club' was by no means an exception.

Most had belonged to their current clubs for some time. Nearly half had been members for two years or more and another quarter for between one and two years; only about one in seven had belonged for less than six months. They also attended fairly frequently; more than three-quarters had been at least once within the previous week and less than one in ten had not attended within the previous month.

They seldom, on the other hand, go every night, and often do not spend anything like the whole evening there; the club is part of a day-to-day round, in which peer group, girls and all sorts of other attachments figure as well. This can be illustrated by a brief review of a week in the life of Roger Best, aged 17, as recorded in his diary. He spent Sunday evening at home; 'My uncle and aunt came from Dagenham for a meal and a drink. I stayed in and watched TV with them.' On Monday evening he went to the cinema with three of his 'mates'. On Tuesday he went round to the youth club, talked to his friends, danced with a girl and took her home. On Wednesday he went to the club again and played billiards. On Thursday he went dancing in the West End with a mixed group of about a dozen. On Friday he 'dropped in at the club, but left early to take one of the girls for a walk over the park'. On Saturday he 'went out with my mates for a drink'. The degree of involvement varied. The diaries suggested that, among the boys who belonged to youth organizations, those of 14, 15 and 16 participated more fully than those who were older.

Whatever their age, their 'mates' were much in evidence. It is hardly an exaggeration to say that every youth club – and, for that matter, every Scout Group or Cadet Corps – is really a federation of peer groups. There are a small minority of club members without close friends and others with only one. It is true, too, that inside a club the peer group may not always be clearly defined: some groups may overlap in their membership, so that it is difficult for boys to draw the line between close and less-close friends – between peer groups and other associates – among those they see at the club. But there is no doubt that for most boys the club is, first, a place where they meet the fellow members of their peer group, and secondly, a place where there are other acquaintances of much the same age as themselves.

The circle of friends were certainly in evidence when boys wrote in their diaries about youth clubs. A 15 year old, for instance, went to his 'local youth club' most nights of the week. He said that on Monday night 'while I was up there I spoke to my friends and we had a laugh. After we left the Club at 9.30 p.m. we hung around talking to some girls until about half past ten, when I went home and went to bed.' Of Tuesday evening, he said: 'At 6.30 I called round to my friend Jack's house to see if he was going up to the Club. He said he was and that he would not be long, so I waited for him. While I was waiting, another friend, Stephen, came round and said he would come up with us. We went up the Club and played table-tennis and snooker, and at nine o'clock we went into the dance-hall for half-an-hour.' So it went on through the week. Another boy, aged 17, only visited his club on one night during the week reported in his diary. He said that on Thursday: 'At 7.30 my mate came round for me and we went up the Club. We met the rest of our mates there, about another six, and at 10.15 we all left and walked home.'

The point was illustrated again in what the boys said when they were asked what they liked about the club or clubs they belonged to. Many mentioned more than one feature. A third spoke about the presence of their friends. 'I see all my mates there,' said one boy. 'The main reason I belong,' said another, 'is because of the other fellows – my mates all meet up there.' And a third: 'I know a lot of people who go up there – my mates and that. It's more like a meeting place.'

Other social assets of club membership were mentioned. A few specifically referred to the opportunity of meeting girls, and more spoke of the 'friendly atmosphere', of liking 'the other people who go' and of the opportunity to meet others outside their immediate circle. As one boy, aged 17, put it, 'You meet people there – not just your own mates, but other people as well. There's an air of friendliness.' These wider 'social' advantages of club membership were mentioned by one in five of the boys who belonged to clubs.

What other things did they like about their clubs? In answer to the question, about a fifth could find little to say: they merely remarked that it was 'somewhere to go' or 'just a way to pass the time'. Sports and games were mentioned most often, by more than a third.

'We play table tennis and billiards.'

'The judo and the weight-lifting.'

'I like the boxing – that's what I go in for.'

'We play football. The main reason I go is to improve at football – my ambition is to play for Arsenal and for England.'

A fifth mentioned dancing and records.

'There are good records there and dancing. That's the main thing I like.'

About one in ten spoke in general terms about the range of facilities offered by their club – 'There's plenty to do there.' 'There are lots of activities going on' – or mentioned other specific interests like art or handicraft.

We also asked what they most 'disliked'. More than half said 'nothing'. Among the other comments, only two stood out. About one boy in five complained of the rules or some other aspect of the club régime.

'They're too strict up there. The way they run it, you pay for a term and you come in late and they say don't do it again.'

'They treat you like a lot of little kids up there. The geezer who runs it is always having a go. He gets on my nerves sometimes.'

And one in ten complained that the club's facilities were inadequate or that they found it 'boring'.

'They haven't really got nothing there. They haven't really got any decent facilities or anything. All that they have got is always being used – table tennis and that.'

'I get bored there. Sometimes you go up there and there's nothing to do – you just stand about.'

Some clubs were particularly criticized on one ground or another. The leader of one, for instance, was frequently mentioned as being 'strict', though many others at the same club spoke warmly about him, saying that the club was 'well-organized' and that they liked it because 'There's a strict leader up there, so there's no mucking about'. One boys' club was especially criticized for its rules: 'It's like an army camp,' said one boy, 'they fine you and things like that. The rules get me down.'

It is clear from all this that the clubs vary in how they are run, in the programmes they offer and in their 'atmosphere'. From observations in some of the local clubs, and from what the boys said, a broad distinction can be drawn between two main types of club. The first was dominated by the younger boys, those aged 14 and 15; the main activities were games and there was a good deal of horseplay and open aggression. Such clubs were sometimes for boys only. The clubs of the older boys, although they had games and sports and other activities, were focused on dancing, girls and talk.

Certainly younger boys more often belong to one-sex clubs. The hundred boys who currently belonged to clubs and other youth organizations belonged to 116 altogether. Of these 116 organizations, just over a quarter were for boys only – including the pre-Service and other uniformed organizations. Among those of 14 and 15 more than half the boys belonged to boys-only organizations, compared with a quarter of those aged 16 and a fifth of those aged 17 and over. As a 19 year old said about his reasons for leaving a boys' club at 15: 'It was a boys' club, you see, and I thought I was getting to the stage where you want to go to a mixed youth club.' This kind of progression is common. About a third of the boys in the sample had joined at least one club or organization after they had left another (and this is counting as 'joining' only those who had belonged for six months or more). Some clubs expressly cater for younger boys – they may, for instance, have a leaving age of 18. Others, though they do not set out to restrict their age range, in practice have younger or older members. Not that the club membership should in any sense be thought of as static; it is clear that the dominant age-group within any one club at a given time may be different from what it was a year or two earlier. In many clubs, groups of friends who join stay together for a few years, setting the tone of the club while they are 14, 15 and then 16, after which they may leave to give way to another batch of 14 or 15 year olds.

Why they leave

The discussion about the function of the clubs, and the part they play in the boys' lives, has led back once more to the theme of a cyclical pattern: clearly the boys' membership of clubs and other organizations is bound up with other aspects of their lives, in particular with the development of their relationships with peers and girls. The question still unanswered is why so many of them stop going to clubs after about 17. How far is this movement away from clubs inevitable, how far the fault of the clubs themselves?

The boys' reasons for leaving clubs give some guide. Between them, they had left 301 youth organizations altogether, and they were asked why they had left each one. They gave a variety of answers, but four main sets of 'reasons' emerged. These are now looked at in turn, the various other answers that applied to only a small minority having been excluded.

About one club in five had been left for reasons that implied some criticism of the club; the boys' remarks echoed the 'dislikes' of those quoted earlier who were still members. They complained about the lack of facilities, the poor organization, the strictness of the rules or the officiousness of the club leader. Amongst these boys were a minority who had left church clubs or Boy Scouts because church attendance had been compulsory.

About two-fifths of the answers were along the lines that the boy had 'lost interest' or become 'bored'. A 16 year old who had left three months before the interview, after belonging for eighteen months, said: 'I found other interests; it was the same old thing again and again. You go for a couple of years and then you get bored.' An 18 year old who had recently left a club said: 'I just lost interest in it. It seemed a waste of time. You get cheesed off going to the same place all the time.' With such comments it is impossible to know whether a criticism of the club was implied or whether the boy felt he had matured. The same thing applied to the answers, something like a fifth, that were in terms of friends leaving. 'You follow your mates,' said a 16 year old, 'They all left and so I did.'

Finally, about a fifth of the answers – mainly from older boys – suggested that leaving the club had been part of the process of maturing. About half of these were put simply in terms of age. Some boys said expressly that they had been 'too old' for the club. One or two had certainly reached the maximum age, but more often the explanation was in the form of a complaint that the other members were 'getting too young'.

'I packed it up because you used to get a load of young mods there. They got on your nerves.' (18 year old, left six months earlier after belonging for two and a half years.)

'I found that in the main the others were getting younger than me – they seemed like a lot of little boys and girls, little kids.' (19 year old, left club two years earlier after belonging for 18 months.)

Sometimes the answers that were to do with 'getting older' mentioned girls.

'I was getting older. I wanted to get out and about more, with the girls.' (19 year old, left two years earlier.)

'I started courting. I did go once or twice after that but the girl-friend had a moan about it and that stopped it altogether. I didn't mind – after I started going with her the club didn't seem to interest me very much any more.' (20 year old, left two years earlier, after belonging for three years.)

Thus, just as some boys at 14 are impatient to move on to mixed clubs, so others of 17 or 18, having formed an attachment with a girl, are ready to leave youth clubs altogether. Of course boys and girls often join up inside clubs, and the couple may continue as members, both of the club and of their circle of friends and acquaintances within it. A number of local club leaders told us, however, that couples often leave when they begin to pair off in earnest. An earlier chapter suggested that when boys start going 'seriously' with a girl, they may be subjected to ridicule by their peers, who see this new relationship as a threat to the unity of the peer group. In the 'public' atmosphere of a youth club, the boy – and the girl, too, for that matter – may be particularly vulnerable. When this happens, the pressures to leave may become powerful.

Apart from those boys who left because of girls, many of the rest left either because they had 'lost interest', implying that they had probably outgrown the club, or because their friends had left, often presumably for similar reasons to those that boys gave for themselves. In other words, most of the leaving was not so much because the clubs 'failed' as because the boys were moving on to another phase.

Those who remained

If most leave youth clubs after about 18, it is worth asking about those who stay on – what kind of boys are they? There were no marked statistical variations between them and others of the same age, but a detailed look at them suggested two interpretations of their different behaviour.

There were altogether twelve boys aged 19 and 20 who belonged to clubs and other youth organizations. First, they differed from younger members in that they more often mentioned a specific sport as their main or even only reason for attending (one boy similarly mentioned the art class). Nine of the twelve answered the question on what they liked about the youth club on these lines.

'I only go for the badminton. I'm practising, trying to improve my game.' (19 year old.)

'Football is my hobby. That's mainly what I go for.' (20 year old.)

The other impression was that some of these boys were highly identified with the organization they belonged to, and got greater satisfaction from their membership than did most of the (mainly younger) members. Though we did not ask specifically about this, they often seemed to be committee members and in other ways associated with the management of the club. A 19 year old who was a committee member of a club said:

'I think that club life is a very good thing, but a club needs all of its members pulling their weight if it's going to succeed. The members, particularly the younger members, don't seem to realize that we all *belong* to the club – it's ours. It's up to us to make a success of it. Personally I don't think there's enough discipline from the committee – some boys get away with too much.'

A 20 year old, who belonged to a church club and was a senior scout attached to the same church, said he liked 'everything' about both and disliked 'nothing'; he remarked, 'I think scouting is a very good thing. I've got a lot of enjoyment out of it, particularly recently, since I've taken up the job of instruction of Cubs.'

A local youth leader suggested that such boys are often those who do not have the opportunity, at work or elsewhere in their lives, to exercise the initiative of which they are capable. To these boys, who are relatively rare, youth clubs and organizations may continue to serve a useful purpose beyond the stage in life at which most leave.

The 'unclubbables'

In public debate about the problems of youth and the contribution of the youth service, much concern is expressed about the youngsters who do not join. This chapter has already shown that in Bethnal Green the proportion of 'unclubbables' or 'unattached' is small. For this reason, our research can say little about what sort of boys stay away.

Though statistical analysis could tell us little, we looked closely at the boys who did not join clubs and others who, though they did join, did not stay long. They seemed to fall into two main categories. Some were painfully shy. They could not bring themselves to go to clubs because it would have faced them with the problem of mixing with others. A 16 year old said:

'People tell me I ought to join a youth club, because I would be able to mix with other people. I can't seem to bring myself to do it. I know I ought to, and perhaps I will some day, but the truth is that I do not get on well with other people.'

Rather more common seemed another type of misfit – the boy who was anti-club. An 18 year old building labourer said:

'I've been to quite a few of these youth clubs. Most of them I left after a couple of months. If you ask me, mate, they're a load of crap.'

Among such boys there seemed a minority who saw each club and each leader as a challenge, an opportunity to 'have a giggle' – or in other words cause some trouble. According to Jimmy Grove, this was the attitude of himself and his friends.

'We go to quite a lot of the clubs round here, but we mostly go for a giggle. We got chucked out of the one along here only a fortnight ago and then we went back again. He said, "Oh, you're back again, are you? You got chucked out, didn't you." He says, "Go on, you can go in, but don't muck about like that", so we all go in like. We're always getting into trouble with these clubs. I start saucing him and all that sort of thing, and he says, "You're being saucy. Go on, get out", like that. One night, when he chucked us out, to pay him back we went round and let the air out of his tyres. Another time we had a lark – he asked us to fit the gym gear up. We said O.K. We fitted up the box and the first one who went over, the lot collapsed. He went nutty, chased us out. When he got us in the gym he used to make us do a sort of course; we had to keep on running round and round. Running round sweating our guts out we were, so we packed it up. Then we went into the boxing and started throwing the gloves about and he chucked us out for that. When we go into these youth clubs it often seems to end up like that. We don't dislike the people there or anything like that. We must do it for fun, it's just that you go in and you mess about and you start getting told off and before long you're monkeying about and playing up.'

There were further examples from boys who had left clubs. The reason a few gave for leaving was that they had been expelled or suspended. 'I got chucked out for mucking about,' said one boy; 'Suspended for throwing bottles,' said another. Again, these boys were often among those who did not get on well at school or at work either.

Other clubs

Some boys belonged to clubs outside the youth service. Unfortunately we did not ask the right questions to enable us to assess accurately the relative importance of these other kinds of club. Fortunately, though, our questions about 'clubs' were often interpreted as including other kinds, and we were therefore given some information about these.

The boys' answers suggest that at the time of interview something like one in ten of them belonged to some kind of club outside the youth service, and rather less had formerly belonged but had ceased to do so. These other clubs were of three principal kinds – commercial 'teenage' clubs mainly for dancing, sports clubs and social clubs, both of the latter being open to people of all ages. About half the clubs to which boys currently belonged were commercial, about two-fifths devoted to a sport, and the remaining tenth general social clubs. Not many of the clubs were inside Bethnal Green, but more than half were elsewhere in the East End; the others were mainly in Central London. Few boys aged 14 or 15 belonged to any of these kinds of club. Above that age, the boys of 16 and 17 more often belonged to clubs offering music or dancing, older boys to sports or social clubs.

In general, there was no evidence that membership of these other clubs was at the expense of the youth service. Of the boys who belonged to such clubs, only two had never belonged to a youth club or youth organization and nearly half the rest were still members. A contrast was sometimes drawn between the atmosphere in a commercial and a youth club. A 16 year old said:

'I like it there. They get some good groups playing and the whole atmosphere is jazzy – it's quite like a night club. It's quite different from the usual youth club. The only thing I I don't like is the bouncers – they do tend to push you about a bit.'

An 18 year old, who had formerly belonged to one of the local youth clubs and had now left, put it more strongly.

'I go to the jazz clubs up the West End. The youth clubs are too dull. You get too many young mods there. To my mind it's a drag.'

This was not the common view. But, since we did not ask systematically about membership of clubs other than youth clubs, may it not be that many more than one in ten of the boys in fact belonged to them? Some other evidence on this is provided by the diaries of the thirty boys who kept them. They included a representative spread of ages and, since the diaries were fairly detailed, other clubs visited during the week for which the diaries were kept are likely to have been recorded. In fact, four of the thirty boys reported going to one or other of these clubs during the week – a proportion similar to the one in ten of the main sample who said they were members. An 18 year old had gone swimming with his (mainly adult) swimming club at the local baths on Thursday night. A 16 year old had gone to a local dancing club with his friends, and another of the same age to a second with his girl. The fourth boy – a 20 year old – had taken his fiancée to a West End jazz club on Friday night. Despite the small numbers, this coincides so closely with what was reported in the survey interviews that there seems no reason to suppose that the commercial and other 'non-youth' clubs have a large unreported membership.

The picture of the youth service presented in this chapter is rather different from how it is usually seen. First, the fact that the overwhelming majority of boys belong to youth clubs during their adolescence suggests that what is lacking in other areas is probably not so much the inclination as adequate provision. The experience of this district indicates that when there are plenty of clubs of different kinds, including a choice of 'open' clubs, then most boys, if not girls, will join. Secondly, whatever other worth-while actvities take place in youth clubs, the cyclical patterns suggest that the principal function of the youth service is social. It provides a setting away from school, work or home, where boys can learn to mix first with each other, then with the girls. One of its advantages, apparently, is that it can help ease the processes of adolescence, by providing an institutional framework in which young people can learn how to begin to behave like adults, while still largely insulated from adult superiority and disapproval. The conclusion, in other words, is exactly contrary to the argument of Musgrove in a recent book, where he asserted that youth clubs were age-segregated institutions imposed by adults on unwilling adolescents in order to exclude them from adult society.[4] At a stage in adolescence, segregation seems to be exactly what they want. Finally, this chapter suggests something about the boys who do not join clubs, or if they do join fit in less well than the others; it seems that often they are the very boys who are also 'rebels' at school or work or both.

[4] Musgrove, F., *Youth and the Social Order*, pp. 154–5.

VIII

DELINQUENCY

The most publicized problem that adolescents, particularly working-class boys, present to adult society is their tendency to misbehave. If court convictions for law-breaking are taken as an indication of anti-social behaviour, it is predominantly the province of adolescents rather than adults, of boys than girls, and of the working rather than the middle class. It is true that the social class difference may be less marked than it seems from the crime figures: delinquency may, for instance, be just as much a feature of middle and upper-class adolescence, but unrecorded because more often dealt with unofficially, by headmasters and university proctors, and treated more leniently by public, police and courts.[1] Even so, there is obviously some delinquency among the subjects of our study. So far, apart from the statement in an earlier chapter that delinquency was not one of the principal activities of most peer groups, the topic has been largely ignored; now to repair the omission.

Our main sample survey does not itself provide any direct information about delinquency. When we tried, in the earliest series of standardized interviews, to ask systematically about the boys' criminal experiences, we could not tell how far they were suppressing the facts, how often they exaggerated or dramatized them. Because we did not feel we could put much reliance upon what they said, we decided to exclude these questions from doorstep interviews. We did, however, discuss delinquency with the boys fairly fully in longer interviews and group discussions; here they talked more freely and, as far as we could judge, frankly. This illustrative material can fortunately be supplemented from two statistical studies of juvenile offenders in East London. The first, by Power and his colleagues at the Social Medicine Research

[1] See two American discussions of this: Cohen, A. K., *Delinquent Boys*, pp. 37–38, and Warner, W. L. and Lunt, P. S., *The Social Life of a Modern Community*, p. 427.

Delinquency

Unit of the Medical Research Council (London Hospital), covered the boys and girls under 17 who appeared before the Courts from January 1958 onwards and who lived in what is now Tower Hamlets – Bethnal Green, Stepney and Poplar.[2] The research workers kindly made available some separate figures for Bethnal Green boys, as well as allowing access to their other data. The second study, by Downes, was an analysis of all the people aged 8 to 25 who lived in Stepney and Poplar and who were convicted by the Courts in 1960 for offences committed during the same year.[3] Downes also carried out some 'informal observation' of boys in Stepney and Poplar.[4] My hope is, by drawing upon these various sources of information, to build up a reasonably accurate picture of the place of delinquency in the lives of the Bethnal Green adolescents.

How much delinquency

As Power points out, 'In London the police do not in general caution juveniles; in almost all instances juveniles found breaking the law are brought before the Courts';[5] this means that his figures, based upon Court appearances, are, in his own words, 'as full as the present system permits' for boys up to 17 (the age at which adult Courts take over from juvenile). When the present book was in preparation, he was able to give us detailed information for Bethnal Green covering the five years 1958 to 1962; the information included the ages of offenders, their offences, number of previous Court appearances, and present or former school.

These figures show that, of the boys living in Bethnal Green who were aged 14, 15 or 16 during those years, about 7 per cent each year came before the juvenile Courts and were found guilty. Just over half appeared only once, a quarter twice, and the rest more often. The annual 'juvenile delinquency rate', measured by the proportion of boys under 17 coming before the Courts for the first time during one year, was about 4 per cent.

These Bethnal Green rates are close to Power's figures for the

[2] The papers so far published on this study are Power, M. J., 'Trends in Juvenile Delinquency', and Power, M. J., 'An Attempt to Identify at First Appearance Before the Courts Those at Risk of Becoming Persistent Juvenile Offenders'. From now on I refer to these as 'Trends' and 'First Appearance' respectively.
[3] Downes, D. M., *The Delinquent Solution*, Chapter 6.
[4] Ibid., Chapter 7. [5] Power, M. J., 'Trends'.

138

East End as a whole. They do not in themselves suggest a very worrying juvenile crime problem. But the figures look more serious if a 'cumulative rate' is calculated – in other words, if we ask how many local boys are likely to come before the Courts at least once at some time during the span of their adolescence. The Tower Hamlets study has been able to follow boys through the years up to 17; its calculations suggest that, by this age, more than one local boy in four – from Bethnal Green, as from Stepney and Poplar – is likely to appear in Court. This still leaves out of account the years from 17 to 20, for which detailed figures are not to hand. If one draws upon national figures for an indication of what happens during these years,[6] it seems probable that something like one Bethnal Green boy in three may appear in Court before his 21st birthday. Measured in this way, delinquency is obviously fairly common.

What crimes do the boys commit? The 14, 15 and 16-year-old Bethnal Greeners who came before the Courts over the five years from 1958 were more often charged with theft than anything else. Altogether 40 per cent of the offences were some kind of theft. The stealing was mainly of a petty kind, but more than a quarter of it was 'breaking and entering'. Stealing was, however, more common among the 14 year olds than the 15 and 16 year olds: 65 per cent of the offences committed by the former were stealing, compared with 29 per cent of those committed by the latter. This age difference fits the pattern of juvenile crime in Tower Hamlets as a whole between the ages of 8 and 17. Power reports that stealing and similar offences rise to a peak at 14 and then fall off.[7]

Among 14, 15 and 16-year-old Bethnal Green offenders, 19 per cent of the offences were 'taking and driving away' (in other words, 'borrowing' a motor cycle, scooter or car), 16 per cent traffic offences, mainly driving a motor cycle or scooter without a licence, and 12 per cent one of the misdemeanours associated with hooliganism and violence – 'insulting behaviour', carrying an 'offensive weapon' and so on. These various offences – 'take and drive away', traffic offences, hooliganism or violence – accounted for 19 per cent of all the offences among boys aged 14, 51 per cent at 15 and 66 per cent at 16. Although there are no figures for

[6] See Little, A., 'The "Prevalence" of Recorded Delinquency and Recidivism in England and Wales', Table 1, p. 261.
[7] Power, M. J., 'Trends'.

Bethnal Green boys aged 17 and over, the evidence from Downes' research near by is that crime in general falls off sharply after about 20, as it does in the country as a whole, and that these offences other than stealing start to become important at about 15 and reach their peak at about 17.[8]

Stealing is general

How does all this match up with what the boys had to say? Their own account suggested that certain sorts of law-breaking – particularly stealing were even more widespread than the official figures indicate. Stealing, it seems, is part of the 'normal' behaviour of boys in Bethnal Green, as it apparently is in other working-class areas.[9] An 18 year old said of himself and his friends a few years earlier:

> 'We used to thieve now and again, same as anyone else, but I don't think we was bad – it was just a normal thing we used to do.'

And a 16 year old was probably exaggerating only slightly when he said:

> 'There's not a boy I know who hasn't in fact knocked something off at some time or another.'

A friend who was present commented:

> 'They're not thieves or anything like that, they're just normal.'

There were many examples of the kind of petty crime that, as the figures suggest, was common at about 13 or 14.

> 'I pinched a load of ball pens, pencils, cycling tools, things like that, when I was younger.' (16 year old.)

> 'We used to pinch ordinary little things, particularly when we were in the last couple of years at school. I remember when we went out on a school party once – there was

---

[8] Downes, D. M., op. cit., pp. 158–64.
[9] See Mays, J. B., *Growing Up in the City*, p. 81; in this study of working-class youths in Liverpool, Mays found that over three-quarters admitted breaking the law, mostly by stealing. Andry, R. G., *Delinquency and Parental Pathology* found that two-thirds of a sample of 'non-delinquents' in London admitted stealing (p. 94).

about sixty of us and we went to this place in the country where there was a little village store that sold souvenirs. I reckon that out of that sixty, about fifty of the kids thieved something out of the store. We laughed about it when we were going away afterwards, saying that the store was almost cleaned out by the time we'd finished.' (17 year old.)

Some of course went on stealing.

'When I was about 10 or 11 I started taking plastic toys and that kind of thing from Woolworths. Then when I was 12 there was a fine little game that a few of us got up to in a warehouse up the Cambridge Heath Road – we used to get in round the back way and take kettles and brooms and saucepans. We took them just for a lark, not to make anything out of it. By the time I was 16 I was stealing all sorts of other things. I used to take leather jackets from outside the clothing shops – just cut them down and walk away. And then a mate and I used to get into warehouses and take electric dryers and mixers and sets of cutlery and things like that.' (18 year old.)

'The first time I was pinched was when I was about 11. It was when my sister was getting married and I wanted to buy her a wedding present. We used to play in the bombed houses and there was this bloke in there – I'll always remember, he was a little bit older than us. He was stripping the lead out of this house and he said to us, "Do you want to earn something?" and we said, "Yes", so he said, "See this lead? I'll just go and stand on the corner and you walk up with it." He had an old wireless set he put it all in. And when me and my mate were walking up to him there were two blokes standing there. They looked just like ordinary blokes, but they turned out to be detectives and they pinched us, and when we looked round this bloke was gone. We told the detectives that some bloke had given it to us, but they never believed us and they found out what house it had come from and it was down to us. We got into trouble over that – up the Juvenile Court and both bound over. After that we pinched all sorts of things out of shops and off stalls. Then when I was about 16 or 17 a mate and I started breaking in. We started with a bicycle shop – we went round the back and climbed over a wall and got in. It looked so easy – just a little wall – and we broke in there and stole quite a few things. After we'd done the bicycle shop, it gave us encouragement and we did some more after that. We used to go round at night and break into shops and cafés. Mind you, all that stopped a couple of years ago. I must sound like a real thief to you, but I don't thieve now.' (20 year old.)

It seems from the figures that most other boys who continue stealing from shops, warehouses and the like after about 14 stop by about 19 or 20. What goes on, up to and beyond this age, is stealing from or defrauding one's employer – often dignified by being described as 'knocking-off' or 'fiddling'. 'I stole a table-top from my firm,' said an 18 year old, 'but I don't call that stealing.' Another said:

'I've knocked off things from work – spare parts, light switches, mirrors and given them to people or sometimes sold them.'

An 18 year old, working for a local trouser manufacturer, explained:

'I work a fiddle if I ever get the chance. Say a load of material comes in, and it's marked on the ticket 45 yards. After a few days that ticket may come away and the governor may say, "What's the yardage?" You tell him you don't know, so you measure it on the machine and you find that it's 50 yards. You look in the book and you find that it's supposed to be 45 yards. You've got five yards over, haven't you? If you tell the governor about it, he'll keep it for himself. He's not going to send it back to the mills and tell them they've made a mistake. So what I do, I take it myself. I don't see any reason why I shouldn't. To take off your governor is the usual practice, I should say. Governors fiddle, don't they? And they cheat each other. So why shouldn't you do the same?'

The same justification was used by others.

'The way I see it is this – the governor's on the fiddle and he's making it out of you anyway. No matter what you do, if you're making something on the side, the governor's making more.' (17, *labourer*.)

'They're out to rook you first, I mean the employers, ain't they? Docking this and that off your money? No, I don't reckon there's much wrong with pinching at work.' (18, *store-keeper*.)

This theft from employers is not by any means an entirely adolescent phenomenon, though it may be more common amongst them. I have heard similar views expressed by their fathers and men like their fathers interviewed in Bethnal Green. Similar attitudes are reported among adults as well as young people in other working-class districts.[10]

Along with this tolerance towards those who take things from employers, there is a widespread view that theft from a friend or relative is morally wrong, as stealing from rich people or large firms is not.[11]

'If you steal off someone who's a friend of yours, someone you know, that's bad. I don't see as there's anything wrong with stealing from a big shop or from a bank or somewhere like that. Ordinary people don't have to find the money out of their own pockets – it's all covered by insurance anyway.' (17 year old.)

'If someone pinches something from a big shop or from the back of a Rolls-Royce, or something like that, and they get away with it, I say good luck to them. What does it matter? It's only a crime against society, so who cares? It's not at all the same thing as knocking down some poor little old lady who's walking along leaning on a stick and with a big purse in her hand. I don't like to think that people around here would knock an old lady like that down for her purse.' (19 year old.)

A few boys did not make this distinction: to them stealing from

---

[10] For instance, Downes in Stepney and Poplar (op. cit., p. 204), Mays, J. B., in Liverpool (op. cit., p. 117) and Jephcott, P. and Carter, M. P., in 'Radby', a Midlands mining and industrial town (*The Social Background of Delinquency*, pp. 67–68).
[11] This distinction, too, was noted in the research in Stepney and Poplar, Liverpool and 'Radby'.

large shops or wealthy people was also wrong. But it seemed as if the two just quoted were expressing the views of the majority.

Attitudes to the offences connected with motor vehicles were more mixed. Some boys talked about their own experiences and those of others.

'I started with scooters. You know, you come home from school and you see a scooter parked there. You've found out how to get it started from your mates and you think "I'd just like to ride one of those things around the block". If it's dark and there's no one about you get on and ride away on it. If nothing goes wrong, you're tempted to do the same thing the next day and the day after that.' (18 year old.)

'It's very common round here – more common to take scooters than cars. The girls go for the scooter boys and they don't care whether the boy owns the scooter or whether he's pinched it. They don't know and they don't care.' (17 year old.)

Most, however, said they would not do it themselves. As one put it, 'It's mad. You might get away with it a couple of times and you might think you're all right, but it's very easy to get caught. I reckon it's a mug's game. I've had two mates who've been nabbed for pinching motor bikes or scooters.' It will be noted that the suggestion here is not that it was wrong to 'borrow' someone else's scooter, only reckless. But, as with the distinction between stealing from friends compared with 'impersonal' organizations, there was widespread disapproval of car or scooter thefts which caused harm or suffering. Several boys, for instance, condemned an incident in 1960, in which a woman of 64 had been knocked down and gravely injured by a 'borrowed' car driven by a 17 year old boy. Another example came from a 17 year old.

'I've done my share of "borrowing" cars and scooters in the past. I don't think it's right, particularly sometimes. Two blokes from round here came out of the Lyceum ballroom one night and pinched a Mini to get home because they reckoned there weren't any more buses running. Well, this car belonged to a young out-of-work actor, who's got polio. It puts him in a right fix. The police find this car abandoned down Bethnal Green and someone grasses about these two blokes and they get pinched. Then the story comes out. Of course the two chaps say they're sorry about the polio bloke and all that, but the beak says they're only sorry because they got caught. Still they only got fined. The point is it just shows how you can hurt people who haven't done anything to you. It's daft really, thoughtless.'

The cult of toughness

Views about violence are also mixed. Some boys were members of groups that sometimes fought others. Jimmy Grove said:

'We like a punch-up now and then. We fight for a reason, we don't just go out to sort somebody out. If one of our people gets hit by a mob, well we go after that group. We go over Victoria Park, there's a mob over there and they grabbed one of our boys, so we went back after them. If they hadn't started on a couple of our mates, we wouldn't have done anything. If I was going along the road tonight and a couple of blokes jumped me and I've got quite a few mates near by, well, what do I do? I jump on *them*. That's how we look at it.'

His friend Alan added:

'We don't go looking for trouble in places outside our area, we don't go up towards Brick Lane because they'd come down and jump on *us*. We don't start on them. Anyone who wants to come in our area, they can as long as they don't start on us. We don't even go over to Stepney, because if we went over there, one night they would come over here, and they've got so many more than we have got that we wouldn't have a chance.'

Others described how conflicts suddenly developed:

'It generally starts through looks. Somebody looks at somebody else and the other bloke says, "Who do you think you're looking at?" Or someone says, "Looking for trouble, mate?" And you say, "Yeah, got any?" And one thing leads to another, he gets a kick somewhere and then it starts.' (16 year old.)

'You're walking along in a crowd, and another crowd is walking along. One of you gets a bit flashy and shouts out, "Who you screwing?" And someone else says, "Why, what you going to do about it?", one starts fighting and then we all join in.' (17 year old.)

Generally, the boys seemed to feel that Bethnal Green was a 'tough' district – in the praiseworthy sense of a 'manly' one. A boy, aged 15, who had moved to Bethnal Green from Suffolk when he was eight, remarked:

'When I first got here I thought all the kids were harder – you know, tougher – than in the village where I used to live. I've got used to it now, and I'm the same myself. I think that East End boys are definitely harder than in other districts.'

And a locally-born boy said:

'Round here, you've only got to look the wrong way to get your head punched in. They're fucking tough, mate.' (16 year old.)

The conventions, among age peers, about loyalty and pride sometimes impose an obligation on a boy to fight, whether he really wants to or not. 'Us two go together,' said one 15 year old. 'If he gets in a fight I help him and it's the same with me.' According to the same boy, this sense of loyalty extends to a wider circle.

'Usually it's just the two of us but we've got a lot of mates on the estate where we live. We live there, you see, and we know them all. If another mob was coming over to hit our mob we would help them, it's only natural.'

Another 15 year old said that he was always expected to support his friends.

'If you don't join in the fight you get called all the names under the sun. "What did you stand there for?" "Why didn't you join in?" Even if two of your mates are on to two others, they still expect you to join in. You must stick by your mates. They call you chicken otherwise.'

Yet another, aged 16, explained how he had been led by

pressure from his friends into a fight he had not particularly wanted:

'I heard this fellow was calling me names – it was over a girl I took off him. He was going round saying I was a cunt and he'd murder me and all that. My mates said, "You going to get him?" sort of thing. So of course I said, "Yes, if I see him." Four days ago I was with eight of my mates and he was with two of his. I called him round the alley and had a fight with him. I only hit him twice and he was on the ground. I was scared beforehand; I always am before a fight. But I had to fight him, because all my mates were backing me up. They were all there. I would have looked small if I hadn't fought him then.'

These examples illustrate the point made in an earlier chapter about the influence of peers. There is, locally and particularly among the adolescent boys, a general 'cult of toughness', a respect for physical prowess and for 'spirit', which sometimes pushes into aggression even boys who have no special taste for it. But in practice the 'toughness' is much more a matter of convention or folklore than of day-to-day behaviour. There was plenty of evidence that most boys seldom fought and disliked violence. Some, for example, said that they had left one or other of the local youth clubs because 'it was too rough there' or 'there seemed to be a lot of fighting'. Some who belonged to another club remarked that its appeal was that 'the manager up there is good – he comes down on anyone who tries to start any rough stuff'. And the answers of the members of the sample, when asked what they thought of the recently reported clashes between rival groups of teenagers at seaside resorts, were revealing. About one in ten seemed to accept or approve of the fighting.

'It's alright. If people like to fight it's up to them to. It's enjoyment in a way. I've been in fights myself – if someone hits you you've got to hit them back, haven't you?'

'Well, you could say it was very good, the fighting. I was down at the coast myself. It was a right laugh down there, some of the things were real funny.'

But as many as two-thirds of the sample firmly condemned the participants.

'It's terrible, It's only a few get together and spoil it for everybody else.' (15, *secondary modern schoolboy*.)

'I think the way they carry on is ridiculous. It shows teenagers up.' (17, *plumber's mate*.)

It's stupid. I don't see how they can go at each other. When it comes to fighting, I don't see that. Anyway, how can you fight someone you don't know?' (18, *shop assistant*.)

In fact, systematic fighting and mob battles are a rare occurrence in the East End. A 16 year old said, 'There are some who say they fight with bottles and knives and go out for big punch-ups and all that, but it's mostly talk.'[12]

The threat to adult order

Just the same, there are other forms of aggressive and destructive behaviour that threaten the orderliness of the adult world and are seen as distinctively 'adolescent'. If there is sympathy amongst the local adults for some of the fighting – on the ground that it is 'manly' to settle a quarrel 'with your fists' – there is hardly any for the apparently senseless rowdyism and damage to property in which some boys indulge.

A 15 year old thought that the habit of destructiveness started at an early age.

'When you're a little kid, you smash up the things people chuck on the bomb sites, like old baths, old prams, old boxes and that. And motor-cars – there's always old motor vans on the bomb sites that the kids smash up. At first they think the bits they pull off are going to be useful for something, but when they get them off there's always something wrong with them, say some bracket won't come off, so then they do some more smashing up. It goes in crazes. After that we used to smash up builder's boards and "House to Let" notices. We didn't do it very much, but I know for a time we was pulling up those "House to Let" boards, and we used to dump them

[12] This is what Downes reported of Stepney and Poplar: 'In both Stepney and Poplar, no inter-gang, and barely any inter-group, fighting was reported or observed, though there was a generally disseminated proclivity towards limited forms of toughness and aggression.' (Downes, D. M., op. cit., p. 212.)

in the canal or in the Victoria Park Lake. I don't know why we did it; it was for a giggle.'

We were also given current examples of characteristic boisterousness. An 18 year old described what happened one Saturday night after he had been to the cinema with a girl:

'11.30 p.m.   On the way back from taking Carol home I saw Rich, Steve, Mike and Fred. We went for a long walk to Liverpool Street Station. We sang and larked about on the way. Walking through Spitalfields Market, we flung old spuds and bits of orange at one another.
'12.30 a.m.   At Liverpool Street we had a drink at the coffee machine and woke up all the tramps sleeping on the benches.
'1.30 a.m.   We started home – tried to thumb a lift but in vain.
'2.45 a.m.   Back in Market Square, Bethnal Green, we played cricket with a piece of wood and a brick. Woke everybody up.
'3.30 a.m.   Went home to bed.'

Another boy, aged 17, described what happened one Sunday afternoon with three friends:

'We decided to go down to Southend in this little van – me and Charlie and Alan and Tom. Charlie was driving. We got down to Southend about 5.30, we jumped out and went in a telephone box to comb our hair in the mirror. We went to the Kursaal and started bilking the dodgem cars, you just jump over the fence, you see, and get in the queue; you say you've lost your ticket and get away with it. Then we went in the bar and had a few drinks. Then we went in the ghost train and Alan got off the train in the dark, I thought he would; we were all waiting for him to jump on us and somebody jumps on the top of us, it's Alan. Then we went on the scenic railway and they wouldn't strap us in (i.e. they were not allowed to ride): they could see what we was like. Then we went on the beach and Charlie shouted out there was a lot of bottles down there. We filled them with water and started throwing them about; they smashed against the stones; I stood there and thought if someone's going to come down in the morning they'll cut their feet to pieces. Then Alan stood on the end of this pier and started swinging round a big tin can on a string, he was going to throw it out to sea, he misjudged it, instead of throwing it upwards he let go too late and it went straight over his shoulder, just missed this old lady. So we ran and jumped in the van and drove away.'

There are, in some of these examples, a number of common themes. First, much of what the boys are doing, is, in strictly rational terms, pointless and senseless – much of the behaviour is an expression of bubbling exuberance, of animal high spirits. As a 17 year old said, 'When you're young you want to let off a bit of steam. It's an attitude everybody experiences – it's a way of expressing yourself.' Secondly, this is almost never done by boys on their own or in pairs; the members of the peer group support each other.

'When they're together there's a sort of devil-may-care attitude. They're all in one bunch and they feel the others don't seem to care – well, they're pretending not to care, anyway – so why should I care. I won't care either. They sort of get carried away with each other. One tries to outdo the other. They say to themselves, if he's not afraid to shout out at that old lady over the road, I'm not afraid to put a stone through that window over there.' (18 year old.)

Finally, much of this behaviour is literally 'anti-social'; property is damaged, other people may be injured, frightened or disturbed. This is why adults, including those in Bethnal Green, disapprove. The boys themselves are either unconcerned or actually want to strike at adult society. Certainly some of them thought this last was true of themselves or their fellows. A 16-year-old grammar school boy said, 'A lot of us feel like it. It's the result of boredom. There's a natural instinct to rebel against somebody'. And a 19 year old, looking back, 'A lot of young people enjoy annoying adults. It may be because other people treat them badly, I suppose – in their work or at home or something like that. They think to themselves we'll do it just for spite. They want to take it out on someone else.'

One boy of 18 suggested that the hostility was often generated by adults.

'Adults tend to hold teenagers down a lot. If a crowd of you go into a pub and you're having a drink, you're with a crowd so you have a laugh. The older people look across at you and stare and say to each other "Mad hooligans" or something like that. They're sort of against us, they're upset by the noise we're making, they're frightened that we're drinking too much. We can take as much as they can, in fact more in some cases. As a matter of fact, one rule we always have in our crowd is that if anybody's driving, they don't have a single drink. If one boy is driving, he sits and drinks lemonade while the rest of us drink beer or spirits. But the older people look across at you and think you're getting drunk and making too much noise and all that sort of thing. It's no wonder that youngsters go a bit wild occasionally, open up now and again.'

A trivial example of an incident provoked by adult intervention was given by a 14-year-old secondary modern schoolboy.

'I went to the Regal with my mate. On the way we bought ten fags and when we got inside we started smoking. There was an old man next to me and he got hold of my fag and stubbed it out and said, "You're too young to smoke." I said, "Mind your own fucking business." So the old man went and got an attendant and we got slung out.'

This sense that adults are sometimes intent upon 'holding them down' seems to be held by a sizeable minority. Their feeling that adult society is against them is expressed in their attitudes to the police. 'I don't like the bloody coppers; I don't think any young boy likes a policeman,' said a 16 year old sweepingly. An 18-year-old carpenter, echoing a suggestion raised at the beginning of this chapter, argued that the treatment of working-class boys was different from that accorded to university students and the like, and that this discrimination was practised by the police and by people in general.

'We don't learn to speak properly. We've been brought up pretty rough. The things these students do are not all that different from what we do. But people don't look at it the same way. They say, "They are studying and they need to let off steam" – you know, exuberance and all that.

But when any of us do it, I mean even the general public –
it's not only the law – people turn round and say, "Look,
they're mad gits, sit on them".'

Examples were given of police discrimination locally against
boys, as they themselves saw it, just because they were adolescent.

'They always push you off the pavement, even though next
door there's a load of older people they don't touch. If you're
a teenager they'll have you for anything; you just stand on
the corner and they have you for loitering. If you're riding
your bike, they stop you and say, 'Where are you going,
where have you been, whose bike have you got?" It happened to me once. Say you have a fight and they come along,
they don't *have* to clip you round the earhole.' (17 year old.)

'One of my brother's friends was standing in the street, and
some boys came up to speak to him, and a copper pulled them
in. They didn't call his mum until three o'clock in the
morning. They said he was loitering, and they were all
fined. There's no reason why you shouldn't stand on a street
corner. They weren't annoying bystanders, only having a
laugh and talking.' (18 year old.)

Given this resentment against the police, it is perhaps not surprising that some boys occasionally, as they put it, 'take the
mickey' out of policemen.

MICHAEL   There was a fight between a couple of people
round in our block, someone went round the phone
box to call the coppers. This copper came up and
we started taking the mickey out of him. Everybody knew the police would be coming round.
We were sort of standing in his way, and he came
up and said, "Is this Norfolk House?" So I said to
him, "You got eyes, mate?" It's up in big letters in
front of him. He says to me, "Don't be funny." I
says, "They're probably expecting you." He says,
"Why?" I said, "How should I know?" He said,
"You just told me they might be expecting me." I
says, "I never said nothing."

PETER   I said, "No, he never said nothing, copper." The

copper said, "Don't you start playing around with me." I said to Michael, "Have you got four coppers. I want them for the telephone box?" The copper went absolutely mad.

MICHAEL Anyway, he went up to the flat, and when he was coming out he said to us, "Watch it", like that. As he was walking away, I shouted out after him. I bawled out at the top of my voice, "You dirty great cunt." As soon as I said it, we turned round and belted off in the opposite direction.

Not that most are seriously antagonistic to the police. But many of them, at least some of the time, do have the sense that adult society is suspicious and hostile, and the police likewise. They in their turn are sometimes anti-adult and anti-police, and this is probably part of the explanation for the occasional defiance and hooliganism.

Family influences

The adults with whom the boys clash may of course include their own parents. But parental attitudes to juvenile crime, and their influence upon their sons, are more complex matters deserving special attention. In a few families fathers in particular themselves openly break the law and are hostile to the police.

'When this copper started shoving my friend around,' said a 17 year old, 'I hit him with a bottle. I was put on probation for two years for that. My old man said, "Jolly good luck – sod the coppers." He don't like coppers because he's a lorry driver; and before he drove lorries he was pinched lots of times for being a street trader.'

Clearly there are some 'criminal families' in Bethnal Green. Power found that, in Tower Hamlets generally, boys were more likely to come before the Courts if one of their siblings had been there already.[13] And we came across families where serious crime was commonplace.

[13] Power, M. J., 'First Appearance'. A study in Glasgow found the same: 'To a remarkable extent the convictions of the boys and of other members of their family run parallel.' (Ferguson, T., *The Young Delinquent in His Social Setting: a Glasgow Study*, p. 151.)

'Look at my family – everyone goes inside from time to time. One of my uncles has just come out after doing six years. Another uncle goes in now and then for three months. Another one is selling stolen goods – he's been doing that for two years and he ain't been caught. He's making loads of money. It runs like that in the family.' (16 year old.)

Such families are rare. Even among the rest, however, minor 'fiddling' or 'knocking off' from employers is commonly tolerated, even approved – probably almost as much, as I suggested earlier, among the adults as the adolescents. The extent of pilfering from the near-by docks is one indication.[14] Many adults in Bethnal Green, too, though they would not themselves steal from large stores or 'impersonal' concerns, are like their sons in regarding such thefts with relative tolerance. It would be wrong to think that this shows manual workers to be particularly immoral. Sutherland has convincingly shown that 'white-collar' crime is widespread;[15] and tax evasion, expense account 'fiddling' and sharp business practice are by no means unknown to many of those who would be quick to condemn pilfering by a dock or railway employee. As Wootton remarks, 'The truth is that the anti-social behaviour of one social circle takes one form, while the members of other circles both behave and misbehave differently.'[16]

In practice the Bethnal Green father who 'lifts' at work comes to terms with his minor thefts in just the same way as his more illustrious fellows with their own forms of misdemeanour – by refusing to regard them as crimes at all. They have not really done anything wrong: they are therefore in their own eyes not 'criminals' and certainly not against the police or the law in general. Similarly fathers who have themselves been 'in trouble' as adolescents are likely to be relatively tolerant of minor transgressions – 'It's just high spirits. Boys will be boys' – but do not, because of this, condone 'serious' law-breaking. All in all, to judge not only from what the boys told us about their parents but also from our earlier studies and our continuing contacts with the district, most adults in Bethnal Green think that the law is in

---

[14] See Downes, D. M., op. cit., p. 193. The studies in Liverpool and 'Radby' cited earlier in the present chapter on p. 143, also bear this out.

[15] Sutherland, E. H., 'White-Collar Criminality'; this is an American article but it seems likely that much of it applies to Britain as well.

[16] Wootton, B., *Social Science and Social Pathology*, p. 70.

general on their side and are ready to uphold it. Even among those who do not wholeheartedly share this opinion, most certainly think that law-breaking should be discouraged because of the risk.

When the boys talked about their parents' views, the commonest attitude they described was one of disapproval of the son's transgressions, with mothers particularly vocal. A 17 year old who had been caught three times and had spent a spell in an approved school, told us what his parents had thought.

'The first time I went up to court I felt horrible, you know. I thought what my old woman would say about it. It didn't turn out too badly, because she didn't say much really – you know, she thought I'd never do it again. The way she carried on when I went up the second and third times, it really shook me. After the last time, she more or less said, "All right, I don't care if you get put away for fucking ten years." My dad doesn't like it either. He's done some jobs in his time – years ago, you know, when the family was hard up. He let it drop once that he'd done some warehouses. He said, "The only time I've ever done something was when I done it for my wife and children." But he went straight off the subject after that – he kind of jumped on to something else. No, I think he'd rather kill me than see me up in court. Anyway, it's all more or less forgotten now. I've got enough sense now not to get caught.'

Others who had kept more at a distance from crime described their parents' influence.

'I used to go with a mob but my mum and dad didn't like it. They thought I'd get into trouble with the law. After I packed it in, some of the others did get pinched for stealing.' (18 year old.)

'I've never really knocked anything off – nothing important. I might have pinched a pencil from school or something like that, but I've never done a job, you know – broken into somewhere and smashed it all up or anything like that. I know people who do do that sort of thing, but I've never done it. I mean, if I'd done it I'd have had the fear my mother would find out and smack me. I've always known my parents disapproved of that sort of thing.' (17 year old.)

If the family is one influence against delinquency, courtship is another.

'You get girl friends, don't you, and all that. If you're going serious with a girl and you get caught pinching, it puts you in a bad way. So you tend to give it up when you start going steady.' (18 year old.)

'There was three of us that used to go out thieving together. But then one of them got married. Once he got married he didn't want to know nothing about it. It wasn't just that he didn't come out with us any more – he got very respectable and all that.' (19 year old.)

The place of delinquency

The theme is by now familiar. What the boys themselves told us corroborates the figures given at the beginning of the chapter. To recapitulate, there are two distinct cycles in juvenile law-breaking. The first is in theft, mainly petty; after the peak at about 14, some boys go on stealing, though most even of these stop by about 19 or 20. 'Fiddling' and 'lifting' from work does persist, and is regarded as fairly trivial by most people locally.

The second cycle is in the offences mainly 'associated with hooliganism and disorder'.[17] This cycle starts later and reaches its peak at about 17. In Downes's words, 'The first stage (of juvenile crime) begins about the age of 9 or 10 and persists to 14–15, i.e. from pre- to mid-adolescence. It involves almost exclusively break-ins and petty larcenies. . . . The second stage begins around 15–16 and persists until 18–19, i.e. from mid- to late-adolescence. It involves take-and-drive-away, rowdyism, some violence. . . .'[18] It is striking that this second stage, in which the law-breaking is predominantly of the disorderly, 'defiant' or violent kind, co-incides with the period of adolescence which earlier chapters have suggested is that of greatest strain and conflict. It seems, how-ever, from what the boys say, that this second sort of delinquency

[17] Power, M. J., 'Trends'.   [18] Downes, D. M., op. cit., p. 164.

is less common than the stealing in which so many indulge when they are younger.

Altogether something like a third of the local boys may come before the Courts during their adolescence. Many others break the law, mainly by shoplifting and other petty theft and mainly in early adolescence or before. Among the older boys, particularly those of about 17, some occasionally do something wild or dangerous. But most of the offences are relatively trivial and for most boys the incident is relatively transitory. Of the boys who come before the Courts about half do so once and another quarter twice, and for virtually all boys the whole thing is over by the age of about 20. The conclusion is that, as an earlier chapter suggested, delinquency is neither one of the main activities nor a continuing activity of most boys or most adolescent groups.

Explanations for delinquency

Is it possible to identify the boys most likely to be delinquent? One finding is that the type of school is related to delinquency. A comparison of the past or present schools of the 14, 15 and 16-year-old Bethnal Green offenders with those of boys of the same age in our sample shows this. The boys before the Courts contained proportionately more boys at secondary modern schools (as defined in Chapter V): 89 per cent of them went to such schools compared with 58 per cent of the boys in the sample.

Downes found the same thing in Poplar and Stepney. He also had information on the occupations of offenders, and he adds:

'Where he is not still at school, the delinquent is most likely to be an unskilled, semi-skilled or unemployed worker. Occupationally, as educationally, the delinquent is "bottom of the heap". . . .'[19]

The 'open' interviews and group discussions in Bethnal Green pointed to the same conclusion about the 'seriously' delinquent. They suggested too that there was, among some boys, a consistent pattern of behaviour and attitudes, into which violence and law-breaking fitted. Earlier chapters have drawn attention to the 'deviants' among the Bethnal Green boys – those who disliked school, who could not settle in their job, who either did not go

[19] Downes, D. M., op. cit., p. 184.

to youth clubs or, when they went, caused so much trouble that they were expelled. It has already been made clear that these are not all the same boys – one who dislikes school does not necessarily find it difficult to settle into a job, nor does the job-changer necessarily stay away from youth clubs. But there is some overlapping, as has been shown in the sets of correlations already reported. Discontent at school and at work, for instance, often go together. The correlation analysis provides evidence of further links also. In particular, boys critical of school or work more often said their parents did not 'understand' them.[20] Andry found, in his comparison of samples of 'delinquents' and 'non-delinquents', that the delinquent boys tended to get on less well than the others with their parents, particularly their fathers.[21] Delinquency, in other words, as some of our interviews seemed to indicate, fits in with other kinds of discontent inside and outside the home.

I can illustrate this by drawing once again on the experience of Jimmy Grove and his friends – the boys who come closest to being a 'gang' out of those we talked to in our research. First, school. Jimmy and his friends all went to secondary modern schools, and most of them disliked school. They described their schools as 'crap schools' and complained about the injustices of the 'eleven-plus'. In the main, they were not successful at school; they resented its discipline; they saw it as something to be accepted rather than enjoyed, a nuisance rather than of any value. In a word, they were in greater or lesser degree the failures and the rebels of secondary education. None of them had gone on to any kind of further education since they had left.

As for work, they were in the main in unskilled jobs, and most of them changed jobs often. Jimmy said:

[20] The correlation coefficients were as follows. Between fathers 'not understanding' and (*a*) criticizing school lessons, ·263; (*b*) criticizing school rules, ·260; (*c*) dissatisfaction with job generally, ·154; (*d*) dissatisfaction with job prospects, ·225. Comparable coefficients with mothers 'not understanding' were: (*a*) ·186; (*b*) ·177; (*c*) no significant correlation; (*d*) ·305.
[21] Andry, R. G., op. cit., pp. 26–27, p. 45, pp. 60–61 and p. 88. A similar connection was noted in a study of eighty-five 18 year olds in an outer London borough: 'There was some evidence that unhappy family relationships were reflected in the boy's choice of job. . . . A group who seemed to be reacting against a disturbed family situation were the "drifters" found working in the semi-skilled and unskilled jobs.' (Logan, R. F. L. and Goldberg, E. M., 'Rising Eighteen in a London Suburb', p. 328.)

'None of us worry what jobs we do. We are all the same, right, boys? We'll do any job as long as the money is high. We don't care what work we do, we don't care what the foreman's like, as long as the money's there at the end of the week.'

About apprenticeships, they said that they could not afford to take them on and that, in any case, they wanted to 'enjoy life, not sit at night school every night'. They were also among those who told stories about misbehaviour in youth clubs and being expelled for it.

They were certainly not content with their lot. For instance, Jimmy said:

'I want to be *it*. I want to be higher than millions of people with my name mentioned every day in the papers – when that happens you are *it*.'

The same boys engaged in organized theft – or as they put it, 'did jobs'. They told stories of breaking into shops and ware-houses, driving away cars and scooters, and so on. They were also more violent than most of the other boys we talked to – 'We go in for punch-ups more than most of the fellows round here.' They spoke more callously about injury to other people.

'I remember the night old Porter broke his leg trying to creep in the club without paying. He tried to creep in there without paying, and he went down with a crash. I was on the floor – I couldn't get up with laughter. He was laying down there with his leg broke. I didn't know it was broke, mind you, but I couldn't get up, I was laying there for hours laughing my head off. What happened, you see, Porter was sneaking up the stairs, he tried to creep in behind the geezer's back, he turns round and sees him and clouts him. Oh, that made me laugh. No one helped him, we were all laughing. Porter does a backward dive down the stairs, didn't he, he fell down screaming to the bottom, no one taking any notice. About half an hour later somebody came down – he's still laying there groaning. It turned out he'd broken his leg. Ah, that was a laugh, that was, honest. That reminds me of the time his father hit the spike. We were fishing down at the canal and his old man came round. To get to us Mr. Porter had to get across this iron tube with a spike at each end, and as he goes across it he hits it. Ah, that was funny. I was on the floor with laughter. He went down the hospital, he had to get it done up. He really injured himself.'

'There was this Irishman who lived in our block of flats. He's got a son, aged about ten, a really spoilt brat. This kid starts setting on one of the little girls who lives in the flats. He slapped her around real bad and she went home screaming her head off. Her father asked who had done it and she told him; he said, "I'm fed up with this." He went down to the front door and he said to the Irishman, "What's this?" "Oh," said the Irish geezer, "We bring them up tough in Ireland." So this fellow pulled him out the door, and he said, "This is how we bring them up in Bethnal Green," and he gave him a crack across the face. He practically killed him. The Irish fellow started staggering down the stairs, staggering along, limping along the road, his mouth all bleeding, he was just about existing. We was pissing ourselves with laughter.'

We have no firm evidence whether these few boys illustrate a pattern that applies more widely. But the elements seem to hang together. The argument is that such boys are consistently rejected; respond with frustration, expressed in aggression; try to kick against society through delinquency and violence. This corresponds closely with a prominent sociological theory on delinquency, that of 'delinquent sub-cultures', which is drawn largely from the United States.[22] In the debate on 'delinquent sub-cultures' there are differences of emphasis in detail, but a broad measure of agreement that the origins of delinquency are to be found in the contrast between the values of a prosperous and democratic society and the lot of the working-class boy within it. These boys live, so the argument goes, in a society which values success, above all material success, and in which, too, advertising and the mass media generally are constantly at work to sharpen

[22] See e.g. Cohen, A. K., op. cit., Cloward, R. A. and Ohlin, L. E., *Delinquency and Opportunity*, Miller, W. B., 'Lower-Class Culture as a Generating Milieu of Gang Delinquency', Matza, D., *Delinquency and Drift*. The whole debate is reviewed and related to the English scene in Downes, D. M., op. cit.

aspirations. But, in a democratic society which prizes achievement, those who do not get on are branded as failures – and this applies most to working-class youngsters. Their sense of failure, according to the theory, is especially sharp when, as now, education is the main ladder of success and when they have been openly rejected by the educational system.

The suggestion is that this sense of failure and frustration is the mainspring of unlawful behaviour, particularly theft, violence and hooliganism. Here the interpretations differ. Some see the lawbreaking as an attempt to get, by illegitimate means, the material trappings that successful people get by legitimate. Some, on the other hand, argue that the motive is above all 'status-frustration' – that is, the boys behave as they do to hit back at the society that has rejected them and to show their contempt for its values.

There has, in fact, been virtually no research in the United States or in Britain to test this theory on a satisfactory scale. Our study cannot provide such a test, but it is none the less instructive to see how the theory stands up to the findings of this research. The attitudes and behaviour of the delinquent boys just described correspond closely to what the theory would predict, and above all to the suggestion that their main motive is a desire to strike at society rather than acquire wealth.

So in broad outline the theory seems to apply. But only to some boys, not to most. Earlier chapters have shown time and again that there is no widespread and continuing sense of resentment, revolt or frustration among the local boys. Many boys are 'delinquent', in the sense that they sometimes break the law, and particularly steal. But, since most boys do not feel rejected or frustrated, the theory does not explain their transgressions. It can help to explain only the delinquency of the minority. My interpretation, though again I cannot demonstrate it, is that such boys engage more often in persistent and 'serious' crime, and are probably more likely to turn into adult criminals. If this is true, it still does not tell us why certain boys respond to a poor school record and a low-status job with a sense of frustration and bitterness, while others whose experience is apparently similar do not. There is no obvious sociological explanation for the difference; we probably have to look instead to psychology.

How, finally, is the relatively trivial delinquency of the majority to be explained? It can, I think, best be interpreted as part of the process of working out adolescent tensions and adolescent resentments against adults. Delinquency is encouraged, too, by the peer group. The process which makes boys withdraw into a peer group of their own sex also withdraws them, to some extent, from the influence of social disapproval. They care less than formerly what their parents think, but have not yet acquired a girl friend whose opinion of them matters. When they do acquire one, and move towards a family of their own, they become once again more subject to the social controls of the local community and the national society.

IX

IN CONCLUSION – GROWING UP IN A WORKING-CLASS COMMUNITY

The preceding chapter ended by suggesting that there is a distinctive pattern of 'rebelliousness' among some boys. This final chapter begins by trying to take the analysis further and distinguish two other more common patterns of response to the problem posed by growing up in a working-class community.

Why, it may be asked, is there a 'problem' at all? For most boys, for most of the time, there is not. But in adolescence they are all facing a series of choices about their future. These are critical years: how they behave – and how they 'get on' – at this stage will probably be decisive for the rest of their lives. As they pass through the last years at school and move on into working life, their actions decide what sort of adult they will become. And this poses a question about their attitude to the local community and its way of life.

This was touched on in the earlier reference to 'delinquent subcultures'. The boys all know, some at a more conscious level than others, that judged by the standards of the wider society their community and its residents are not 'successful'. They know that, despite the 'affluence', local people are relatively poor financially and relatively low in status. They know that the national society to which they belong – and for that matter, 'western society' generally – values 'success' largely in terms of money, fame, yachts and Rolls-Royces; that these things are relatively scarce in East London; and that if they themselves are to succeed in these terms they need to break with the local way of life.

Most of those to whom we talked about this in any detail – they amounted to about fifty, of whom something like a third were in the main sample – recognized clearly enough that social class came into this. There are of course the entertainers, the pop stars and the professional footballers who achieve success and, in some sense at least, retain contact with their origins; occupations like this were mentioned by about one in ten of the boys as what they would 'like' to be doing ten years hence. There are also the adults who get a profitable living from crime or near-crime. These are, however, exceptional; in the main to get on in anything but the most modest sense depends upon belonging to, or joining, the middle or upper classes – what a 17-year-old garage mechanic described as 'the very rich, the top class, and the people with money, the middle class, the people who live in Woodford and places like that'. A 16-year-old sprayer said:

'You get these so-called "middle-class" people, who think they are higher than you because they live in higher-class places. People with bowler hats and umbrellas. They think they own the world. They look around with their noses in the air and talk to you as if you were nobody.'

The boys knew that membership of these 'superior' classes could be inherited – 'They're born to money, they've got every chance,' said an 18-year-old warehouseman, 'They're thorough-breds, we're mongrels.' But they also knew that a 'higher' social position could be achieved; said a 17-year-old tailor's presser, 'The governor of our firm comes from our class but he's pushed himself up. He's nearly middle-class already.'

Though membership of the 'successful' classes can be won on merit, it does not depend simply upon achieving financial success. It demands too – and indeed the financial success itself may turn on – different values, different attitudes, different modes of behaviour from those common to the East End. The issue can be illustrated by what some of the boys said about accent. Many were aware that a 'Cockney accent' could be a draw-back.

'At work, you're dirt. I'm a Cockney and there's classes, isn't there? And when people know you're a Cockney, they think, "Oh, he isn't much good, he's from the East End." That's the point – there's classes in this world, you've got to have a big house and a big car and speak the right way.' (16, *apprentice telephone engineer*.)

'If you try hard, you can speak as good as any Englishman, though you're a Cockney. If you speak posh you have more chance of a job; if you speak Cockney you get a dirty job, a barrow-boy and that sort of thing.' (18, *shop assistant.*)

This focuses the issue with which the boys are posed – though, as I suggested earlier, it is hardly a real choice for most of them. They can decide that they want to succeed in middle-class terms and set out to make themselves into middle-class kinds of people.

'There's a proper way of speaking everyone should have,' said a 17-year-old clerk, 'and I'm trying to get it. I'm trying to change my accent, to sound my aitches and say "Good evening" instead of "Wotcher" and "Goodbye" instead of "Ta-ta".'

'You have to talk a bit different to what you do at home,' said a 15 year old, a would-be bank messenger. 'That's if you want to get on well. Because you're in the City and talking to all posh people. You want to be able to mix with the right sort of people.'

Such a path was renounced by most. They insisted that they would not – or could not – make the kind of changes exemplified in 'trying to talk posh'.

'I don't want promotion. I just want to stay ordinary,' said an electrician's mate, aged 19, 'A friend of mine went into a bank. He had to change his voice and now he says "*H*allo"; you'd think he was a poof.'

'I couldn't change the way I spoke,' said a butcher's boy, aged 18. 'I've been brought up like that. I know my way around here, anywhere else I feel out of place.'

This illustrates what I mean by the boys' 'choice', the dilemma posed by growing up in a working-class community. Broadly, there are two ways of responding, and in the course of the research we came to recognize two general categories of boy. The first were those whose values, sentiments and aspirations were essentially like those of their working-class fathers; they had manual occupations and they expected to stay in them. They were, in the main, content with their lot and looked forward to the same kind of job as they had now. They could be called 'working-class' boys. Secondly, there were those who looked beyond

Bethnal Green for their inspiration, who criticized it and renounced its values, and whose ambitions and sentiments were closer to those of the middle class. They could be called 'the boys more middle-class in outlook' or 'middle-class' boys (as long as it is borne in mind that I mean 'middle-class' only in this special sense). These two types correspond to those described by Whyte[1] in his classic study of 'Cornerville', an Italian working-class district of Boston in the United States; Whyte called the first 'corner boys', the second 'college boys'.

Both sorts of boys – 'working-class' or 'corner boys', and 'middle-class' or 'college boys' – were, in their different ways, making an adjustment to their condition. They were coming to terms with society, either accepting their status in a manual occupation or seeking for advancement in a non-manual one. But there was also the third group already referred to: the 'rebels', who rejected both the standard 'working-class' values of the local community and the 'middle-class' values that predominate in the wider society.[2] Despite what has been said earlier, the boys who rejected standard 'working' and 'middle-class' values were not all delinquent or even potentially so; this is discussed later, but meanwhile I describe all the deviants collectively as 'rebels'.

The three types

Two questions follow – what proportions are there of the three types in Bethnal Green and what are the main characteristics of each? In an attempt to answer these questions, we used two methods of analysis described in more detail in Appendix 4.

Briefly, the first method took twenty-one items from the survey questionnaire and gave each of the 246 boys a score according to his answers. Each boy was then assigned to the category – 'working-class', 'middle-class' or 'rebel' – on which he had the highest score; those on the borderline were, after careful examination of the interview, assigned to the category we judged most appropriate. The second method, like the series of correlations referred to in earlier chapters, had to be confined to the 177 boys at work; using a computer and drawing on a total of thirty-four items from

---

[1] Whyte, W. F., *Street-Corner Society*, p. xx.
[2] This three-fold distinction is similar to that of Cohen who, in his *Delinquent Boys*, added to Whyte's 'corner' and 'college' boys a third category of 'delinquent' boy. (Cohen, A. K., *Delinquent Boys*, pp. 128–30.)

the interview, it used 'component analysis' to calculate for each boy two statistically weighted scores – one on 'social class' attitudes and behaviour, the other on 'rebelliousness'.

The results of these two methods of analysis were then compared.[3] They showed some variations but also a good deal of consistency. The computer analysis, in other words, broadly confirmed the findings of the more arbitrary and subjective method: that there were 'clusters' of behaviour and attitudes among the boys and that our three-fold distinction reflected some real differences.

The boys obviously vary widely in the consistency of their answers. Many are 'middle-class' in some respects, 'working-class' or 'rebel' in others. For this reason, it is difficult to say with any precision what proportions of local boys are of each type. But, on the basis of the two sets of analysis, it seems that something like a fifth could be described as 'middle-class', a tenth or less as 'rebels' and about two-thirds or three-quarters as 'working-class'. The principal characteristics of each 'type' are shown in the following 'profiles'.

The 'working-class' boy   He goes to a secondary modern or possibly 'comprehensive' school and leaves at 15. He did not dislike school; on the whole he was not critical of the teachers and he approved of most of the rules, though he thought the lessons of little value and school generally rather remote from life. He is most likely to have a skilled or semi-skilled manual job which he is broadly content with. When he is asked what job he would like to do in ten years' time if he could choose, he will probably say the job he has now, which is also the one he 'expects' to have in the future: 'Plumber's mate now, expect to be a plumber, and if I could choose, that's what I'd like to be.' He expects to marry, probably before he is 25. He is more likely to spend money than to save it, and to say that one should 'enjoy oneself' rather than 'work hard'.

The 'middle-class' boy   He went to a grammar or 'comprehensive' school, and left at 16 or over. He liked school and approved of the teachers and the school rules; unlike his 'working-class' counterpart, he regarded the school curriculum as 'useful'. If he is not still at school – as he may be until 18 – his present job is as a clerk,

[3] See diagram 1, p. 214.

167

a salesman or a junior executive. His father is often a shopkeeper or clerk. The boy likes his work, and is looking forward to moving up the career-ladder as he gets older. He believes in saving money, and in studying and working hard so as to 'get on'. He expects to marry, but this is likely to be after 25 rather than before. His work and interests are outside Bethnal Green; he does not particularly like the district and looks to the day when he will live somewhere 'better'.

The 'rebel' He went to a secondary modern school and, like the 'working-class' boy, left at 15. But he did not like school: he disliked the teachers and the school régime, as well as thinking the lessons 'useless'. His job is manual, and is more likely to be unskilled or semi-skilled than skilled. He is discontented with his work and particularly the lack of prospects. He has probably had at least three jobs since leaving school, sometimes many more. He does not get on too well with his parents and he dislikes the police. He is more likely than other boys to say that he does not intend to marry at all or that he does not know whether he will. He rejects, even more firmly than his 'working-class' fellows, the idea of 'deferred gratification'. It is probably from boys like this that the seriously delinquent are drawn.

To this much simplified typology some important qualifications have to be added. First, about the 'working-class' boy: the suggestion that he is 'content' with his life should not be made too much of. His contentment is relative, and there is little doubt, from what the boys told us in the longer interviews, that many feel bored and frustrated at work; the point is that they do not express any serious rebellion, because they do not think of their condition as being something that can be changed. In other words, what I report should not be taken as an excuse for neglecting the problems of such boys at school or at work. Secondly, if they are less 'aspiring', in occupational terms, than the 'middle-class' boys, this does not mean that they have no aspirations. For some, as has been suggested, the aim is to become more skilled, a craftsman. And outside the occupational sphere, many have other aspirations: they would like to move out of Bethnal Green when they marry, want a semi-detached house with a garden in the suburbs, look forward to having a car, washing-machine, refrigerator and holidays abroad. 'The people of Bethnal Green,' said an 18-year-old apprentice instrument maker, 'are more homely and easy to get on with, but I'd like to get away to raise a family. Out in the suburbs, with a nice little house, it's better to bring up children.' If one chose to define 'middle-class' in terms of aspiration to higher consumption standards, together with some limited aspirations at work (mainly towards a more skilled job or sometimes a more technical one), then many of these boys could indeed be described as somewhat 'middle-class' in outlook, and more so than earlier generations of East Enders.[4]

As for the boys described as 'middle-class', I do not want to give the impression that they are uniformly content with their lives. Some of them had experienced, or were still experiencing, the problems of grammar school boys described in an earlier chapter. Such boys were the victims of 'culture-conflict' – the pull of loyalties towards the grammar school and its values on the one hand and their family and local community on the other. Of course those who were themselves the sons of shopkeepers and white-collar workers were less subject to these pressures. The others were the 'scholarship boys' described by Hoggart and by Jackson and Marsden. Examples of the resistance of some of these boys to school have been cited earlier in the book; the conflict the other way round, from a boy who had largely accepted the school, was expressed by an 18-year-old grammar school boy:

> 'There is a social stigma in Bethnal Green about staying on at school and going to university. They think you are a stuck-up so-and-so because you've got intelligence, because you want to improve yourself. This stigma of doing something different from the rest, it's the big conflict in my life. My grandmother still thinks you should go out to work when you're 15 – that you should work for your living and if you want to improve yourself the only thing is to become an apprentice. I'm in the sixth form now, and if I go on to university it will be worse.'

Finally, a qualification about the 'rebels'. There were few enough of them in our sample, and it seemed reasonable to include in one category all those who showed marked indications of

---

[4] Though the whole matter is more complicated; see, for instance, Goldthorpe, J. H. and Lockwood, D., 'Affluence and the British Class Structure'.

deviance. I have already suggested, what cannot be proved from our figures, that being a 'rebel' of the kind outlined is associated with more serious delinquency. But it seemed to us in the interviews that there was another kind of rebel. One such was Robert Young, aged 19 when interviewed.

He was alone, playing records by Billie Holiday and Miles Davis. He said, 'Just a minute, I'll turn this down,' and then flopped on to the old rexine-covered sofa, where he spread his long arms and legs. He was wearing a light-blue shirt with a tab collar, open at the neck; close-fitting silver-grey slacks, fawn suède boots. He went to a secondary modern school, left at 15 and worked at two other jobs before he got his present one as a lorry driver's mate. About school, he said, 'At that age I had a mad feeling that nothing was worth it. I didn't take much interest in nothing at school. Now I think I was silly. I really regret leaving school.' He does not like his job; 'It's not the sort of thing I want at all. The best you can hope for is when one of the drivers dies you take over his job. I'd like to be a journalist, but I don't know how to get into that line. I've been thinking about going to evening classes but I don't know where to go.' He says of his parents, 'They couldn't understand me in a hundred years. Like most ordinary East End people, their idea of living is to have a steady job and settle down with a nice little wife in a nice little house or flat, doing the same thing every day of your life. They think the sort of things I do are mad.' What sort of things? 'Well, I might decide to take the day off and go up the park and sit and meditate. Or go round my friend's pad for an all-night session. A group of us drink whisky and smoke tea (marijuana) and talk about what's happiness and things like that.' He says that he and his friends regularly take Purple Hearts too: 'It may seem sinful to some people. But we're just young people who like to enjoy ourselves and forget the Bomb.' He reads Jack Kerouac, Norman Mailer, James Baldwin – 'That's the sort of thing I dig. I suppose I'm really searching.'

As far as we can make out, there were only four such boys in the sample of 246, and, although we met a handful of others, the total numbers were too small to build up a clear picture of their characteristics. But they were hardly 'delinquent'. Although tending to be critical of school, unhappy in their job, at odds with their parents and disinclined to marry, they had no disposition towards violence, theft or other crime. They were, rather, inclined to cultural, intellectual and artistic pursuits. They were left-wing or anarchistic in their politics; they read 'serious novels' and some of them tried to write or paint. Their friends and their interests, like those of some 'middle-class' boys, were outside Bethnal Green – usually in the West End. Although, with numbers so small, the following fact could well be due to sampling variations, it is worth putting on record: all four of the boys in the sample that we judged as of this kind said they spent their weekends 'right outside Bethnal Green', compared with about a third of the boys generally.

These boys had attended secondary modern schools or the lower streams in grammar schools, and, although they seemed intellectually lively, had been passed by in the educational system, which had failed to win their co-operation. As it is, they may well, like the boy quoted, drift for a while into drug-taking and heavy drinking, in an attempt to resolve their sense of frustration against a society whose opportunities seem closed to them.[5] Only further research, with a much larger sample, could provide a check on these impressions.

Withdrawal and return

'Rebelliousness' is not just an attitude of certain sorts of boy: it is also a phase through which many pass. There were 'rebels' at all ages but they seemed to be concentrated in mid-adolescence. The numbers in the group distinguished as 'rebels' by our first method of analysis were too small for us to be able to say confidently whether 'rebelliousness' was in fact related to age. We therefore drew instead upon the special analysis of the 177 boys at work, comparing the quarter who had the highest scores on the 'rebel scale' with the others. The more 'rebellious' boys, measured in this way, amounted to a sixth of those aged 15 and 16, over a third of those aged 17 and 18, and a fifth of those aged 19 and 20.

[5] In terms of the delinquency theory of Cloward and Ohlin, they could be said to have chosen the 'retreatist' solution. (Cloward, R. A. and Ohlin, L. E., *Delinquency and Opportunity*, especially pp. 25–27.)

This is no surprise: it sums up the findings of chapter after chapter and the main theme of the book. This study has demonstrated in detail what has long been known in a general sense: that during adolescence most boys withdraw from the mixed-age society of childhood into a one-age society of their fellows, and that as they mature and particularly as they move towards courtship and marriage, they rejoin the mixed-age society as adults.

The reasons why this withdrawal takes place are obviously complicated, but some of the threads can be disentangled. In any society, the transition from child to adult involves a dramatic change in social roles; during adolescence the child has to prepare himself to behave differently towards others and become a different sort of person.[6] He has to learn to be more independent, more self-reliant, more confident, more authoritative. Authority, in particular, presents a crucial problem of role-change. A child is subordinate to the authority of adults; on the whole children do, and expect to do, what parents and other adults tell them. This relationship of subordination must give way to one in which the adolescent can himself exercise authority. Not only does he find, as he gets older, that he *wants* to assert his independence; it is actually *essential* for him to do so, as part of the preparation for his new role as an adult and a potential husband and father. This process underlies the clash between adolescents and their parents or other adults. It also partly accounts for the withdrawal; in feeling their way to their new independence and authority, young people keep their distance from parents and other adults. Their parents, particularly, are bound to try to exercise authority over them and constant challenges are likely to be painful or at best embarrassing.

There is of course more to it than this. The physical changes in puberty and the rapid rate of growth themselves impose psychological strains: young people understandably feel physically 'odd' and 'awkward', and therefore self-conscious.[7] And the boy's awareness of these manifest physical and social changes reinforces the big questions of his future adult role: 'Who am I?' and 'What sort of adult am I going to become?'[8] In simpler societies, where adult

[6] Ten major 'developmental tasks' that adolescents have to undertake are set out by Havighurst, R. J., *Human Development and Education*, pp. 111-58.

[7] See, for instance, Wall, W. D., *The Adolescent Child*, p. 5; Miller, D., 'Adolescence'.

[8] Erikson in particular has drawn attention to this 'crisis of identity' in adolescence. See e.g. Erikson, E. H., *Childhood and Society*, pp. 261-2.

roles are clear-cut and settled in advance, and where choice is limited, such questions are seldom posed with any urgency. In complex industrial societies like our own, where choice is, at least in theory, almost infinitely open, there is more of a problem.[9] It is complicated by the awakening of sex; a boy's questionings about his adulthood become mixed up with anxieties about his sexual potency and 'normality'.

When young people are trying to grapple with this problem of 'identity' – assessing and re-evaluating themselves, trying to resolve who they are – what is, again, more natural than that they should draw back for a while from adult society? As we have seen, they do not merely withdraw: they associate with age-mates more than at any other stage in life, looking to them for company and moral support. Since the boys are going through the same processes, they feel they can understand and sympathize with each other. And the informality and equality of the peer group makes it a setting in which its members can assert and test together their new independence. The peer group, in other words, provides a social context in which boys can help each other work through the processes of adolescence.[10]

A war of the generations?

This withdrawal into the peer group is only a matter of degree. Most boys in Bethnal Green remain members of their family and of the wider kin-group. Their lives are set in a locality in which they know many other people, including shopkeepers, stallholders and publicans. Though some are antagonistic to school and others unenthusiastic, there is little sign of widespread hostility to the schools or teachers. Many boys work in small local factories, having secured their job through relatives or friends, and even those in large concerns share a common life with workmates of mixed ages; more than a quarter of them – probably something like the national average for their age – are trade union members. Then, too, most belong or have belonged to youth clubs and similar organizations. In other words, they are very much

[9] Eisenstadt, S. N., *From Generation to Generation*, argues that adolescent age-groups figure more in societies that are relatively 'open' than in others (see especially pp. 52–53 and p. 270).
[10] This function of peer groups is described by Mays, J. B., *The Young Pretenders*, pp. 46–47.

members of their society, linked to it in a host of other ways as well as through their membership of peer groups.

There is little sign either of what one sociologist has called 'the war of the generations',[11] nor of any widespread feeling of resentment against adult society. When the boys in the sample were asked if they thought they had 'as much chance to enjoy life as you should have', over four-fifths said they had. Asked whether they thought they had 'as much chance to get on in life' as they ought to, nearly nine out of ten said 'Yes'. Even allowing for a tendency to make the best of things, the consensus is impressive.

These findings are broadly in line with other studies in, for instance, Sheffield,[12] a north Midlands town,[13] Stepney and Poplar.[14] Such research as has been carried out does not support the more gloomy or dramatic accounts of working-class adolescent rebellion. Not that one should be complacent. Nor that today's Bethnal Green boys or young people generally are just the same as those in earlier decades. Obviously they have more free time and are wealthier; their lives are less circumscribed, their opportunities greater in all sorts of ways. Obviously, too, their emergence as 'consumers' with relatively large disposable incomes, and the resulting commercial 'teenage culture', have helped to make them more aware of themselves as a distinct section of the population. For these reasons, they may be more confident, more assertive and somewhat more inclined to challenge adult authority.

Scepticism about more highly-coloured interpretations of contemporary adolescence is supported by such evidence as there is from the past. Besant wrote in 1901 of the East End boys:

'Their own idea of employing their idle time is to do nothing, to amuse themselves. . . . They begin by walking about in little companies of two and three . . . they occupy a great deal of the pavement, regardless of other people; they get up impromptu fights and sham fights; they wrestle; they make rushes among the crowd; they push about the girls of their own age. . . . The boys gather together and hold the street; if anyone ventures to pass through it they rush upon him,

[11] Wilson, B., 'War of the Generations'.
[12] Carter, M. P., *Home, School and Work*, Chapter 4 and Chapter 10.
[13] Musgrove, F., *Youth and the Social Order*, Chapter 5.
[14] Downes, D. M., *The Delinquent Solution*, pp. 230–31.

knock him down, and kick him savagely about the head; they rob him as well.'[15]

A quarter-century later, in 1927, Harris wrote:

'Leaving school and plunging straight away into factory life, with an eight-hour day or longer, they arrive back to Bethnal Green tired, often noisy, and undisciplined, a reaction from the pressure of their work. . . . Groups of them pass up and down the Bethnal Green Road, three and four abreast on the causeway, making no effort to get out of the way of other pedestrians, making a nuisance of themselves. . . .'[16]

However one interprets these observations, the conclusion is not that today's East End adolescents are more troublesome, more rebellious, more at odds with adult society, than their predecessors. Indeed, one would hardly expect them to be if one remembers what things were like when their fathers and grandfathers were boys. With high unemployment and low wages, with overcrowding and large families, adolescents surely had more reason to feel resentful against adult society in general and their parents, who took most of their earnings, in particular. The contemporary youth, with his greater financial independence, more space at home, and a background of more exclusive parental care and attention,[17] might be expected to have sweeter relationships with the parental generation.

What, though, of the well-known 'fact' that juvenile delinquency is increasing? Wootton has pointed out the difficulty of interpreting criminal statistics (quoting, by illustration, an 'increase' of 48 per cent in crime in one district, which turned out to be largely due to a change in the system of police reporting), and she comments: '. . . we probably ought to refrain from the tempting and common practice of quoting movements in the criminal statistics as evidence of the ups and downs of criminal behaviour.'[18] This does not mean that delinquency is nothing to

[15] Besant, W., *East London*, p. 173 and p. 177. Besant also reported: 'In the autumn of last year (1899) an inoffensive elderly gentleman was knocked down by such a gang, robbed, kicked about the head, and taken up insensible; he was carried home, and died the next day.' (p. 177).
[16] Harris, C., *The Use of Leisure in Bethnal Green*, pp. 51–52.
[17] The fall in family size in Bethnal Green, and the rise in the status of children, are discussed in *Family and Kinship in East London*, pp. 5–7, pp. 13–14.
[18] Wootton, B., *Social Science and Social Pathology*, p. 24.

worry about: only that the crime figures do not in themselves prove that the present generation of adolescents in Bethnal Green (or elsewhere) constitute more of a problem.

Implications for policy

Given the process of withdrawal from adult society described in this book, the problem is how to deal with it. How can the adjustments of adolescence be carried through in a way that inflicts least damage upon the boy, the local community and the wider society? More speculatively, I end by offering some suggestions, on the subjects of the last four chapters – education, work, youth clubs and delinquency.

The study shows that there are two crucial influences in the boys' lives. The first is the peer group, which rises in importance and then falls off as the altar begins to beckon. The second is the local community, which stays important to the great majority of boys and becomes even more so as they move into adulthood. Any suggestions for policy must take these two social forces into account.

It is sad that education has so little influence. The lessons, particularly in arts subjects, bore many boys; they sit through the ritual with better or worse grace, thinking it all a waste of time and effort. The power of the school is weakened because of its conflict with the peer group and the local community. To take advantage of educational opportunity, particularly through the grammar schools, boys usually have to give up the benefits of peer group membership and turn their back on their parents and the local community as well. As a result, some pass up the chance of further education, and later regret it.

The peer group presents one obstacle to education. Our study suggests that the decision whether to go on with education comes near the stage when the boys are most involved with peers, least sympathetic to parents, and probably least likely to accept the idea that they will soon 'settle down'. The boys, in other words, are at the point of maximum withdrawal from the influence of adult society. This very withdrawal may itself be encouraged by the school's tendency to treat them as children. 'Where society does not permit the adolescent to assume a social role compatible with his physical and intellectual development, but keeps him dependent . . . adult maturity is come by with more difficulty.'[19]

If the diagnosis is right, the first step is to find some way of treating pupils differently as they mature. Adolescents in education need to be treated more like young adults, less like overgrown children; they need too a greater freedom so that the peer group can exist as an association of near-independent students rather than a counter-system to a school régime geared to disciplining 11 and 12 year olds.

I do not know how this could best be done. The boys' own experience in further education indicates that there, already, something like the right atmosphere exists. This might suggest that young people should switch and take their last one or two years of compulsory education in technical colleges, colleges of further education and the like. This would have the added advantage that it would often pave the way for them to continue at the same institution in part-time study after starting work. Boys might be more sympathetic to education if they saw more clearly the relevance of its contribution to their growing up. From as early as is reasonable, therefore – say at 13 or 14 – the curriculum needs to be geared to future careers, and non-vocational subjects likewise should be taught in ways that connect up more with the boys' own lives and interests.[20]

The family and local community need to be brought in more. Schools could forge stronger links than at present with parents and others.[21] The process might be aided by special arrangements to provide council homes in the locality for teachers who work there. And the decision to stay on at school in particular would be helped by more realistic maintenance grants for the families of pupils; at present the arrangements for students of 16 and 17 are miserly compared with those for students of 18 and over.

Even with such changes, there would still be the problem of re-entry into education for those who realize their mistake after they have left. For these boys, there will always be a need for a

[19] Tanner, J. M., *Growth at Adolescence*, p. 145.
[20] See Chapter 14 of the Newsom Report (*Half Our Future*), which makes the same recommendations.
[21] See Young, M., *Innovation and Research in Education*, Chapter V; Mays, J. B., *Education and the Urban Child*, Chapter 6; and a forthcoming report, by my colleagues Michael Young and Patrick McGeeney, on an experimental study of the relationship between a particular primary school and the local parents.

second chance, an opportunity to get back into the educational system, whether full or part-time. It is important that the channels should be kept open to enable them to do this and that they should be able to find out what they need to do to re-enter. A few of the boys we interviewed spontaneously asked us for advice about further education. They were only a tiny minority, but it is likely there were others who had problems but did not raise them, and altogether there must be thousands of young people every year who need advice of this kind. There should probably be a special educational advisory service to help them.

As for work, the youth employment service does not seem anything like as helpful as it might be. In some other parts of Britain, the employment opportunities are more limited than in London. In districts like Bethnal Green, however, there are plenty of jobs in great variety within a few miles, and the major problem is 'placement' – that is, fitting the boy to a job that suits his abilities and interests. Many boys, as we have seen, get jobs through relatives and friends. But this informal system, operating in and through the local community, does not seem to connect up with the official service. As with the schools, the need is for the youth employment officer to link up with family and other informal contacts. He should see his task, not as 'finding a job', but as offering to lend his advice and skills to boys and their families, especially since the latter, as reported in Chapter VI, seem to do a better job of 'placing' young people.

Bethnal Green, though relatively 'deprived' in most respects, is strikingly well-off for youth clubs, both in quantity and variety. It is of course difficult for a survey like ours to judge the 'quality' of the youth work; there is no doubt that the local clubs could be improved, particularly with better buildings and more money spent on them. The study does show, however, that the clubs can perform a useful function in helping young people to mature, and that, where there are plenty of clubs, with a wide range of choice, the overwhelming majority of boys join at some stage in their adolescence. The Bethnal Green clubs are for the most part regarded with affection by adults and young people alike; they are thought of, not as hostile institutions, but as part of the local way of life. Since so many young people do attend them, the clubs might themselves run advisory bureaux, linked with the schools and the youth employment service, on further education and on jobs. In this way, boys could feel free, in a familiar setting, to turn for help and advice.

Finally, about delinquency. I have suggested that the withdrawal into the peer group is inevitable; and at least some of the boisterousness of youth is inevitable too. Most of the delinquency is relatively trivial – sweets or a pencil stolen from a store, a scooter borrowed, 'insulting behaviour' or 'rowdyness'. This sort of behaviour should not, of course, be condoned; but it hardly threatens the fabric of society. Most boys who appear before the Courts do so only once or twice and, in terms of their own future development as responsible adults, their adolescent transgressions are not much to worry about. The exceptions are those boys (about whom we know far too little) who commit more serious and systematic crimes, or who go on to an adult criminal career. But even the misbehaviour of the majority is a social nuisance and it sometimes leads, often unintentionally, to serious harm. Cars are stolen, windows smashed, cinema seats ripped up, public telephones put out of order, girls assaulted and other people, boys or adults, dangerously injured.

If the answers to this were easy they would have been found and applied long ago. Three proposals, modest and undramatic, seem to flow from our research. The first has to do with the fact that, though most local boys are not seriously delinquent, they apparently have little positive sense that theft or vandalism are 'wrong': the result is that in such a district it is incredibly easy for adolescent boys, in Matza's phrase, to 'drift into delinquency'.[22] They do not usually set out to break the law; the opportunity presents itself and, since their resistance is weak, they succumb fairly readily. One way to counter this, as the police constantly argue, is simply to make crime more difficult. Stores could make shoplifting harder, people could be encouraged to fit their cars and motor scooters with thief-proof devices, and more could be done to discourage vandalism with, for instance, less vulnerable public telephones and public lavatories.

A second approach would be to try, as with education and job-finding, to work more actively with the local community. Most parents are against law-breaking and most boys influenced by parents. Since a boy's first offence is usually trivial, it might make more sense to warn him and his family, rather than taking him to

[22] Matza, D., *Delinquency and Drift.*

Court. This might be done by the police or by special Juvenile Liaison Officers (as has been tried in Liverpool[23]); the so-called 'family councils', proposed in a Government White Paper in 1965, might have similar effects, since they would try to work with the family, outside the Courts.[24]

A third line might be to recognize the boisterousness of adolescence and provide more in the way of legitimate outlets for it. I have quoted the Bethnal Green boy who complained that, while the high spirits of students were tolerated, the reaction to himself and his fellows was 'Mad gits. Sit on them'. One advantage of being a student is that his need to 'let off steam' is acknowledged and much of his horse-play channelled into university 'rags' and the like. New ways might be found to provide equivalent outlets for working-class adolescents. One suggestion is that the local youth clubs might combine for an annual 'rag' of their own on behalf of local hospitals, old people's clubs and so on.

No policies can hope to do more than ease the course of adolescence. To restate the main theme of this book, adolescent boys need to draw away from the all-age society into a one-age society of their own, and some tension between the two is inevitable. The tension is not necessarily harmful and seldom causes lasting damage; there is no evidence, as far as I can see, of any more serious estrangement between the generations than in earlier decades. But the withdrawal into the peer group is clear enough, as is the fact that like adolescence itself it is transitory. If there were wider recognition of the processes – and above all of the reasons why they are bound to produce some strain – the transition to manhood might become less distressing to both generations than it sometimes is at present.

[23] Mays, J. B., *Growing Up in the City*, pp. 139–46, described the work of Juvenile Liaison Officers in Liverpool.
[24] *The Child, the Family and the Young Offender*, pp. 5–8.

APPENDIX I

METHODS OF RESEARCH

As the Introduction explains, much of the information in this book was drawn from relatively free interviews and group discussions with boys we got to know well, from our observation in Bethnal Green, and from the diaries.[1] Most of the quantitative data, however, came from what I have described as the 'main sample', and most of this Appendix is devoted to a description of the sample survey and a discussion of the sample interviewed.[2]

There is no sampling frame from which one can select a random sample[3] of boys aged 14 to 20. We therefore had to spend some time and effort locating such a sample. We began by selecting a sample of *addresses* from the electoral registers covering what was then the borough of Bethnal Green. These had been compiled in October 1963 and published in February 1964. Using the procedure suggested by Gray, Corlett and Frankland,[4] we picked from these lists a random sample of 2,310 private addresses.

The first task for the interviewers was to see whether there were eligible boys at the selected addresses. Forty-five of the addresses were unoccupied or in process of demolition (14 and 31 respectively). This left 2,265. At these addresses there were 279 eligible young men. In order to decide how many addresses to select initially, we had calculated from Census data for 1961 that we would need to call at seven or eight addresses to find one boy; in practice this turned out to be about right – the ratio of addresses to eligible boys was 8·1.

Of the 279 young men selected by this method, nine could not be contacted – they worked out of London for much of the time

---

[1] The diaries are discussed in Appendix 3.
[2] Appendix 2 reprints the interviewers' instructions and the interview schedule.
[3] The word 'random' is used in the statistical sense, to mean that every eligible person had an equal chance of selection.
[4] Gray, P. G., Corlett, T. and Frankland, P., *The Register of Electors as a Sampling Frame*, pp. 10–11.

(two), were on their holidays and would not return before we stopped interviewing (three), or they were simply never in although we called six or more times (four). Another three could not be interviewed for special reasons – one was deaf, one had a speech defect, and the third was mentally defective. This left 267 boys. Of these, twenty-one refused an interview;[5] and the remaining 246 made up the sample interviewed. The response is summarized in Table XXIII.

TABLE XXIII
Response in youth survey

	Number	Percentage
Interviewed	246	88%
Refused	21	8%
Not contacted	9	3%
Not able to be interviewed	3	1%
Number eligible	279	100%

If we assume that the initial information – about the presence or absence of boys at the selected addresses – was correct, the response was reasonably good. Those interviewed amounted to 88 per cent of the sample of boys, and the proportion who refused was 8 per cent.

Bias in the sample?

It is difficult to form any judgements about possible ways in which the sample interviewed might differ from the relevant 'population' – boys aged 14 to 20 living in Bethnal Green at the time of the survey. However, the sample almost certainly included a smaller proportion of married young men. In the sample of 246 only one was married, and Census data suggest that we might have expected more. Some married men would have been excluded from our initial sample of addresses; since these were

[5] In fact sixteen refused themselves and five refusals were from parents. Where parents said that they did not want their son interviewed – or that he would not want it – we did what we could to persuade them to allow us to see the boy and let him decide for himself. Unfortunately four parents – one of whom had two sons – would not allow this.

drawn from electoral registers, they could not include any addresses at which there were only people under 21 – say a young married couple. As for losses after this stage, we know that one man who refused was married; others who refused and those who were not contacted may also have been married, but it is unlikely, since the interviewers were on the look-out for them.

To make some sort of comparison of the ages of the boys in our sample with those in Bethnal Green generally, we projected forward the age figures from the 1961 Census. Thus boys aged 11 in October 1961 were counted as age 14 in June 1964, and so on. (Doing this involved the reasonable assumption that there had been no net migration in or out of Bethnal Green of boys of these ages).[6] The ages of Bethnal Green boys aged 14 to 20, calculated in this way, are shown in Table XXIV, together with the ages of the boys in the sample interviewed.[7]

There seems to be a fairly broad correspondence between the

TABLE XXIV

Ages of Bethnal Green boys
(Census 1961 adjusted and sample interviewed)

	Census 1961 (adjusted to 1964)	Sample interviewed
14	12%	13%
15	15%	15%
16	15%	21%
17	18%	16%
18	14%	15%
19	14%	9%
20	12%	11%
Total %	100%	100%
Number	2,334	246

[6] The total population of Bethnal Green changed hardly at all between 1961 and 1964, according to the estimates of the Medical Officer of Health: the estimated figures were 46,490 for mid-1961 and 46,420 for mid-1964. (*Annual Reports of the Medical Officer of Health*, Metropolitan Borough of Bethnal Green, 1961 and 1964.)

[7] We also recorded the ages of the boys who could not be contacted or who refused; the interviewers asked the ages of eligible boys at the selected addresses and were able to get those of all but eight. The age distribution of the initial sample of boys is not shown because it matched almost exactly that of the sample interviewed. This suggests that there was in fact no specially heavy loss at this stage among 19 or 20 year olds or among married young men in particular.

sample interviewed and the adjusted Census figures. It looks as if our sample contains a rather high proportion of 16 year olds, and the 19 and 20 year olds together may be rather under-represented – the proportions were 26 per cent in the Census and 20 per cent in the sample interviewed. This discrepancy would fit in with the suggestion earlier that our initial sample may well have under-represented married men, who would probably have been aged 19 or 20. To sum up, our sample slightly over-represents boys of 16 and under-represents men of 19 and 20, particularly those who were married.

Statistical analysis and interpretation

When the interviews were completed the information was transferred to punch-cards and analysed on a 'counter-sorter' machine. Many more analyses were, of course, undertaken than are – or could be – presented in the book. In deciding what to include, I was naturally guided first, by what particular tabulations seemed to 'show' in the way of differences or similarities, and secondly, by the drift of the other data of various kinds.

In considering whether an apparent difference in the figures – for example, between the club membership of boys of different ages – reflected a real difference, I have been guided by the results of appropriate tests of 'statistical significance'. I pointed out in an earlier book that the use of such tests had been criticized by a number of social scientists, and I said that these arguments had convinced me.[8] I still think that there is a good deal of force in the criticisms. First, there may well be 'non-random' errors in the sampling, interviewing or coding that the tests cannot throw light on. Secondly, 'hunting' for significant differences, as distinct from testing previously stated hypotheses, is bound to give some apparently 'significant' results that have arisen by chance.[9]

It is, however, a great advantage to have some objective criterion to measure 'probability'. The statistical tests do, after all, take into account the two crucial factors – the numbers involved and the size of the differences – and do give some indication of

[8] Willmott, P., *The Evolution of a Community*, pp. 132–3. Examples of critical writings are Selvin, H. C., 'A Critique of Tests of Significance in Survey Research'; Selvin, H. C., 'Survey Analysis', pp. 26–28. Coleman, J. S., 'Methodological Note' in Lipset, S. M., Trow, M.A. and Coleman, J. S., *Union Democracy*.
[9] See Selvin, H. C. and Stuart, A., 'Data-Dredging Procedures in Survey Analysis'.

whether a particular difference is so small or is based on such small numbers that it might well have arisen by chance alone. All in all, it now seems to me right to use the tests, applying standard levels of probability, as long as one points out the limitations: a test does not *prove* that the difference in question reflects a real variation; it only establishes some sort of (admittedly shaky) base.

This is the approach adopted in the present book. The results of the statistical tests have not been reproduced 'to avoid the appearance of spurious precision which the presentation of such tests might seem to imply'.[10] But, since the tests do 'provide some indication of the probability of differences occurring by chance',[11] they have been carried out and in general attention has not been drawn to any difference which statistical tests suggest might have occurred by chance one or more times in twenty (where P is ·05 or greater).

[10] Cartwright, A., *Human Relations and Hospital Care*, p. 248.
[11] Ibid., p. 248.

INTERVIEW SCHEDULE AND INTERVIEWERS' INSTRUCTIONS

INTERVIEW SCHEDULE

Serial No. ☐ ☐ ☐

INTRODUCTION: I am from the Institute of Community Studies here in Bethnal Green. We are doing a survey of young people – to find out what jobs they do, what they do in their leisure time and so on. It's for a book about what it's like growing up in Bethnal Green. Can you tell me whether there are any young men aged 14–20 at this address (I mean boys who've had their 14th birthday and not yet had their 21st). CHECK ELIGIBLE SUBJECTS. THEN TO SUBJECT: REPEAT EXPLANATION AND ADD: We've picked a cross-section of addresses and yours is one of them. Can I interview you? It's all confidential: no names will be published and no information will be passed on to anyone else.

1. Can I first check your age?

(ON 1 JUNE 1964)

14........ 4
15........ 5
16........ 6
17........ 7
18........ 8
19........ 9
20........ 0

2. When did you first come to live in Bethnal Green?

Born here.................. 1
10 years + ... 2
5 < 10 years................. 3
2 < 5 years 4
Less than 2 years ago 5

IF NOT BORN HERE (2–5)
Where did you come from?

Other East End 6
Other Greater London 7
Outside London 8
Outside Britain (specify)...... 9

3. Are you still at school or at work?
Still at school 1
Other full-time education 2
At work 3

IF STILL AT SCHOOL (1) PUT
Qs 4–12

IF OTHER FULL-TIME EDUCA-
TION (2) GO ON TO Q 13

IF AT WORK (3) GO ON TO Q 22

186

TO THOSE STILL AT SCHOOL (1)

4. What school are you at?

5. Have you passed any exams at all?
   Yes...................... X
   No .... O
   IF YES Which exams?
   CODE ALL THAT APPLY
   G.C.E. 'O' level 1
   G.C.E. 'A' level 2
   Other (specify)............. 3

   IF G.C.E. (1 or 2) How many sub-
   jects did you pass in?
   At 'O' level ——————
   At 'A' level ——————

6. Do you intend taking any (more)
   exams while still at school?
   Yes...................... X
   No .... O

   IF YES Which?
   CODE ALL THAT APPLY
   G.C.E. 'O' level 1
   G.C.E. 'A' level 2
   Other (specify)............. 3

7. Are you by any chance attending
   evening classes?
   Yes...................... X
   No .... O
   IF YES (X) Where is that?

8. What age do you expect to leave
   school?
   15........ 5
   16........ 6
   17........ 7
   18........ 8
   19........ 9

9. On the whole, are you looking
   forward to leaving school or not?
   Looking forward to it 8
   Not looking forward to it 9
   Don't know, can't say 0
   COMMENTS:

10. What do you feel about school in
    general?
    (a) How well do you feel you are
    getting on there?

    (b) Do you feel on the whole that
    the lessons at school are:
    Very useful to you 1
    Quite useful 2
    Not much use 3
    No use at all 4

    (c) Why do you feel that?

11. (a) What do you think about the
    teachers at your school?

    (b) About how many of the teachers
    would you say you like?
    All 1
    Most 2
    PROMPT About half 3
    A few 4
    None............. 5

12. And what about the rules at school —
    how many of them do you think
    have got good reasons behind them?
    All 1
    Most 2
    PROMPT About half 3
    A few 4
    None............. 5

(b) Can you give me any examples? (GOOD OR BAD)

GO ON TO QUESTION 39

13. TO THOSE IN OTHER FULL-TIME EDUCATION Where are you studying?

14. Can I ask you about your last school. What school was it?

15. Did you pass any exams at school?
Yes.........................X
No ....O
IF YES Which exams?
    G.C.E. 'O' level 1
    G.C.E. 'A' level 2
    Other (specify).............. 3

IF G.C.E. (1 or 2) How many subjects did you pass in?
    At 'O' level ——————
    At 'A' level ——————

16. What age did you leave school?
             15........ 5
             16........ 6
             17........ 7
             18........ 8
             19........ 9

17. I'd like to ask about your feelings about leaving school – what you felt about it at the time and what you feel now. (a) First, *at the time* were you, on the whole, glad or sorry to leave?
    Glad 8
    Sorry...................... 9
    Don't know, can't say 0

(b) Do you feel the same about it now?
    Yes........................ X
    No .... Y
IF NO Are you, on the whole, glad or sorry *now* about having left?
    Glad 1
    Sorry 2
    Don't know, can't say 3
COMMENTS:

18. What do you feel about school in general?
(a) How do you feel you got on there?

(b) Do you feel on the whole that the lessons at school were:
    Very useful to you 1
    Quite useful 2
    Not much use 3
    No use at all............... 4

(c) Why do you feel that?

19. (a) What did you think of the teachers at your school?

(b) About how many of the teachers would you say you liked?
        All 1
        Most 2
PROMPT About half 3
        A few 4
        None............. 5

20. And what about the rules at school – how many of them do you think had got good reasons behind them?
        All 1
        Most 2
PROMPT About half 3
        A few 4
        None............. 5
(a) Can you give me any examples? (GOOD OR BAD)

21. Can I ask what you think about the atmosphere at your college compared with your last school?

    GO ON TO QUESTION 39

    TO THOSE AT WORK

22. Can you tell me where you work?
    Bethnal Green 1
    Other East End 2
    City of London 3
    Other Central London 4
    Elsewhere in Greater London 5
    Outside Greater London 6

    (*b*) What does the firm or organization do?

23. What is your job there?

    CHECK: Apprentice or trainee .. 9

24. (*a*) Do you belong to a trade union?
    Yes...................... 1
    No 2

    (*b*) Why is that?

25. About your job, would you say that on the whole you are satisfied with it or not?
    Satisfied 1
    Dissatisfied 2
    Other (specify)
    IF DISSATISFIED (2) Why is that?

26. Would you say you are satisfied with the money you get or not?
    Satisfied 1
    Dissatisfied 2
    Other (specify)
    IF DISSATISFIED (2) Why is that?

27. Would you say that on the whole you are satisfied with the prospects in your job or not?
    Satisfied 1
    Dissatisfied 2
    Other (specify)

    IF DISSATISFIED (2) Why is that?

28. What *are* the prospects of promotion or advancement in your present job?

29. How many other full-time jobs have you had since leaving school, including your present one?

    Number————————

30. How did you get to know about:
    (*a*) your present job (*b*) your first job after leaving school (if not present).

	Present	First
Youth Employment Officer	1	1
Employment Exchange	2	2
Advertisement	3	3
Through father......	4	4
Through other relative	5	5
Through friend	6	6
Through school or teacher	7	7
Made own inquiries..	8	8
Other (specify)	9	9

31. Can I ask about your last school. What school was it?

32. Did you pass any exams at school?
    Yes....................... X
    No .... O
    IF YES Which exams?
    G.C.E. 'O' level 1
    G.C.E. 'A' level 2
    Other (specify)............. 3

IF G.C.E. (1 or 2) How many sub-
jects did you pass in?
At 'O' level ————————
At 'A' level ————————

33. What age did you leave school?
15........ 5
16....... 6
17........ 7
18........ 8
19........ 9

34. (a) I'd like to ask about your feelings about leaving school – what
you felt about it at the time and
what you feel now. First, *at the time*,
were you, on the whole, glad or
sorry to leave?
Glad 8
Sorry...................... 9
Don't know, can't say 0

(b) Do you feel the same about it
now?
Yes....................... X
No....................... Y
IF NO Are you, on the whole, glad
or sorry *now* about having left?
Glad 1
Sorry...................... 2
Don't know, can't say 3
COMMENTS:

35. What do you feel about school in
general? (a) How do you feel you
got on there?

(b) Do you feel on the whole that
the lessons at school were:
Very useful to you 1
Quite useful 2
Not much use 3
No use at all 4

(c) Why do you feel that?

36. (a) What did you think of the
teachers at your school?

(b) About how many of the teachers
would you say you liked?
All 1
Most 2
PROMPT About half 3
A few 4
None 5

37. (a) And what about the rules at
school – how many of them do you
think had got good reasons behind
them?
All 1
Most 2
PROMPT About half 3
A few 4
None 5

(b) Can you give me any examples?
(GOOD OR BAD)

38. Are you attending any day or
evening classes at present?
Yes....................... X
No .... O
IF YES (X) (a) Where is that?

(b) Do you go in the evening or
daytime?
Day 1
Evening 2
Both 3

(c) Can I ask what you think about
the atmosphere there compared with
your last school?

IF NO (O) Have you attended any
day or evening classes since leaving
school?
Day 6
Evening 7
Both 8
Neither 0

Interview Schedule and Interviewers' Instructions

TO ALL

39. Can I ask a few questions about your family?
    Are you living with:

    Your own parents 1
    Father and stepmother........ 2
    Mother and stepfather 3
    Father 4
    Mother 5
    Other (specify) 6

IF NOT OWN PARENTS (i.e.
IF 2–6) What happened to your
parents/father/mother?

    Parents divorced 1
    Parents separated 2
    Father dead 3
    Mother dead 4
    Both parents dead 5

40. Can you tell me what job your father (stepfather) does?

IF FATHER DEAD OR PER-
MANENTLY ABSENT FROM
HOME AND NO STEPFATHER
What job did your father do?
WRITE IN ABOVE

41. How many brothers and sisters have you got living at home here?
    Brothers ——————————
    Sisters ——————————

42. Including brothers and sisters who don't live here, as well as those who do, where do you come in the family? And where among the boys only?

	All family	Boys only
Only one ..	1	5
Youngest ..	2	6
Eldest	3	7
Others	4	8

43. Have you got any relatives (outside your own household) living in Bethnal Green?

    Yes........................ 1
    No........................ 2

IF YES Which relatives?

CODE ALL THAT APPLY

    Grandparent(s) 1
    Aunt(s), Uncle(s) 2
    Married brother(s) 3
    Married sister(s) 4
    Cousin(s) 5
    Nephew(s), niece(s) 6
    Other (specify) 7

44. And when was the last time you personally *saw* any relative (whether they live in Bethnal Green or not)?

    Last 24 hours 1
    Over 24 hours – week 2
    Over week – month 3
    Over month 4
    CHECK: That isn't someone who lives in your own household, is it?

45. At evenings and weekends, do you *usually* stay in and around Bethnal Green, or go right outside it?

	Evening	Weekends
In and around B.G.	1	4
Right outside it....	2	5
About half and half	3	6

46. When was the last time you went to the West End?

    Last 24 hours 1
    Over 24 hours – week 2
    Over week – month 3
    Over month – year 4
    Over year 5
    Never 6

47. Can I just run through a list of things – I want to ask how many evenings, if any, you have done each of these things during the past week (seven days)?

Stayed in for evening ...... ——
Watched TV .... ——
Went to pictures .... ——
Went to café .... ——
Went to pub .... ——
Went dancing .... ——

<u>IF 16 OR OVER</u>

48. Have you got a motor scooter, motor bike or car?

Scooter 1
Motor bike 2
Car........................ 3
None .... o

49. Do you do *most* things in your spare time:

Alone 1
CODE With one particular friend,
ONE same sex 2
ONLY With one particular friend,
opposite sex 3
In a group 4

<u>IF NOT IN A GROUP (1–3)</u>
Are you ever in a group?
Yes........................ X
No .... O

<u>IF NO (O) GO ON TO</u>
<u>QUESTION 55</u>
<u>TO THOSE EVER IN GROUP</u>

50. How many of you are usually together?

51. Is it:
All boys 1
Mixed 2

52. Is it more or less always the same crowd of people, or do they vary?
More or less the same 3
PROMPT Varies a little 4
Varies a lot 5

53. And is there a recognized leader or or leaders, or not really?
One leader................. 1
Two or more............... 2
No real leaders 3

54. When you are together – what things do you mostly do?

55. Have you got a 'best friend' or particular 'mate'?
Yes....................... 1
No 2

<u>IF YES</u> (*a*) Where does he live?
Within 5 minutes walk........ o
Elsewhere in Bethnal Green .. 1
Other East End 2
Elsewhere (specify) 3

(*b*) And how did you get to know him?
Grew up together ⎱
Neighbour ⎰ 1
Same primary school ⎰
Same secondary school 2
Work 3
Other (specify)

192

56. Do you belong to any youth clubs or youth organizations? Yes....Y No....X

IF YES (Y) How many?————

RECORD FOR EACH

(*a*) Name				
(*b*) Where is that?				
(*c*) How long have you been a member? Less than 1 month .... 1 month < 6 months .... 6 months < 1 year .... 1 year < 2 years .... 2 years + ...	1 2 3 4 5	1 2 3 4 5	1 2 3 4 5	1 2 3 4 5
(*d*) When was the last time you went? Within last 7 days .... 1 week < 1 month ago .... 1 month < 6 months ago .... 6 months + ago	6 7 8 9	6 7 8 9	6 7 8 9	6 7 8 9
(*e*) What do you like about it?				
(*f*) What do you dislike?				

57. Have you been a member of any (other) youth clubs or youth organizations in the past? Yes....1 No....2 IF YES (1) How many————

RECORD FOR EACH

(a) Name				
(b) Where is that?				
(c) For how long were you a member?				
Less than 1 month	1	1	1	1
1 month < 6 months...........	2	2	2	2
6 months < 1 year	3	3	3	3
1 year < 2 years	4	4	4	4
2 years + ...	5	5	5	5
(d) When did you leave?				
In last 6 months	1	1	1	1
6 months < 1 year ago	2	2	2	2
1 year < 2 years ago	3	3	3	3
2 years < 3 years ago...........	4	4	4	4
3 years < 5 years ago...........	5	5	5	5
5 years + ...	6	6	6	6
(e) Why did you leave?				

58. How about girls? Which of these applies to you?

PROMPT
- Married 1
- Engaged 2
- Have regular girl friend 3
- Take girls out sometimes 4
- See girls around .. 5
- Have little to do with girls 6

IF NOT MARRIED (2–6) What about marriage later on? Do you think you will ever get married?
- Yes........................ 1
- No 0

194

IF YES (1) (*a*) At about what age do you think you are most likely to get married?

19 or under 1
20–24 2
25–29 3
30–34 4
35 or more 5

(*b*) Why do you think you'll get married?

IF NO (0) Why do you think you won't get married?

59. Can I now ask your opinion on one or two other things? Which of these two statements, if you had to choose, would you say is closest to your own view of life?

When you're young you ought to enjoy yourself and not worry too much about the future 1
When you're young you ought to work hard, and keep at things even if you don't enjoy them 2

Don't know, can't say 3

IF LIVING WITH PARENT(S)

60. How well do you feel your parents really understand you?

	Fa.	Mo.
Very well	1	6
Fairly well	2	7
PROMPT Quite well......	3	8
Not too well ..	4	9
Not much at all	5	0

61. If you won, say, £50 on the pools or something like that, what do you think you would do with it?

Spend it all 1
Spend most of it 2
Spend half, save half 3
Save most of it.............. 4
Save it all 5

IF SPEND ALL, MOST OR HALF (1, 2 or 3) What would you spend it on?

62. What kind of work do you expect to be doing in ten years time?

63. If you could choose, what would you like to be doing?

64. Do you think you have as much chance to enjoy life as you should have?

Yes........................ 1
No......................... 2

COMMENTS:

65. Do you think you have as much chance to get on in life as you should have?

Yes........................ 1
No......................... 2

COMMENTS:

66. (*a*) There's been all this talk recently about 'Mods' and 'Rockers', fighting at Margate and Brighton and so on. What do you think about all that?

(*b*) Who do you think is really to blame for the trouble?

TO THOSE AT WORK

67. Finally, can you tell me how much pay you get on the average each week (that's including overtime and bonus earnings, but leaving out income tax, national insurance, and so on)?

Under £5 1
£5 < £10.......... 2
PROMPT £10 < £15 3
£15 < £20 4
£20 or over 5

IF LIVING WITH MOTHER

68. How much do you give your mother each week?

	Under £2	1
	£2 < £3	2
PROMPT	£3 < £4	3
	£4 < £5	4
	£5 or more	5

TO THOSE AT SCHOOL OR IN OTHER FULL-TIME EDUCATION AND LIVING WITH PARENT(S)

69. How much money do your parents give you to spend each week?

	Under 5s	1
	5s < 10s	2
PROMPT	10s < 15s	3
	15s < £1	4
	£1 or more	5
	(specify)	

70. Do you have any job outside school/college?

Yes X
No .... O

IF YES (X) (a) How many hours a week do you work?

———

(b) How much do you earn on the average?

Under 5s 1
5s < 10s 2
10s < 15s 3
15s < £1 4
£1 or more 5
(specify)

Thank you for your help. (GIVE THANK-YOU LETTER)

Willing to do diary?

Yes 1
No 2
Possibly 3

Willing to be interviewed at Institute?

Yes 1
No 2
Possibly 3

Subject's name:

Subject's address:

Who present?:

Alone 1
Brother(s) 2
or friend(s)
only present 3
Parent(s) present 4
Others present 5

Interviewer:

Date:

Day of week

Monday 1
Tuesday 2
Wednesday 3
Thursday 4
Friday 6
Saturday 6
Sunday 7

NOTES

Interview Schedule and Interviewer's Instructions

INTERVIEWERS' INSTRUCTIONS

1. *Organization of survey.* We want to interview a cross-section of adolescent boys in Bethnal Green, and since there are no lists from which we can pick such a sample, we have to use a rather tedious method to get one. What we have done is to pick, from the Electoral Registers, a sample of *addresses* in the borough of Bethnal Green. You will be given lists of these addresses and your first task will be to check whether there are any young men aged 14 to 20 inclusive living there. If there are, you should ask to see them, explain about the survey and interview them. Note that at each address *all* the young men of the right age should be interviewed. On the lists, you should show clearly (*a*) how many eligible people there are at each address, putting 'o' if there are none and 'DK' if after repeated efforts you are unable to find out whether there are any; (*b*) how many have been interviewed; (*c*) the reasons for failure – i.e. never in, in hospital, refusal – if (*b*) differs from (*c*). The important thing is for us to be able to say at the end how many young men there were at the selected addresses, how many were interviewed, and why the others weren't. The names of people shown as living at each address are included, by the way, because this may help you in making the initial contact; but it is the address that matters, not the name, and, if the people with the name listed have moved since the Electoral Registers were compiled last October, you should still interview any young men of the right age living at that address.

2. *Interview subject alone.* The young men whom you interview – what we call the 'subjects' of the survey – should be interviewed on their own. It should not be difficult to arrange this; you should say something like: 'Is there somewhere I could interview you on your own. We want to get your own views, and if there is someone else there that might influence your answers.' We have tried this out in the 'pilot' interviews and found it works well. This is so important that we would *almost* rather have no interview than one in someone else's presence; but if you simply cannot arrange to see the subject on his own, make sure you record, on the last page of the questionnaire, who else was present.

3. *Filling in the questionnaire.* You should go through the questionnaire putting the questions exactly as worded, and in the order in which they appear. The answers are to be filled in either by ringing the appropriate pre-code, or by writing the answer in the space provided. If for any reason the pre-code numbers do not apply, or the person is exceptional in some way that is important, you should write a full explanation of this on the questionnaire.

4. *Detail.* We are, in any case, wanting to get answers as full as possible, particularly on the 'open' questions like opinions of school, work, youth clubs, 'Mods' and 'Rockers', and so on. With these questions, you should write in people's answers as fully as possible, quoting their remarks verbatim wherever you can, and putting quotation marks to show that it is a direct quote. If there is not enough space on the page you should use the back of the previous page, putting an asterisk opposite the question, and another asterisk together with the question number opposite the remarks quoted. If, for instance, you got a very full answer about the informant's attitude to 'Mods' and 'Rockers' on Question 66, you would write this in on the back of page 6, putting an asterisk and the figure 66 opposite what you write and another asterisk opposite Question 66 itself.

5. *Descriptions.* We would also like each of you to write physical descriptions of at least two of the boys you interview. These should be as detailed and factual as you can make them – if necessary, ask them the exact name of the type of shoes they are wearing or the style of shirt. Also note haircuts, colours and patterns of ties, socks and the like.

6. *The subject's age.* Note that, when we say we want boys aged 14 to 20 inclusive, we mean on 1 June 1964. Eligible subjects are, in fact, those who on 1 June had passed their 14th birthday but had not yet passed their 21st. You should therefore check that the boys really are eligible to start with, and when you check their age in Question 1 you should make sure that the age you record is what they were on 1 June; the best way might be to ask 'when was your birthday?'

7. *Subject's number.* Each address on your list has got a number of its own – e.g. BN 23. Would you record this number just above the boxes at the top right-hand corner of page 1 of the questionnaire; if there is more than one boy interviewed at that address, please put e.g. BN 23a, BN 23b. Don't put the number inside the boxes marked 'Serial No.'; we shall be giving each person interviewed new serial numbers later on.

Detailed notes on the questions

Question 1. The question of age has already been mentioned in Paragraph 6 above.

Question 2. (*a*) The sign '$<$' means 'less than', as you probably know. So code '3' is 'five years or more but less than ten years'; someone who had lived in Bethnal Green for exactly ten years would be coded '2', not '3'. Note that this sign is used in other questions, e.g. Question 67, and the same warning should be borne in mind.

(*b*) Some definitions:
'Other East End' = Hackney, Poplar, Stepney and Shoreditch.

'Other Greater London' = anywhere else in the new Greater London Council area.

'Outside Britain' = outside England, Wales and Scotland.

If in any doubt, write in what the subject tells you and let us sort it out later in the office.

Question 3. The question is put in the form of a straight choice between school and work; we assume that there will be very few in full-time education other than school, and that those who are will tell us. Note that the questionnaire 'branches' after this question. You put Question 4–12 to those still at school; 13–21 to those in 'other full-time education'; 22–38 to those at work.

Question 4. Write in the name of the school. (This applies also to Questions 14 and 21.)

Question 5. 'Code all that apply' means that if, e.g. the subject has passed both some 'A' levels and some 'O' levels, you should ring both '1' and '2'. (See also Questions 6, 15 and 32.)

Question 7. If they go to evening classes, write in the name of the institution they go to and where it is. (See also Questions 13 and 38a.)

Question 9. Note that this question says 'On the whole'. Obviously most people have mixed feelings about leaving school: we don't want you to ring 'O' ('Don't know, can't say') unless they really can't choose. So if people seem to be mixed about this, try to press them gently – by saying, e.g. 'Yes, but *on the whole* are you looking forward to it or not?' (Questions 17 and 34 are similar, and there are other questions later in the schedule, particularly on p. 7, to which the general point applies.)

Question 10. The first part of this question is 'open'; write in whatever the subject says, bearing in mind the point made in Paragraph 4 above. (Questions 18 and 35 are basically the same, and there are other similarly 'open' questions elsewhere in the questionnaire; always *something* should be written in, unless of course the question has not been put because it doesn't apply.) With 10b, you should read out the alternatives, as with a 'Prompt'. (See Question 11 below.)

Question 11. The word 'Prompt', which appears in other questions also, means that you have actually to *read out* the alternative answers.

Question 22. 'Other East End' has been defined above (Question 2). 'City of London' means just that. 'Other Central London' means the following boroughs – Holborn, Finsbury, Westminster, St. Marylebone, St. Pancras, Lambeth, Kensington and Chelsea. 'Elsewhere Greater London' again means the rest of the G.L.C. area.

Question 23. Please get the answer here in plenty of detail. 'Works in a factory' won't do; we want to know just what he does. Nor will 'Civil Servant'; what grade is he? And so on. (This applies also to Question 40, about the father's job.) Check finally if the job is as an apprentice or trainee, and ring '9' if it is.

Question 30. Note that the second column applies only if the subject's present job is not his first job since leaving school. If it is also his first job, something will be ringed in the first column and nothing in the second. Note, too, that we want only *one* code ringed in each column; if he says it was both through a friend *and* an advertisement, try to get him to say which was the *main* source of information.

Question 40. See note to Question 23. We want the occupation of the father, or – if there is a stepfather in the home – the stepfather. If there is no stepfather and the father is dead or has gone away, ask about the father's former job.

Question 42. This is about the subject's 'birth order', first among all his brothers and sisters, then among the boys only. If, e.g. the boy was the eldest in the family and had sisters but no brothers, he would be coded '3' in the first column, '5' in the second.

Question 45. Note the word *usually*.

Question 47. We want to know, not how many *times* they did these things in the past week (i.e. the seven days before the interview) but on how many *evenings* they did them.

Question 49. Note that it's *most* things and that we say 'Code one only'. We want, in other words, only one of the codes 1 to 4 to be ringed.

Questions 50–54. These apply to people who have said 'In a group' in answer to the first part of Question 49 or 'Yes' in answer to the second part.

Questions 56 and 57. With each of these questions the idea is that you should fill in at the top the name of the youth club or youth organization and then ask the series of questions about each in turn.

Question 58. You should 'prompt', i.e. read out, only the last five possibilities. 'Married' will apply to very few, and they will certainly tell you so.

At the end of the interview, thank the subject and hand him a copy of the 'thank-you' letter. You should then explain:
    (a) 'We are going to ask some people later if they would be willing to keep a detailed diary for a week. We would explain the kind of thing we want, and would pay £2 as a fee. Do you think you would be willing?' (Ring accordingly.)
    (b) 'We are also going to ask some people if they would be willing to come to our office at the Institute and be interviewed with a tape

recorder – having a chat on one or two particular topics. Do you think you would be willing?' (Ring accordingly.)

At the end of the interview. Fill in the subject's name and address, your name and the date. If anybody is worried about their name and address being put on the questionnaire you should explain that this is simply in order to provide a check on their number – once it has been checked, they just become a number and their name no longer comes into it at all. It is a good idea, finally, to check through the interview before you go on to the next one, to see if you have missed anything out or anything is unclear, adding any notes or expanding any points.

Completed interviews. We would prefer you not to hang on to completed interviews for too long. Please either bring them to the office before 6 p.m., at the beginning of the next evening, or put them through the letter-box in the envelopes we shall provide.

Peter Willmott
27 May 1964.

DIARY INSTRUCTIONS AND SAMPLE DIARY

The boys in the general sample were asked whether they would be willing, if asked, (*a*) to keep a week's diary, (*b*) to come to the Institute of Community Studies for further interviewing. Three-quarters said 'Yes' to each question and all but a handful of these said 'Yes' to both. We grouped the boys who were willing to do a diary into one-year age-groups and then selected seven at random from each group. Of the forty-two picked in this way, thirty finally did write diaries for the same week in July 1964. Later, to get more diaries from boys still at school, we selected another six boys and asked them to do a week's diary for us in October 1964: five agreed.

The rest of this Appendix reproduces the instructions that were given to the diarists and a sample diary.

NOTES ON KEEPING DIARIES

You will remember that you were interviewed recently in the survey we are doing about growing up in Bethnal Green. We are now going to try to get diaries to fill out the information we got from the interviews. The idea is for people to write detailed diaries of next week – that is starting on Sunday, 12 July and going on to Saturday, 18 July. We have picked some of the people interviewed, and you are one of them – we hope that you will be willing to do one of these diaries for us.

How to fill in the diary

Enclosed are a number of sheets of ruled paper. We would like you, at the end of each day, to write up that day's diary on these sheets. You should start on Sunday, putting 'Sunday' at the top; then you should put the time you got up, on the left-hand side, and go on through the day, putting the time at the side and what you did opposite it. The beginning would look like this:

Sunday

9.00 a.m.   Got up and went downstairs to breakfast. Read the *News of the World* and had an argument with my sister about the picture – 'Girl with Green Eyes' – that was on at the Ritz last week.

9.40 a.m.   Went round to call on Fred, my mate who lives round the corner . . .

And so on. You should go right through the day like this, ending up with the time you went to bed. Then the next day (Monday) would start at the time you got up and go right through the day. And so on throughout the week.

What we want to know

The main thing is to put in plenty of detail. We want to know what you do in as much detail as possible. We would particularly like to know about what you do at work – who you see and who you talk to as well as the actual work. And about the evenings and week-ends. Please say where you went, who with, what you did, how long you stayed in each place. Mention any contacts with girls and say something about them. If you go out with a crowd, tell us something about them – their ages, whether they are all boys or mixed, where they live and so on. We specially want something about your friends and when you see them, so please put in names (or initials) so we can see if you are spending a lot of time with the same people. *Remember that all the information will be treated as confidential; it will only be seen by us at the office and we shall only use it for the book. Your name will not be published, and nor will anyone else's name or anything else that would give away who you or they are.* We shall be quoting some extracts from the diaries in the book, but with names and other details changed. This means that you needn't worry about putting down the actual name of your friend, but if you would prefer to do so you can just put an initial instead.

Payment

We shall pay a fee of £2 after we get the completed diary, which should be posted to us on 20 July. Use the large enclosed envelope to post the diary to us – or bring it round, if you would prefer to. Don't bother to return unused sheets of paper. Will you please show on the enclosed sheet, posted in the small stamped envelope addressed to us, first whether you are going to do a diary at all, and secondly how you would like to be paid – by postal order through the post, or in cash by one of us calling at your home or by calling here. We would like you to post this off straight away, so that we shall know, before next week begins, how many are taking part.

Thank you for your help.

Peter Willmott

SAMPLE DIARY

Diary of 'Arthur Rose', aged 15
(Names and other details have been altered)

Sunday

I am staying at a caravan which is owned by my mate's parents.

6.50 a.m.   Sunday morning, am awakened by the noise of a kettle boiling. It was Frank's (my mate's) dad making an early morning cup of tea. After having a cup of tea I went back to sleep again.

9.00 a.m.   I was awoken with another cup of tea.

9.15 a.m.   I decided to get up, washed and dressed.

9.30 a.m.   Breakfast was on the table which consisted of egg, bacon, and tomatoes, bread and butter and another cup of tea. After breakfast went out to have a look at some people fishing in a nearby lake.

10.00 a.m.   Went with Frank to one of his mate's chalet to see if he was going swimming with four girls we met on Saturday night.

10.15 a.m.   Met the girls at their caravan, got changed for swimming in the river.

3.00 p.m.   We went back to the van for dinner. After dinner sat outside the van and went to sleep.

4.00 p.m.   I was awakened by Frank's dad who was saying that another friend had broken a record by fishing a 4 lb. 4 oz. bream from the river; he had beaten the record by 2 ozs.

4.30 p.m.   I suggested that we go and say Goodbye to the girls. When we arrived at their van the girls asked us to go for a walk; anyway two said that they were too tired. Jill, that is the name of the girl that I was with, said, 'Let's have a game of cards', which we did.

6.00 p.m.   I said Goodbye to Jill but before I left I got her home address so I am able to write to her during the week.

7.30 p.m.   We left the van at about 7.30 p.m. in my mate's dad's car. We arrived home at about 8.30 p.m. Had tea round Frank's house, then left for home, arrived home at 9.00 p.m. Sat writing diary, then went to bed at 11.45 p.m.

Monday

6.30 a.m.   Was woken by Mum, got up and had a cup of tea, then got dressed.

7.00 a.m.   Left home to go to work. Got on the bus with Frank at 7.15 a.m. (Frank is one of my mates at work).

7.25 a.m.   Arrived in work, clocked myself in. Then I went round the café for a cup of tea.

7.30 a.m.   Started work. I had to do drilling, and bolting trusses together (trusses are beams which go on roofs which help to support them).

10.30 a.m.   Had just finished my tea break. (I had cheese rolls, and a cup of tea.) I then started work on some more trusses.

12.30 p.m.   I washed my hands. I then went round to the café for my dinner. I had liver and two vegetables. After I had my dinner I went to the park at the back of the firm. I met some girls I know who work near where I work. We talked as we sat on the grass.

12.55 p.m.   I said Goodbye to the girls and I went to work.

1.00 p.m.   Started work on painting the trusses.

3.00 p.m.   Had tea and started work.

5.00 p.m.   Stopped for another cup of tea; started work at 5.15 p.m.

7.30 p.m.   Finished work and went home with Frank.

8.00 p.m.   Had to wait ages for a bus, but when I got in I had a wash, then had my tea.

8.30 p.m.   After tea I got dressed, had a shave. I then went out. I went up the local youth club.

9.00 p.m.   I done some modern dancing up the club.

9.15 p.m.   My mate Jimmy came up the club.

10.30 p.m.   When it was time to go home I was just going to say Goodbye to some girls I knew when a bottle came through the window. When we looked out we saw about 30 boys from another club hanging around outside the club. Then me and my mates went out to sort out the boys; there were about 30 of us. There wasn't a fight because when the boys saw all of us they ran. We stood and talked for awhile. I then decided to go home. When I got in I had a cup of tea and then went to bed about 11.30 p.m.

Tuesday

6.30 a.m.   Got up, had a wash, got dressed, had my breakfast and went to work. I did the same as yesterday morning. In the afternoon I helped my mate Albert to make a Bar B.Q. spit for one of the governors. We got all the metal cut out and marked up.

7.30 p.m.   I clocked out and got a bus home.

8.00 p.m.   When I got in tea was ready; I had egg salad.

8.45 p.m.   I decided to get washed and dressed and go swimming at the York Hall baths. As I got round the corner I saw a bus at the lights; I ran to the bus stop and caught the bus; when I got on it I saw Jimmy, my mate. We arrived ten minutes late, but we got in. When we got changed we did some diving on the diving-board. The time seemed to fly past. Then we went back to the club and had a drink of Pepsi and a game of darts.

10.30 p.m.   We left the club and walked down the road to the bus stop where we talked until a bus came along. My mate Jimmy caught the bus, so I walked to the fish shop and bought some fish and chips. When I got home I made a cup of tea and went to bed about 11.30 p.m.

Wednesday

6.30 a.m.   I was wakened by Mum with a cup of tea and some biscuits.

7.10 a.m.   Was washed and dressed and had my breakfast.

7.15 a.m.   Caught the bus with Frank.

7.25 a.m.   Got in work. Started at 8.00, was finishing the governor's Bar B.Q. spit about 2.00 p.m. Then I started on another job; I had to cut up 120 pieces of 1" by ¾" flat. I finished that about 6.00 p.m.

6.00 p.m.   My mate wanted me to help him make a saucepan rack for his caravan, so I did. We finished at 7.15. I then sat down for 15 minutes.

7.30 p.m.   I clocked out and went home.

8.00 p.m.   I did not fancy any tea so I got washed and changed.

9.00 p.m.   I decided to have a night in and so I just watched television. Then I had a cup of tea and a cheese sandwich and went to bed about 11 p.m.

Thursday

6.30 a.m.   Was woken up by Mum with a cup of tea. After I had my tea I got up and got dressed and washed. I had egg and bacon for breakfast.

7.17 a.m.   I was a bit late and had missed my usual bus, but a few minutes later another bus came along. I supposed Frank had caught the 7.15 bus.

7.29 a.m.   Arrived in work just in time to clock in at 7.30.

7.30 a.m.   I was not working with Albert. I was working with Gerry. We were making a balustrade. I had to cut up the bars.

10.17 a.m.   Had tea break as usual.

10. 30 a.m.   Started work again.

12.30 p.m.   Stopped for dinner, went to the café. After I had dinner I went to the park; sat in the park until 12.58. Gerry had the afternoon off because he had to go to the hospital about his eyes, because he kept getting headaches.

1.00 p.m.   Started work.

1.30 p.m.   I finished cutting up the bars then I drilled them with a $\frac{2}{32}$" drill.

3.00 p.m.   Had another cup of tea.

3.12 p.m.   Started work again.

3.30 p.m.   Had finished drilling, started on tapping with a $\frac{1}{4}$" tap.

7.30 p.m.   Finished work and went home with Frank on the bus.

8.00 p.m.   Got home, had fish and chips for tea. I decided to get washed and dressed and go to the 'Beat Club'.

9.00 p.m.   Arrived at the club. When I got in the club I saw a lot of my mates, so I went with them. We talked about the group. They said it was the worst group they had up there for a long time. I agreed with them.

9.45 p.m.   One of my mates, Roger, said, 'let's go over the fair', so we went over the fair. When we got over there we saw some more of our mates and they tagged along with us. We stood on the side of the whip and listened to the records.

10.45 p.m.   We all decided to go home.

11.00 p.m.   Got in and had a cup of tea, then I went to bed at 11.45.

Friday

6.30 a.m.   Got up, got washed, dressed and had a cup of tea. Then I had my breakfast.

7.00 a.m.   Left home to go to work. I had to go to a firm up in the City to work on a job. When I got to the place where I was to work, I saw Albert my mate.

8.00 a.m.   Bill Burgess and Fred Worth arrived; they are fitters from our firm. Started work on maintaining a rolling machine.

11.15 a.m.   Went to have our tea break in the café down the road.

1.00 p.m.   Went to have dinner.

4.15 p.m.   Had my tea break.

6.30 p.m.   Packed up and went home; Bill gave me a lift home.

7.00 p.m.   Had my tea, got washed and dressed and went up the club.

7.45 p.m.   When I got up the club I went in the hall. I saw some of my mates; they were playing darts. After they had finished their game of darts we went and sat down and talked. One of the blokes on the staff was sitting with me and someone said something about boats, and the bloke on the staff started telling us how much it cost to insure a liner, and all about the *Queen Mary*. All her war record and how she was changed into a liner.

9.45 p.m.   Frank arrived late, he had been to an A.E.U. meeting. I bought him a solo drink. Then we went into the dance hall to watch the girls dancing.

10.30 p.m.   Left the club and made our way home.

10.45 p.m.   When I got in had a cup of tea and went to bed at 11.30 p.m.

Saturday

6.30 a.m.   Got up, got dressed and washed in some good clothes, put my old jeans in a bag, as well as my boots and shirt.

6.45 a.m.   Had my breakfast, then I sat in the armchair and read a book.

7.30 a.m.   Left home to go to work. I am going on my holidays next week and I want the money.

8.00 a.m.   Got in work, started work about 8.15. Starting making a brachet for a pipe which sprays water over the copper after it is treated with acid.

10.30 a.m.   Had our usual tea break. Started work at 11.00.

6.30 p.m.   Got home. When I asked Mum when tea would be ready, she said 'about 7.30'. So I said 'I won't be long. I am just going to pick up my coat from the menders' (as I have had my collar of my coat altered).

7.15 p.m.   Got in and Mum was just cooking tea. After I had my tea I got washed and I went over the fair.

7.45 p.m.   I met my mates and we walked round the fair. We went on a couple of things.

8.30 p.m.   One of my mates Dave said 'let's all go up the "Beat Club".' When we got there we found that some girls we knew were there and we danced with them. The two groups were really good.

10.30 p.m.   The club closed and me and my mates made our way home. We got outside the cinema. There we stopped and talked until 11.00. I then walked home as the buses had stopped running.

CLASSIFYING BOYS INTO 'TYPES'

As Chapter IX explains, this analysis was done in two stages. In the first, a rather arbitrary method was used to assign each of the 246 boys in the sample to one of three categories. The second analysis, using a computer, had for technical reasons to be confined to the 177 boys at work;[1] its purpose was to provide a more systematic check on the grouping produced by the first method. The two stages are described in turn.

First analysis

After some preliminary analyses, 21 items were selected as indices. They are listed on pp. 212–3, together with the answers that we regarded as appropriate to each 'type'. The items included two questions which had been asked as an indication of what is thought to be a crucial difference between working and middle-class attitudes – the extent to which people are prepared to 'defer gratification' on the one hand or prefer to live for the present on the other. One question asked what the boys would do if they won some money, the expectation being that the 'middle-class' boys would be more likely than the others to say they would save. The second question posed two alternative 'views of life' to the boys and asked them which they favoured; one emphasized the importance of enjoying oneself in youth, the other the need to work hard. The expectation was that 'working-class' boys, and even more 'rebels', would be disposed to opt for the first statement, 'middle-class' boys for the second. As will be apparent from

---

[1] This analysis, like the 'correlation matrix' referred to in Chapters V, VI and VIII, had to be restricted to the boys at work because both analyses depended on having standardized information for each boy. Since the battery of information about work was not available for the sixty-nine still at school, we could include these boys only by dropping the data on work or by giving some sort of notional scores to them on these questions. We decided that it was better to confine the analyses to the majority at work than to adopt either of these unsatisfactory alternatives.

these examples and from the list of the responses by which boys were classified, on some questions we postulated that 'working-class' boys and 'rebels' would be alike, 'middle-class' boys different; these were the questions that particularly emphasized differences in social class behaviour or values. But on other questions we expected the 'working-class' and 'middle-class' boys to be like each other and unlike the 'rebels'; these were questions which emphasized the extent of rejection or rebellion.

First Analysis – Indices Used

| Item | Reponses according to which boys were classified into different 'types' | | |
	'Middle-class'	'Working-class'	'Rebel'
1. Opinion of lessons	'Very' or 'quite' useful	'Very' or 'quite' useful	'Not much use', 'no use at all' or 'don't know'
2. Opinion of teacher	Like 'all', 'most' or 'about half'	Like 'all', 'most' or 'about half'	Like 'few', 'none' or 'don't know'
3. Opinion of reasonableness of rules	'All', 'most' or 'about half'	'All', 'most' or 'about half'	'Few', 'none' or 'don't know'
4. Occupational class	Non-manual	Skilled manual	Semi-skilled or unskilled
5. Job satisfaction (general)	Satisfied	Satisfied	Dissatisfied or 'mixed'
6. Job satisfaction (prospects)	Satisfied	Satisfied	Dissatisfied or 'mixed'
7. Job prospects	Non-manual	Manual	Few
8. Number of jobs	1–4	1–4	5 or more
9. In Bethnal Green evenings	'Right outside it'	'In and around it' or 'about half and half'	'In and around it' or 'about half and half'
10. In Bethnal Green weekends	'Right outside it'	'In and around it' or 'about half and half'	'In and around it' or 'about half and half'
11. Last visit to West End	Last 24 hours	Not in last 24 hours	Not in last 24 hours
12. Local friend	Lives outside Bethnal Green	Lives inside Bethnal Green	Lives inside Bethnal Green
13. Age expects to marry	'Expect to marry after 24'	'Expect to marry by 24' or already married	'Don't expect to marry' or 'don't know'
14. 'View of life'	'Work hard'	'Enjoy life' or 'mixed'	'Enjoy life'

Classifying Boys into 'Types'

Item	'Middle-class'	'Working-class'	'Rebel'
15. Father understands	'Very well', 'fairly well' or 'quite well'	'Very well', 'fairly well' or 'quite well'	'Not too well' or 'not much at all'
16. Mother understands	'Very well', 'fairly well' or 'quite well'	'Very well', 'fairly well' or 'quite well'	'Not too well' or 'not much at all'
17. 'Spend or save' £50	Save 'half', 'all' or 'most'	Spend 'all' or 'most'	Spend 'all' or 'most'
18. Job aspirations	'Expect non-manual, choose non-manual' or 'expect manual, choose non-manual'	'Expect manual, choose manual' or 'expect non-manual, choose manual'	Other answer
19. Chance to 'enjoy life'	'Yes'	'Yes'	'No', 'don't know' or 'mixed'
20. Chance to 'get on'	'Yes'	'Yes'	'No', 'don't know' or 'mixed'
21. 'Mods and rockers'	Condemnation of fighting or 'It's exaggerated'	Condemnation of fighting or 'It's exaggerated'	Approval, acceptance or other answer

Each boy's set of answers was considered in turn. He was given a score of one point in the appropriate column each time his answer matched that indicated. For instance, a boy who had said, on the first item, that he thought 'most' of the lessons 'useful', would receive one point on the 'middle-class' scale and one point on the 'working-class'. If a particular item did not apply – items 4 to 8, for instance, did not apply to boys at school, nor 15 to a boy whose father had died – no score was recorded on that item.

At the end we added up the scores. If a boy had a score two or more points higher on one 'type' than either of the others, he was classified accordingly. If the scores were the same on two 'types', or if there was a difference of only one point, we looked at the interview schedule in detail and made our own subjective assessment of the appropriate category. Twenty-one boys had equal scores in different 'types', and another thirty-five a difference of only one; seventeen of the latter were, after examination, assigned to a different 'type' from that on which they had scored most. In making our decision, we were particularly influenced by a boy's job and by his career aspirations.

The main disadvantages of this method were first, it was based

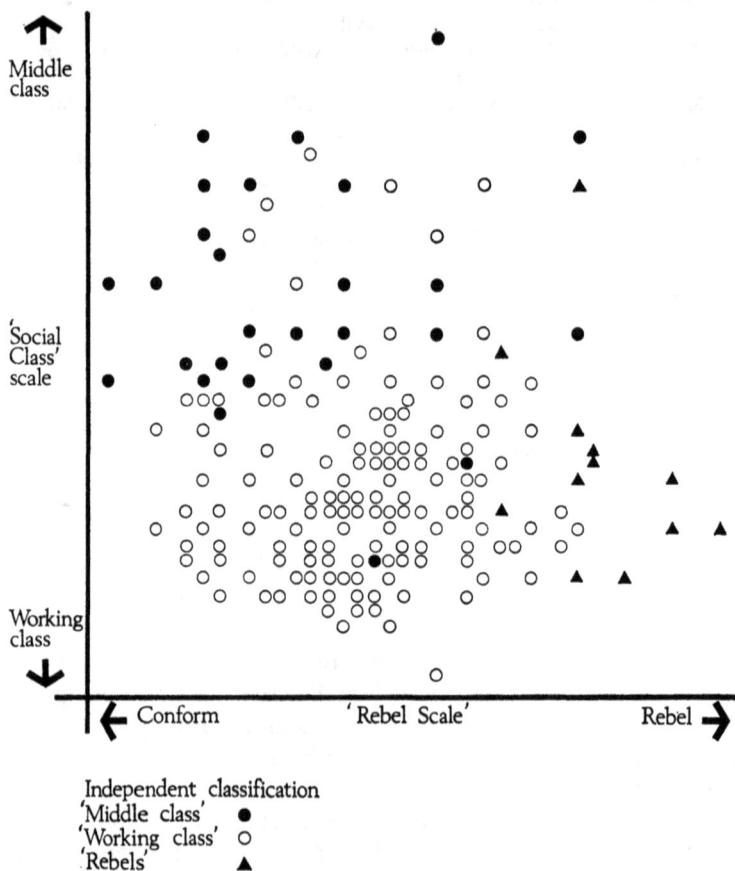

Independent classification
'Middle class' ●
'Working class' ○
'Rebels' ▲

on crude measurement, one that gave equal weight to each item on the scale; and secondly, it involved subjective and often somewhat arbitrary decisions over the boys who had borderline scores. Hence our attempt at a statistical check.

Second analysis

The second method used what is known as 'component analysis'. It set out to determine statistically a score for each boy on two scales – one of 'social class' and the other of 'rebelliousness'. With each scale, statistical analysis was used to find the weighted combination of the answers to the relevant questions which would account for most of the variability, and then produce a score for each boy. A wider range of information was drawn upon for this analysis than the first – there were sixteen items in the 'social class' scale and twenty-one in the 'rebelliousness' scale (four items were included in both scales). These are listed on p. 216. Using these items, scores on both scales were calculated for each of the 177 boys at work. The results are plotted on a graph (see p. 214), which also indicates the category to which each boy had been assigned by using the first method. The diagram shows that our 'rebels' had a higher 'rebelliousness' score than the others, and that most 'middle-class' boys had a higher 'class' score. The two analyses produced a few striking variations; the explanation for these is two-fold – the computer analysis drew upon more items and, instead of simply giving a score of one point for each item, it calculated weighted scores based upon the items which accounted for most of the variability. Despite the differences, there was a broad correspondence in the results. The diagram shows three fairly distinct clusters – in our terminology, 'middle-class', around the top left-hand sector of the graph; 'working-class' around the bottom left-hand; and 'rebel' around the bottom right-hand. The top right-hand sector is almost empty, indicating that few boys are both 'rebels' and 'middle-class' in outlook.

How many of each type?

The first analysis allocated each boy to one of the three categories, but the method left much to be desired. The second analysis provided a check, at least for the 177 boys at work, but could not indicate how to assign boys to categories. The main impression from the second analysis was that the proportions of 'middle-class' boys and 'rebels' might reasonably be regarded as somewhat larger than the first analysis had suggested. In the light of both analyses, our view was that the proportions were roughly as follows:

'Working-class' – about two-thirds or three-quarters.
'Middle-class' – about a fifth, possibly less.
'Rebels' – a tenth or less.

Classifying Boys into 'Types'

Second Analysis – Items used to Produce Weighted Scores

'Social class scale'	'Rebelliousness scale'
Type of school	Occupational class
Examinations	Apprentice
Age left school	Number of jobs
Works East End	Evening classes attended
Works West End	Size of group
Occupational class	What group does
Apprentice	Opinion of lessons
Father's occupational class	Opinion of teachers
In Bethnal Green in evenings	Opinion of school rules
In Bethnal Green at week-ends	Satisfaction job, generally
Last visit to West End	Satisfaction job, prospects
Friend lives outside East End	Expects to marry
Friend met locally	'View of life' ('Work hard'
Expects to marry late	or 'enjoy life')
'View of life' ('Work hard'	Father understands
or 'enjoy life')	Mother understands
'Save' or 'spend' £50	'Save' or 'spend' £50
	Job aspirations
	Chance to 'enjoy life'
	Chance to 'get on'
	Mods and Rockers

APPENDIX 5

LIST OF REFERENCES

ABRAMS, M., *Teenage Consumer Spending in 1959*, Part II. London, London Press Exchange. 1961.

ALLCORN, D.H., *The Social Development of Young Men in an English Industrial Suburb*. University of Manchester. Ph.D. Thesis. 1955.

ANDRY, R. G., *Delinquency and Parental Pathology*. London, Methuen. 1960.

BESANT, W., *East London*. London, Chatto and Windus. 1901.

BIERSTEDT, R., *The Social Order*. New York, McGraw-Hill. 1963.

CARTER, M. P., *Home, School and Work*. Oxford, Pergamon Press. 1962.

CARTWRIGHT, A., *Human Relations and Hospital Care*. London, Routledge and Kegan Paul. 1964.

CLOWARD, R. A. and OHLIN, L. E., *Delinquency and Opportunity: A Theory of Delinquent Gangs*. London, Routledge and Kegan Paul. 1961.

COHEN, A. K., *Delinquent Boys*. Glencoe, The Free Press. 1955.

COLEMAN, J. S., *The Adolescent Society*. New York, The Free Press. 1961.

DOWNES, D. M., *The Delinquent Solution*. London, Routledge and Kegan Paul. 1966.

EISENSTADT, S. N., *From Generation to Generation*. London, Routledge and Kegan Paul. 1956.

ERIKSON, E. H., *Childhood and Society*. New York, W. W. Norton. Second edition. 1963.

FERGUSON, T., *The Young Delinquent in his Social Setting: a Glasgow Study*. London, Oxford University Press. 1952.

FLOUD, J. and HALSEY, A. H., 'Intelligence Tests, Social Class and Selection for Secondary Schools'. *British Journal of Sociology*, Vol. VIII, No. 1. March 1957, pp. 33–39.

FREUD, S., *Two Short Accounts of Psycho-Analysis*. Harmondsworth, Penguin Books. 1962.

FYVEL, T. R., *The Insecure Offenders*. Harmondsworth, Penguin Books. 1963.

GOLDTHORPE, J. H. and LOCKWOOD, D., 'Affluence and the British Class Structure'. *Sociological Review*, Vol. II, No. 2. July 1963, pp. 133–63.

GORER, G., *Exploring English Character*. London, Cresset Press. 1955.

GRAY, P. G., CORLETT, T. and FRANKLAND, P., *The Register of Electors as a Sampling Frame*. The Social Survey. Central Office of Information. November 1950.

HARRIS, C., *The Use of Leisure in Bethnal Green*. London, Lindsey Press. 1927.

HAVIGHURST, R. J., *Human Development and Education*. New York, Longmans Green. 1953.

HOGGART, R., *The Uses of Literacy*. Harmondsworth, Penguin Books. 1958.

HOLLINGSHEAD, A. B., *Elmtown's Youth*. New York, John Wiley. 1949.

JACKSON, B. and MARSDEN, D., *Education and the Working Class*. London, Routledge and Kegan Paul. 1962.

JEPHCOTT, P., *Girls Growing Up*. London, Faber and Faber. 1942.

JEPHCOTT, P., *Rising Twenty*. London, Faber and Faber. 1948.

JEPHCOTT, P. and CARTER, M.P., *The Social Background of Delinquency*. University of Nottingham, unpublished. 1954.

KINSEY, A. C., POMEROY, W. B. and MARTIN, C. E., *Sexual Behaviour in the Human Male*. Philadelphia, W. B. Saunders. 1948.

LIPSET, S. M., TROW, M. A. and COLEMAN, J. S., *Union Democracy*. Glencoe, The Free Press. 1956.

LITTLE, A., 'The "Prevalence" of Recorded Delinquency and Recidivism in England and Wales'. *American Sociological Review*, Vol. 30, No. 2. April 1965, pp. 260–63.

LOGAN, R. F. L. and GOLDBERG, E. M., 'Rising Eighteen in a London Suburb'. *British Journal of Sociology*, Vol. IV, No. 4. December 1953, pp. 323–45.

MATZA, D., *Delinquency and Drift*. New York, John Wiley and Sons. 1964.

MAYS, J. B., *Education and the Urban Child*. Liverpool, Liverpool University Press. 1962.

MAYS, J. B., *Growing up in the City*. Liverpool, Liverpool University Press. 1954.

MAYS, J. B., *The Young Pretenders*. London, Michael Joseph. 1965.

MILLER, D., 'The Seven Ages of Man – Adolescence: Personality'. *New Society*, No. 112. 19 November 1964, pp. 11–12.

MILLER, W. B., 'Lower-Class Culture as a Generating Milieu of Gang Delinquency'. *Journal of Social Issues*, Vol. 14, No. 3. 1958, pp. 5–19.

List of References

MORRISON, A., *A Child of the Jago*. London, Methuen. 1896.

MORSE, M., *The Unattached*. Harmondsworth, Penguin Books. 1965.

MUSGROVE, F., *Youth and the Social Order*. London, Routledge and Kegan Paul. 1964.

POWER, M. J., 'An Attempt to Identify at First Appearance Before the Courts Those at Risk of Becoming Persistent Juvenile Offenders'. *Proceedings of the Royal Society of Medicine,* Vol. 58, No. 9. September 1965, pp. 704–705.

POWER, M. J., 'Trends in Juvenile Delinquency'. *The Times.* 9 August 1962.

RADCLIFFE-BROWN, A. R. and FORDE, D., *African Systems of Kinship and Marriage*. London, Oxford University Press. 1950.

SCHOFIELD, M., *The Sexual Behaviour of Young People*. London, Longmans Green. 1965.

SELVIN, H. C., 'A Critique of Tests of Significance in Survey Research'. *American Sociological Review,* Vol. 22, No. 5. October 1957, pp. 519–27.

SELVIN, H. C., 'Survey Analysis'. University of Rochester, unpublished. February 1966. (Prepared for *The International Encyclopedia of the Social Sciences,* to be published by the Macmillan Co., The Free Press of Glencoe and Collin's Encyclopedia in 1967.)

SELVIN, H. C. and STUART, A., 'Data-Dredging Procedure in Survey Analysis'. University of Rochester, unpublished. 1964.

SHERIF, M. and SHERIF, C. W., *Reference Groups*. New York, Harper and Row. 1964.

SPINLEY, B. M., *The Deprived and the Privileged*. London, Routledge and Kegan Paul. 1953.

SUTHERLAND, E. H., 'White-Collar Criminality'. *American Sociological Review,* Vol. 5, No. 1. February 1940, pp. 1–12.

TANNER, J. M., *Growth at Adolescence*. Oxford, Blackwell Scientific Publications. 1955.

THRASHER, F. M., *The Gang*. Chicago, University of Chicago Press. 1963.

VENESS, T., *School Leavers*. London, Methuen. 1962.

WALL, W. D., *The Adolescent Child*. London, Methuen. 1948.

WARNER, W. L., HAVIGHURST, R. J. and LOEB, M. B., *Who Shall be Educated?* London, Kegan Paul, Trench, Trubner. 1946.

WARNER, W. L. and LUNT, P. S., *The Social Life of a Modern Community*. New Haven, Yale University Press. 1941.

WHYTE, W. F., *Street Corner Society*. Chicago, The University of Chicago Press. 1943.

WILLMOTT, P., *The Evolution of a Community*. London, Routledge and Kegan Paul. 1963.

WILSON, B., 'War of the Generations'. *Daily Telegraph*. 24 August 1964 and 25 August 1964.

WOOTTON, B., *Social Science and Social Pathology*. London, George Allen and Unwin. 1959.

YOUNG, M., *Innovation and Research in Education*. London, Routledge and Kegan Paul. 1965.

YOUNG, M. and WILLMOTT, P., *Family and Kinship in East London*. London, Routledge and Kegan Paul. 1957.

ZWEIG, F., *The British Worker*. Harmondsworth, Penguin Books. 1962.

Census 1931. County Report – London. London, H.M.S.O. 1932.

Census 1951. County Report – London. London, H.M.S.O. 1954.

Census 1961. County Report – London. London, H.M.S.O. 1963.

The Child, the Family and the Young Offender. Home Office, White Paper (Cmnd. 2742). London, H.M.S.O. 1965.

Classification of Occupations 1960. London, H.M.S.O. 1960.

The Demand for Places in Higher Education. Appendix One to the *Report of the Committee on Higher Education* (Robbins Report). London, H.M.S.O. 1963.

Early Leaving. (A Report of the Central Advisory Committee for Education, England). London, H.M.S.O. 1954.

Half Our Future (A Report of the Central Advisory Council for Education, England) (Newson Report). London, H.M.S.O. 1963.

L.C.C. *East End Housing*. Publication No. 4213. London, London County Council. 1963.

Metropolitan Borough of Bethnal Green. *Annual Report of the Medical Officer of Health for 1961*. London. 1962.

Metropolitan Borough of Bethnal Green. *Annual Report of the Medical Officer of Health for 1964*. London. 1965.

Ministry of Education. *Circular No. 144*. 16 June 1947.

The Work of the Youth Employment Service, 1959–1962. National Youth Employment Council. London, H.M.S.O. 1962.

The Youth Service in England and Wales (Albemarle Report). London, H.M.S.O. 1960.

INDEX

School, identification with—*contd.*
  mixed, 73
  parents and, 177
  peer groups at, 92, 95
  primary, 73–4
  rebelliousness, 117–18, 158
  record, 98–9, 117, 133, 136
School, secondary modern, 73
  criticisms of, 79–80, 86, 95
  examinations at, 73
  influence of eleven plus, 76–7
School, type and attitudes to education, 79
  and criticisms, 94
  and delinquency, 157
  and type of work, 104
  'working-class' boys' views, 167
Scouting, 123, 132
Seaside, 17, 149–50
Sex, group attitudes to, 41–2, 49
Sexual experience, 42, 48–52
Sheffield, 80
Siblings, 57, 58, 65
Society, adult, attitudes, 174
  modern, 160, 172–3
  western, delinquent sub-cultures, 163
Spending, 14–15
Sports, 127, 131, 134, 135
Status frustration, 161
Stealing, age, 139, 141–2
  attitudes to, 140, 142–3 and n.
  peer group influence, 34
Stepney, 25 n., 138, 148 n., 157, 174
Success, material, 94, 160, 163–4

Teachers, 82–3, 94 n., 167, 177
Television, 54–5
Toughness, 145–6, 147
Trade union membership, 173
Trainees, 98, 103
Training, technical, 104

Uncles, 46, 66 and n., 67
Unclubbables, 132–3, 136
Unemployment, 175
University delinquency, 137
  settlement, 121

Values, material success, 160–1
  middle-class, 164
  rejection, 164
Violence, 147, 148, 159–60

Wealth, 13–14, 175
West End, 16, 18, 32–3
Withdrawal, 172, 176, 180
Work, 100–20
  attitudes to, 20, 118–19, 167, 168
  change of, 115–16, 117
  clerical, 113, 114
  expectations, 111
  job getting, 105, 106, 116
  place of, 18, 103, 104, 173
  prospects, 113–17
  rebelliousness at, 117, 158
  satisfaction, 110–11, 119–20
  skilled, 102, 113
  type, 103–4,
    and school record, 104, 117
    and occupational class, 168
  unskilled, 20, 115
Workers, skilled, 103, 114
  unskilled, 106, 112, 120, 157–9

Youth clubs, 31, 121–36
  ages of members, 29, 123–4, 128–9, 173
  attendance at, 125
  authority in, 127, 128
  criticisms of, 127–8, 129, 178–9
  expulsions, 133
  facilities, 127, 129
  girls in, 38–9, 122–3
  identification with, 131–2
  junior, 124
  leaving, 129–30
  male, 128
  mixed, 128, 130–1
  organization, 129
  peer groups in, 125
  pre-Service, 121, 128
  Recreational Institutes, 121
  rules, 128
Youth employment service, 106, 178
Youth service, Bethnal Green, 135

For Product Safety Concerns and Information please contact our EU
representative GPSR@taylorandfrancis.com
Taylor & Francis Verlag GmbH, Kaufingerstraße 24, 80331 München, Germany